Malcolm Saville
A Friendship Remembered

ViV Turner

Girls Gone By Publishers

Published by

Girls Gone By Publishers
4 Rock Terrace, Coleford, Bath, Somerset BA3 5NF

First Edition
Published by Girls Gone By Publishers 2010
Text © ViV Turner 2010
All uncredited photographs © ViV Turner 2010
Photographs on pages 44, 56 and 159 © the estate of Malcolm Saville
Photographs on back cover (bottom) and pages 28 and 29 © Len Timbrell 2010
Photographs on back cover (top) and pages 33, 58, 59, 128 and 162 © James Turner 2010
Photograph on page 62 © Myra Moody 2010
Design and layout © Girls Gone By Publishers 2010
Cover design by Sarah Woodall

The moral right of ViV Turner to be identified as the author of this book has been asserted by her in accordance with the Copyright, Designs and Patents Act 1988.

All rights reserved.
Without limiting the rights under copyright reserved above, no part of this publication may be reproduced, stored in or introduced into a retrieval system, or transmitted, in any form or by any means (electronic, mechanical, photocopying, recording or otherwise), without the prior written permission of the above copyright owners and the above publisher of this book.

Girls Gone By Publishers, or any of their authors or contributors, have no responsibility for the persistence or accuracy of URLs for external or third-party internet websites referred to in this book, and do not guarantee that any content on such websites is, or will remain, accurate or appropriate.

Edited by Tig Thomas
Typeset in England by Little Pink Cloud Limited
Printed in England by Antony Rowe Limited

ISBN 978-1-84745-095-1

The Publisher and Author acknowledge the kind permission of the Estate of the late Malcolm Saville for the use of some quotations in this book, and in return a donation has been made to the Alzheimer's Society.

Malcolm Saville's Christmas card (see page 150)

Advertising flier from Knight Books

CONTENTS

Introduction		7
Acknowledgements		8
Preamble		9
I.	Malcolm Saville … My Friend	11
II.	*Mystery at Witchend*	25
III.	*The Gay Dolphin Adventure*	35
IV.	*Jane's Country Year*	47
V.	Holidays	55
VI.	Quizzes	77
VII.	Index	90
VIII.	Lone Pine Wales	106
IX.	*Home to Witchend*	113
X.	Publishing and Publicity	130
XI.	Mr and Mrs Saville	156
Malcolm Saville Today		172
Answers to the First Quiz		173
Answers to Fun Quiz		174
Answers to *Home to Witchend* Quiz		175

For Brian

INTRODUCTION

'For our time is a very shadow that passeth away.' These words, which sit between the 'Quarter Boys' on St Mary's church clock in Rye, remind me of the passing years. It is over a quarter of a century since Malcolm Saville died, and I am one of the diminishing number of people who were privileged to have known him. I have thought long and hard before writing this book as a tribute to Mr Saville. I believe that he would have liked me to share my recollections of him with his family and the many people, young and old, who enjoy his books.

Malcolm Saville is not a chronological account, charting the history of my contact with Mr Saville from beginning to end, nor is it attempting to be a biography. I have instead taken a thematic approach, using the different chapters to celebrate some of the important and significant moments in our lengthy friendship. This book is based on my personal memories of Mr Saville over a span of some thirty years. I have done my best to be accurate, but it may be some errors have crept in and I apologise if I have inadvertently included any inaccuracies or misrepresentations.

It has been my endeavour to donate to posterity my memories of this great children's author, with the help of extracts taken from Mr Saville's letters. His books were written in a different age from this fast-changing world, and my reminiscences should give an insight into the way of life of those times. Mr Saville and I had a friendship which was based on understanding, loyalty and trust. This book is the story of that friendship, the memory of which will remain with me forever.

ViV Turner
2010

ACKNOWLEDGEMENTS

I would like to express my thanks to the following people:

Clarissa and Ann at Girls Gone By for publishing the book,
Tig Thomas for editorial help and for being such a joy to work with,
Sarah Woodall, for her superb cover design, and her work on typesetting and designing the inside of the book,
John Allsup for providing scans of dustwrappers and illustrations,
Sarah Mash for her meticulous proofreading,
My husband Brian for his patience in typing my manuscript,
My son James for his computer expertise and for taking photographs,
Darren Cresswell for scanning photographs and always being willing to help me,
Len Timbrell, my serendipity friend, for allowing me to use his photographs,
Myra Moody, a friend from school days, whose husband comes from Whitby, also for a photograph.

PREAMBLE

Leonard Malcolm Saville was born on 21 February 1901 in Hastings, Sussex, the son of a bookseller and grandson of a missionary and minister of Rye Congregational Church. He went to boarding school at the age of nine and never regretted this. He also went to other private schools. He left school at sixteen and began working for the Oxford University Press, his initiation into a career in the book trade, where he sorted stock for booksellers' orders. Two years later he joined Cassell & Co where he worked in their publicity department. After a further two years he moved to Amalgamated Press, again in publicity. His writing started with football reports for which he received a pound a match. He told me that this was excellent training as he had to write at a fast speed. It was at this time he learned many of the writing skills which were to serve him in good stead when he began work on his own books. He also became editor of two magazines, *My Garden* and *Sunny Stories*, taking over the editorship of this latter title from Enid Blyton.

In 1926 he married Dorothy May McCoy. They were to have four children, Robin, Rosemary, Jennifer and Jeremy, and many grandchildren. His significant career move came in 1936 when he joined George Newnes Limited in London as sales production manager. At this time, the Saville family lived in Harpenden, Hertfordshire. In the late 1930s, the Saville family visited Shropshire for a holiday and this county came to mean as much to them as his home county of Sussex. They continued to visit Shropshire, and during the war years it was an inevitable choice for Mr Saville to evacuate his wife and young family there. These were lonely times for Mr Saville as he remained at home in Hertfordshire as a deputy night controller for the ARP. It was during this time that he wrote *Mystery at Witchend* which was published by George Newnes, as were many of his Lone Pine stories. *Mystery at Witchend* was later broadcast on *Children's Hour*. Mr Saville was a prolific author who wrote nearly one hundred titles and sold well over a million books. The attraction for many of his readers was that they could visit the majority of the locations used in the books. Most of these were set in Britain, although some of his later stories were set abroad. His most popular locations were Shropshire and Sussex, which featured in what were to become his bestselling books, the Lone Pine series. Mr Saville encouraged children to write to him and they would always receive a handwritten reply. Any children who visited him in his various homes—usually to have books signed by him—were always made welcome. A deep Christian faith, family life and a career in the world of books were the most important elements of Mr Saville's life. He always wrote books that he knew children would like to read, and running unobtrusively through all his books were his Christian and moral beliefs.

In the early 1940s Mr Saville and his family moved to Westend Farmhouse in Wheatonhampstead, which became the setting for some of his stories. Amongst his many house moves was one to Chelsea Cottage in Winchelsea, where he lived for ten years. His final home was in Ringmer, Lewes.

Mr Saville died on 30 June 1982 in Hastings, at St Helen's Hospital. He told me that he hoped one day that his old bones would be buried in Winchelsea churchyard (Mr and Mrs Saville worshipped at this church when they lived in Winchelsea and Mr Saville was a member of the Parochial Church Council). He would be happy that his ashes (and later those of his wife) were scattered in the garden of remembrance of Winchelsea Church.

Chapter I

Malcolm Saville … My Friend

I was eight years old before I appreciated the joy of reading, and then it was thanks to the picture of a fastidious cat's face on the spine of Paul Gallico's *Jennie*. This book became a treasured birthday gift from my much loved maiden aunt, Ada, (affectionately known by me as 'AA'). Discovering *Jennie* began my lifelong passion with words. As a little girl, what I looked forward to most at school was the period when the teacher would read a story to the class in the afternoon. It was during one of these quiet times that I first became entangled within the branches of *The Magic Faraway Tree*.

Because I lived in the country, everywhere that I went involved a long walk to an infrequent bus service. This gave me an early appreciation of nature, and the small group of children with whom I grew up were important people to me. We attended the same infant and junior schools. On the rare occasions when we meet, the years roll away as we recall those early days.

I had long wanted to join the library and I felt much anticipation when one Saturday morning my father said that he would take me there, so that I might become a member of the Junior Library. This involved a walk along country lanes with high hedges obscuring the cornfields from my view, although I was always conscious of the wind rustling in the grasses. We passed a smallholding where the pigs snorted noisily, and a gentle rise brought us to the terminus of the bus service. I constantly craned my neck to watch for the bus coming, and my patience was rewarded as it turned round for its return journey with my father and me as passengers. We alighted in the town of Dudley, part of 'the backbone' of England. At its highest point sit the extensive ruins of a Norman castle, which since 1937 has been surrounded by a zoo. The town centre has a bustling open-air market from which strands of often narrow streets and passages wind their way to the town's suburbs. The town is internationally famous for its fossils, to be found amongst the limestone hills and excavated caverns of the Wren's Nest. There are also many canals, along some of which narrowboat rides may be taken, including a fascinating journey through tunnels to the eerie world of the vast caverns.

A short walk brought us to our local library. We climbed the impressive staircase, pushed open the heavy door and walked into the Children's Library. We walked across what seemed to be an endless floor and I was duly registered as a member.

Saturday mornings were my treat after that and a few months later my parents decided that I was sufficiently mature and well acquainted with the route to make this journey by myself. This was to be the highlight of my life for many years. I became familiar with the routine in the library and was always watchful of the time when the librarian would wheel the heavily loaded wooden trolley of the books returned that day and place them on the appropriate shelves. An undignified scuffle would ensue because this was the best way to gain the choicest returns of the day. One particular morning, on entering the library, I gazed at this shelving and with disappointment noticed that it contained only one book. I walked slowly towards it and picked it up. It was a dilapidated copy without a dustwrapper and I read the title without much interest. It was called *Mystery at Witchend*, written by someone named Malcolm Saville. I flicked through it and put it down on the shelf. I looked at it again and picked it up. I noticed the illustrations and decided that I would take it. I was fortunate to begin at the beginning and from that day to this Mr Saville's books and in particular the Lone Pine series were to be an integral part of my life.

For several years I was content to read Mr Saville's books and discuss them with my friends, but as I grew older I felt that I wanted to contact this man who was so important to me. I wrote to him and was delighted to receive his reply by return. In that first letter, he told me how important his readers were to him and how much he enjoyed receiving their letters; he said that he always replied to them himself. He was interested in my collection of his books and sent me details of the Lone Pine Club in case I wished to join. Of course I did, and I still have my badge with its solitary pine tree logo. That first fan letter was to grow over many years into an enduring friendship. At Mr Saville's request, I continued to write to him, send him postcards from holidays and, when he asked, was delighted to send him photographs of myself. He did the same and I have a pile of correspondence from him, including postcards and photographs that have pride of place in my albums.

My Lone Pine Club Badge

For a long time now I have had a complete set of Lone Pine stories in hardback which includes all of the Newnes editions. Not all the books in my collection are pristine copies, but this has never mattered to me, and still does not. A battered Newnes edition classified as a reading copy would mean far more to me than a brand-new later edition and I treasure every one of my books. Many have stories in their own rights. Some were gifts to me from AA, now long since departed, and some were the result of searching through second-hand bookshops. A few are ex-library copies of Newnes editions that I obtained with the help of a sympathetic librarian in exchange for new books. Both the librarian and I were delighted with these transactions. Mr Saville himself put me in contact with helpful dealers who sought out hard-to-find copies for me and, of course, he did give me some himself including a most treasured possession, a hardback copy of *Home to Witchend*. As many of my second-hand books came minus their dustwrappers, Mr Saville assisted in the search for these. In a letter from him of 21 April 1975, I was pleased to read: 'I've just found an Australian edition of LP5 ... the jacket is the same as Newnes so you are welcome to this one. See what perseverance will do for you!' This jacket only differs from the Newnes copies in that it has the word 'Dymock's' at the base of the spine.

When I married in December 1971, our honeymoon hotel was the Mermaid in Rye and my wedding present from Mr Saville was a selection of old photographs which included Lone Pine locations. I truthfully told him that this was the most exciting gift that I had received. Although we had talked on the telephone we had never met, but during my visit to Rye Mr Saville invited me to visit him in Winchelsea the following summer and offered to be my guide to his Lone Pine locations, if I would like that. I assured him that I would very much and it was with great eagerness that, the following year, my husband and I left our holiday home in Hastings to journey to Mr Saville's home, Chelsea Cottage in Winchelsea. Of course, in true Lone Pine tradition the sun shone at its brightest and as we drew up in front of the neat lawn Mr Saville came out to greet us.

All these years I had held a picture of him in my mind of what he would really be like and here he was before me smiling in welcome. He took my hand in a warm grasp and his eyes were direct as he looked at me. We were of a similar height, and I was instantly aware of how alive and vibrant this man was. Photographs were fine but they had not been able to tell me of the dynamic interest in life that emanated from the person standing before me. As he smiled at me, I suddenly realised that he was just as curious and interested about me as I was about him. I relaxed as we followed this slightly stocky, casually dressed gentleman into his home. We were not to meet Mrs Saville until later in the day.

Chelsea Cottage, in the ancient town of Winchelsea, was an elegant building and I recall that it had lots of stairs. Mr Saville led me up many of these until I was in the room, quiet and high, where he did his writing. It was an awesome experience and one that I will always remember. This was not a large room, but it was dominated by a wall of shelving tightly packed with books. Facing away from these, so that it would catch the maximum amount of light, was Mr Saville's desk where he wrote his books, always by hand. It was a very full room and obviously a working environment. He drew my attention to the well-lined shelves containing all of the books that he had written. At his bidding, I examined the shelf of Lone Pine books, neat and smart in their dustwrappers. He was clever enough to know that talking about Lone Pine stories was a sure way to make me lose my shyness of him and before long we were chattering eagerly while examining the precious books. I was delighted when he said that he would be happy to sign the pile of my Lone Pine books that I had brought with me, as having his signature on them made them so much more special.

I gazed around and noticed the photographs that he had pinned up, which I knew were from his readers. I was particularly pleased to see one that I had sent him. He showed me a letter he had received from a young fan that had made a lasting impression on him, as it explained how much the books were enjoyed because 'they do not give me bad dreams'. I had never thought about this aspect of his stories, but it was true they were not scary. It was a considerable feat to be able to write exciting adventure stories that were not frightening to readers, although they were littered with shady characters. Mr Saville was an expert at this.

As I sat beside Mr Saville at his desk, he described his procedure for writing the books. He explained to me that his initial interest was always in a real place. Sometimes he would read something in a newspaper or hear a chance remark, but there was always a place that was the start of a story. He had visited, and had researched carefully, every setting in the Lone Pine series, learning about its history, places of interest and dramatic happenings that could become vital in a storyline. I learned that Mr Saville's books were planned with the precision of a military campaign, and only when he was completely satisfied did he start to write. In the early days all of his work was handwritten and he liked to write a chapter at a time. The next day he would correct this in a contrasting colour. Only then did he despatch this by post to his secretary to be typed and returned. They never met, but apparently the system proved satisfactory for many years.

He said that it was time for him to take us out to lunch and that he had a surprise for us. This intrigued me, but I had to be patient as Mr Saville said that first of all, he wanted to show us Winchelsea, the smallest town in England. We walked along the elegant streets and were surprised when Mr Saville told us that the majority of these innocent-looking houses had cellars beneath them which, in the days when smuggling was rife, would often contain contraband. He talked at length and with knowledge about this illegal occupation, which he brings to life for his readers in a passage in *The Elusive Grasshopper*.

In the evening, following the events in Dungeness earlier that day, Jon, Penny and Arlette sit round the fire in the secret room 'under the roof' in the Dolphin Hotel with their guest, James Wilson. James Wilson says: 'I suppose you know all about the smugglers of Romney Marsh in days gone by, and I expect you've read plenty of stories about them …'

'In the old days, of course,' Wilson went on, 'it was brandy, lace and wines which were smuggled in from France and the wool of the Romney Marsh sheep which went out. I was reading myself the other day that no part of England was so continually active in smuggling through the centuries as this little stretch of coast between Hastings and Hythe. This is easy to understand, of course, because it is very thinly populated, handy for landing goods and once the bales were safely on the back of the pack-ponies it was convenient country for evading pursuit. I'm told that in autumn and winter the mist lies a few feet thick over all the Marsh, and although I've never seen it, I can imagine that the Marsh-men who would know every track and every dyke would be able to guide their ponies for many miles without even being seen by the watching Redcoats. No stranger would have a chance in these parts, and I've no doubt that many a mother's son trying to do his duty as a Preventive Officer or a dragoon finished his young life at the bottom of one of the dykes which cross the Marsh. I was thinking to-day as I drove these girls home that I wouldn't care to be out on the Marsh on a winter's night—not even in a car.

'There was a lot of money to be made out of smuggling, and even when a few of the "owlers", as they were called, were caught it was difficult to find a local magistrate who would convict them, for it was said, with some truth, I believe, that the magistrate who sat on the bench by day and the parson in his pulpit on Sunday rode with the smugglers at night … Another thing I was reading was that the big, lonely churches on the Marsh—and if you look carefully you will see that they are all far too big for the size of the villages they are supposed to serve—were often used for storing contraband. There's one quite near to you here at East Guldeford which is an obvious example, for it stands by itself nearly three hundred yards from the road and from the nearest house … And you saw for yourselves to-day at Dungeness how suitable that place is for smuggling and any other secret operation.'

We gazed at the noble Church of St Thomas and then walked to the look-out from where our guide pointed out the former location of Miss Ballinger's beach bungalow. After collecting his car Mr Saville drove us slowly down the steep hill taking us out of Winchelsea and on the way to Rye. I told him that I felt the magic of this town and that it had cast a spell over me just as Miss Ballinger says it does when she first meets Jon and Penny. Mr Saville said that he always felt the same on entering the town and that this sense of excitement never left him.

The best guide in all the world showed me Lone Pine Rye. As we walked in complete harmony over the cobbles of Watchbell Street, I could hardly believe that I was really here walking along what I will always think of as Trader's Street with the man who had given me years of pleasure through his writings.

We hesitated and looked at the sign that to me should have been the Gay Dolphin and I made Mr Saville laugh as I tried to guess which would have been the window of Jon's room. We then walked slowly to the end of the street and leaned on the wall warmed by the sun where the Lone Piners love to lean. We stayed in companionable silence, following Mr Saville's gaze down to the sluggish River Rother making its lazy way to the sea, after negotiating Rye Harbour and skirting Camber Castle. We then looked towards where Winchelsea sat dreaming on its hill before gazing at the endless expanse of marsh, which was just as I had imagined it from Mr Saville's description. He looked at me sympathetically and of course knew exactly how I was feeling. I had soon learned that he had the ability to make you feel that you were the only person who mattered when he was with you. It was good to feel that important. Our visit to Rye culminated in the surprise, which was Mr Saville taking us to the Hope Anchor for lunch.

Immediately on entering the Hope Anchor, Mr Saville disappeared and whilst I was standing wondering what to do he reappeared, light and agile, and whispered to me conspiratorially that he had been to look at the visitor's book to see whether any suspicious characters had registered. He said that as a writer he should be alert to such things, and I could believe this as his eyes darted with interest around the room. It was obvious that we were expected as we were led to a table and, although I wanted to savour every precious moment, I cannot recall what we had to eat that day. We all received VIP treatment and I was told that anything that I wanted I could have. Of course Mr Saville was well known and I could see he thoroughly enjoyed his celebrity status. I felt more than a little embarrassed when I was introduced as 'his oldest Lone Piner who knew more about his books than he did'. I was to learn that when certain members of Mr Saville's far-flung family came to stay, he would often take them to the Hope Anchor where they would 'enjoy a beer or two'. He mentioned such occasions many times, but never once similar visits to the Mermaid.

Over lunch I bombarded him with questions, and he did the same to me. I told him that my favourite Lone Pine characters were Jon and Penny and he said that his was Jenny. When I asked which of his own books he liked best of all he replied *Jane's Country Year*. We discussed letters that he had received from children and how one child had had the temerity to tell him how much she loathed Peter. I asked whatever did this girl mean and he said it was because Peter was so perfect. I had to smile at this and said that I knew exactly what was meant as it was hard to find any fault in Peter. When I said that maybe I liked Penny so much because she did have many faults, Mr Saville said that this was a shrewd remark. I was to learn over the years that, whatever adulation he received, any criticism was keenly felt and, if at all possible, the problem was resolved. Another child complained of the lack of brunettes in his books and so he had introduced Harriet.

After lunch we had a whirlwind tour that took my breath away. We drove along the road which ran parallel to the Military Canal where Jon and Penny go swimming. Even on a summer's day the water was dark and sullen and did not look particularly inviting. I was not surprised that Penny had cut her leg, as the murky depths looked as if they could be full of hidden perils. In a letter sent by Mr Saville prior to our visit he had said: 'I'll show you where Amorys might have been,' and as we drove on I asked him to clarify this statement. He said that one day, as he had stood on the gently sloping land rising from the left of the Military Canal, he had decided that this was where he wanted Major Bolshaw's old farmhouse to be. It was only then that he had looked for a suitable building in the vicinity, but he stressed that on this occasion the siting was what mattered to him. However, I wanted to know the exact property he had chosen and, when he had pointed this out to me, I took a photograph of it.

'BOARD RESIDENCE *available in old farmhouse. Delightful situation in Isle of Oxney overlooking Romney Marsh. Three bedrooms available. No telephone. Write for details or call and inspect. Bolshaw, Amorys, Stone-in-Oxney.*'

We had lots of fun and it turned into a treasure hunt when Mr Saville asked whether I could be as clever as the twins and find The Grasshopper. He was quite gleeful as he taxed my brains, and I pleaded with him not to make it too hard as we had so much to see, but his answer was that someone who read his books as often as I did should not find this too difficult. He knew that I would rise to the challenge! We drove slowly through the attractive village of Appledore, which was the setting of Dore Street and it was not long before I pointed triumphantly to an imposing building that looked exactly like the one drawn in the endpapers in *The Elusive Grasshopper*. He smiled and said: 'Well done' and I looked with interest at the door through which James Wilson and his 'fiancée' Arlette walk for their part in the search for the stolen watches.

The Grasshopper (above)—'It was a beautiful house of warm red brick, with a central porch and tall windows, whose frames were painted white.'

Mr Saville and Brian outside Stone-in-Oxney church after our visit (see p19). Their serious faces reflect our sombre mood after Mr Saville had shown us the altar stone that represented pagan worship.

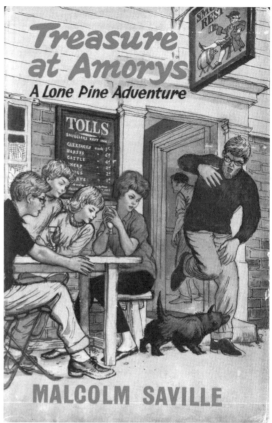

Mr Saville took this photograph of Brian and myself (above left) outside the Ferry Inn which was the setting of the Smugglers Rest in Treasure at Amorys. *He was particularly pleased with this photograph.*

Right: relaxed and happy sitting outside the Smugglers Rest just as the Lone Piners did

The Ferry Inn, which was the setting for the Smugglers Rest, was not difficult to find (see opposite) as there was an old notice on the wall listing the toll charges just as on the *Treasure at Amorys* dustwrapper and I had my photograph taken with Mr Saville beside this. Like the Lone Piners, we sat outside and enjoyed cool drinks on a hot day.

We continued exploring the Isle of Oxney where there were so many Lone Pine locations to visit, all so different from each other, and none more so than what we were to find in Stone church. Within the cool and quiet of the little church, Mr Saville took us to the belfry, where we gazed upon the stone which was a Roman altar to the heathen god Mithras and traced the outline where we could see the rough carving of a bull. It was hard to realise that there was once pagan worship in our Christian country. As we stood quietly listening to Mr Saville's words of explanation, I understood how much his faith and beliefs, which shone clearly from the pages of his books, meant to him. It was easy to recall Mr Saville's vivid description of the bull sacrifice in Penny's dream and I was aware of the cold floor beneath my summer footwear. Mr Saville glanced at me and, realising how I was feeling, walked towards the door. It was a relief to be outside in the sunshine again, but I did take a photograph of him with Brian (see p17), and the normality of the action eased the tension.

Our host seemed to share all of my excitement and promised that what we were to see next we would never forget. I sat in expectant silence as we were driven to the lonely mass of shingle which was Dungeness. The desolate waste was a shock after the mellow green and white to which now we were accustomed and as I gazed around, I wondered that anyone would come here out of choice. It was hard work walking over the endless pebbles as we followed Mr Saville to the lighthouse which rose, a welcoming beacon in this inhospitable place. We were surprised to see how close were the ships, which appeared to be sailing along the shingle until we scrambled up to where we could look down and watch them moving slowly along the channels of water. We peeped into the café where Jon and Penny with Arlette had tea, but we did not go inside as it looked rather dingy. Mr Saville pointed in the direction of where the old school was, but I was relieved when it was decided to leave this for another day (and besides, the possibility of being hit over the head by a bogus birdwatcher did not conjure any enthusiasm within me). Of course I knew that my companions were far more interested in looking at the little train which was now puffing into the station where it disgorged its many passengers. We

Standing on the endless shingle beside the railway line at Dungeness

examined the gleaming miniature engine and chatted with its proud driver before I stood exactly where Arlette did to have her photograph taken. With unspoken agreement we waited to see the train start on its return journey to Hythe, with a shrill whistle and smoke and steam almost obliterating it; we watched until it was out of sight.

Dungeness—Standing beside the locomotive just as Arlette did

It was time to retrace our steps to Chelsea Cottage, where we were welcomed by Mrs Saville who waited for us with a superb, dainty English tea. As we sat in the homely sitting room, we told her all the exciting things that we had done. The room was of medium size and welcomingly cool away from the heat of the day. It was a relief to sit in one of the comfortable chairs and relax. I sat with my back to the window next to my hostess. She was small and softly spoken and soon put me at my ease. I told Mr Saville truthfully that this had been one of the most marvellous days in the whole of my life. He hesitated before answering and I felt quite choky when he said that for him it had also been 'quite a day'. By this time I felt that I had known Mr Saville all of my life and, indeed, to a large extent I had. Our exciting day was nearly over, but not before Mr and Mrs Saville had promised to come and visit us at our home. Mr Saville had said he was delighted that I wished to call it Witchend. During our holiday in Hastings we had found a woodcarver at Rock-a-Nore who had made a nameplate for us, which was to hang outside our home for many years. Inevitably, this weathered and lost its early brightness, so that when we moved house we had a new one made of wrought iron. Wherever we live, our home will always be called Witchend as it stands for so much that I hold dear. Mr and Mrs Saville also asked us to visit them when they came to stay with their great friend Mrs Tyley at Cwm Head in Shropshire. Of course we promised to do this. There was no sadness on our departure as we had cemented a friendship that had begun years ago in our early letters. We knew that this would last always.

We journeyed back to Hastings, and I fervently hoped that Mr and Mrs Saville would now spend the rest of their lives in Chelsea Cottage at Winchelsea, which I knew they loved.

It was, of course, unthinkable to leave this exciting holiday without a ride on the Romney, Hythe and Dymchurch Railway. We commenced our journey on it a few days later from Hythe. Surprisingly, it actually started early from the station and we were just in time to see it disappear. We looked around Hythe until the next train was ready to leave; it was well worth the wait. The ride was bumpy and uncomfortable, but I realised with a thrill that this could have been the ghost train that had played such an important part in *The Elusive Grasshopper*. Whilst waiting for our return journey, we again walked over the difficult terrain which made our ankles ache and it was without regret that we boarded the train and left this isolated part of the world.

While I knew him I always felt that Mr Saville seemed contented at Chelsea Cottage; he told me that, although he enjoyed travelling, he was always happy to return home. In December of 1972 I wrote to Mr Saville saying that we had decided to spend Christmas at home and had invited both of our families, and this was the kind response: 'There is a Christmas card on the way to you and we both send our love to you and Brian and wish you many, many happy returns of your wedding anniversary. It is a wonderful idea to spend your second Christmas together as you are doing. We shall be alone here together—our choice—on Christmas Day.' I could understand that, with such a hectic life, sometimes Mr and Mrs Saville just wanted to shut the door on the world and enjoy the peace and contentment that a happy marriage could bring. On this occasion it was only to last a few hours as on Boxing Day they would be welcoming some of their family.

I also detected something of a restless spirit in Mr Saville, but maybe it was just his enquiring mind wishing to soak up the atmosphere of new places. He encouraged us to visit Mallorca, the setting of his exciting Marston Baines story *White Fire*. Mr Saville wrote, 'You should see Soller, Puerto Soller, Porto Cristo, Valdemosa and Deja (where Robert Graves lives). I hear though that there have been tremendous developments in the Island but it should be wonderful in November. I remember that you can hire a car for self-drive in Palma. Send me a postcard!' We did all of these things. It was a surprise when Mr Saville once told me that he had considered the possibility of going to live in Soller.

One day 'out of the blue' Mr Saville asked whether I would like to devise a quiz based on his Lone Pine series for his young readers, to be sent out with the Newsletter for the Lone Pine Club. As this proved to be popular, I did others. They were also used at Mr Saville's many public appearances. I was flattered and after some misgivings as to my ability to do this to his satisfaction I agreed and thanked him for asking me. This proved to be an unusual and rewarding experience and I had the added pleasure of knowing that I was being of assistance. The quizzes are discussed in greater detail in Chapter VI.

As Mr Saville trusted me with such an important aspect of his work, I decided to mention to him something that had been bothering me for a long time. Hesitantly, I pointed out certain discrepancies that had occurred throughout his books, such as the colour of hair and eyes of certain characters changing. It amazed me that Mr Saville had not noticed this himself, but as he pointed out, once a story was written and had gone to press, he was already involved in another story which could even be in a different series. He trusted other people to sort out these details. Mr Saville said that he fervently hoped that other readers had not been as observant as me and that these errors had gone undetected, but, although I did not say anything to him, I doubted this very much as it was so obvious. I said that he needed the equivalent of a continuity girl to stop these errors happening and he promptly gave me the job! It was when he was writing *Home to Witchend* that Mr Saville asked me to do an index for him of everything that was in the Lone Pine books. This proved to be a marathon and rewarding task and over the years, as I matured, our friendship deepened and he turned to me more and more for advice. And so I shared his frustrations and anxieties and we became very close.

With my involvement in so many aspects of Mr Saville's work, we were communicating on almost a daily basis and it always gave me pleasure to recognise the familiar distinctive handwriting on the envelope as I went downstairs each morning and picked up the post. From 1971 and in the ensuing years, I really did live what was a Lone Pine life, involved in my research for Mr Saville, particularly in relation to the Index and the Quizzes which needed to be checked meticulously and took up more and more of my time. Housework became neglected and our dining table was constantly filled with papers, Lone Pine books, Ordnance Survey maps and, of course, my old manual typewriter. Somehow, in the midst of this, we had hurried meals, just as Jon and Penny do during their search through old Uncle Charles's box, before returning to the most pleasurable work that I have ever undertaken and that I would not have missed for anything.

I was completely captivated when Mr Saville told me of his great idea to write the Lone Pine Story, which would explain how the first book and its sequels evolved. He would start by describing how this series began after a 'glimmering of an idea' that he had about a story to be set in Shropshire, and then how he was almost compelled to continue the series because of popular demand … He would explain that some of his ideas came from real incidents, like the great storm in 1953 for *Sea Witch Comes Home*; or objects, like the stone which is a Roman altar to the heathen god Mithras in Stone church for *Treasure at Amorys*. With others, it was a place that he had visited that inspired the story—for *Mystery Mine*, the town of Whitby in Yorkshire and the moorland country with the Roman road. This was to be a biography of the Lone Pine Story. It would begin with the ideas, places, characters and plot that became *Mystery at Witchend*. Although he found the Index useful in many ways, the real reason why he had urged me to compile it was because it would give him all the groundwork for what he would write. I felt humble and honoured that he should share this with me and immediately I agreed to continue to be what I knew I was to him—his Girl Friday. Mr Saville was so serious about this project that I felt that he meant this to be the swansong of his writing career and, if this was the case, then this autobiography (I use this word because Mr Saville and the Lone Pine Series were so inextricably merged) had to be right in every detail. I vowed to help him as much as I could. I asked him whether he would sit under the

Lone Pine tree for his inspiration and this made him laugh, but the only answer was to 'wait and see.' Sadly, this project was never to be written, but I do know that he made many notes for what was to be probably his most important work and maybe some day these notes will come to light.

Once Mr Saville excitedly told me that he was to be interviewed on the BBC television programme *Late Night Line Up* and that, as it was to be broadcast nationally, I would be able to watch it. On my showering him with questions he conceded that he had no idea what he would be asked, but it was obviously because he was an author that he had been invited to be on the programme. It was many years ago, long before we had a video recorder, and yet I wanted a permanent record of the programme, so Brian brought home one of his office dictating machines, which had to suffice. Eventually the great day arrived, and Brian and I sat silently, hardly daring to breathe so that we did not miss anything. It was wonderful to see Mr Saville, but, as the programme progressed, we both became disappointed at its content and felt that in no way did it do Mr Saville justice. The two other people who were interviewed at the same time were allowed to dominate the programme and seemed unaware that they were in the presence of a gentleman and a well-known author. Mr Saville was allowed little time to speak. I was in a quandary as to what to say to him about it, but when I did speak to him, he asked me what I thought of the interview and I had to be honest and say that I felt let down. It was almost a relief when he said that he felt exactly the same and that when you were on the air live you just had to go along with the interviewer however you were feeling. He added, 'There was no rehearsal, but my family are all disgusted.' Mr Saville did say, 'I was glad to have the chance to voice my views and have offered to do the same again if they could get together a team of real *writers*—not TV adapters who steal the creative ideas of authors.' At the time of the interview he had a terrible cold and he did 'wonder whether I was able to pass it on to my two mates on Thursday night'. He informed me that 'when I have a cold (which is very rare) I'm not worth living with. I am impossible.' I tried to console him by saying that any publicity had to be good and that no interview could detract from his excellent stories. I do not think that I was able to convince him, but, of course, this was put behind us and we never spoke of it again. I still have the recording.

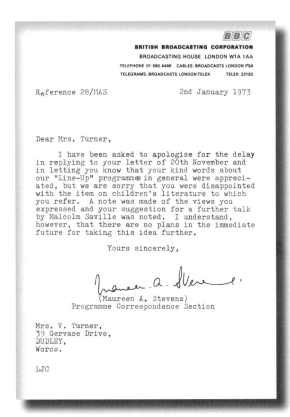

Letter from the British Broadcasting Corporation

It seems a lifetime ago when my young, inquisitive fingers had picked up the well-thumbed copy of *Mystery at Witchend* as it sat isolated on the library shelf. I count that as one of the most significant moments of my life and I have never stopped being grateful for it being the catalyst for one of my most enduring friendships. Mr Saville became my mentor and a beacon of light and hope in a tarnished world. I could never thank him enough for this.

Mr Saville was almost a contradiction in that he loved people, was inquisitive, outwardly so extrovert and a keen conversationalist and yet, as he would tell me, needed to spend many hours alone. In later years he would tell me of his doubts about his writing, and his publisher's wish to omit the descriptive passages. I thought the worst cut was the omission of the chapter heading 'Daughters are the Thing' from *Sea Witch Comes Home*, and Mr Saville agreed with me. There is a description of Rose sitting on the steps of the veranda of Heron's Lodge shelling peas in the original version which is so true to life that I was sorry to see this go. I knew that Mr Saville had to agree to these cuts for the books to remain in print. Incredibly, one edition of *Saucers Over the Moor* was incorrectly titled *Saucers over the Moon*.

When Mr Saville died, I feel that he would have been glad that I kept in touch with Mrs Saville; she said that my letters and telephone calls gave her joy. I like to feel that I gave something to Mr Saville because he gave so much to me and I believe that I did, as he called me his favourite fan and a trusted and loyal friend.

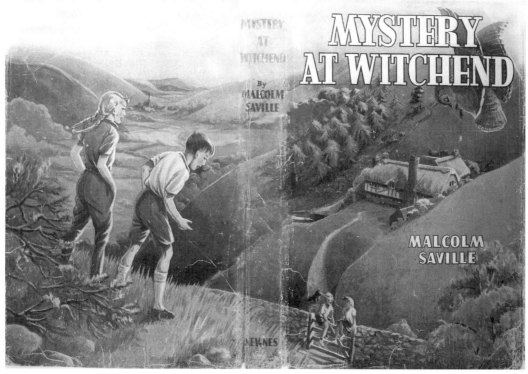

The first edition dustwrapper of Mystery at Witchend: *illustration by G E Breary*

Chapter II

Mystery at Witchend

Mr Saville first visited Shropshire with his wife in the late 1930s; and it could be that, if there had never been a war during which he evacuated his wife and young family to the safety of Shropshire, *Mystery at Witchend* would never have been written. It was when Mr Saville worked in London during the war years that he started to write this first Lone Pine story. Each chapter on completion was sent to his family in Shropshire where it was eagerly awaited and enjoyed. When the story was finished it was accepted for publication by George Newnes Limited who proceeded to publish all of the Lone Pine books up to and including *Man with Three Fingers*. *Mystery at Witchend* was dramatised for radio and broadcast on *Children's Hour* where it was a great success.

Mr Saville told me that when he wrote *Mystery at Witchend* he had no idea that he would be urged to write further books about the same people, nor that the series would span more than three decades. I once had the temerity to say that to me the early Lone Pine stories were the best that he had written and I was relieved when he was gratified by this and understood how I felt. I told him that the Secret Seven, the Famous Five and Biggles were all discarded for anything that he had written, and that I always returned to the Lone Pine series. There is a timeless quality about these books which are filled with energy and humour, perhaps because Mr Saville was fascinated by life, and his characters, however unintentionally, have so much of himself in them.

In the foreword of *Mystery at Witchend*, Mr Saville writes, '… you will not find Witchend.' There is no house called Witchend, but there is one on which it was based. Leaving Marshbrook (Onnybrook in the stories), taking the B4370 west-south-west, a right turn points to Priors Holt. Journeying along this lane you pass Hamperley Farm (this is the setting for Ingles Farm). At the end of the narrow lane is Priors Holt, the house known in the books as Witchend. It is as described in the book, although it has since been modernised and turned into a family home. When in Shropshire Mr Saville and his family stayed close by at Cwm Head House, owned by Mrs Tyley. This is how he discovered Priors Holt and decided to use it in his first Lone Pine story, as Witchend. He never stayed in the house itself. Mr and Mrs Saville continued to visit Shropshire and Mrs Tyley for the rest of their lives whenever time permitted.

I was lucky enough to read my first Lone Pine book at exactly the right age—that is, when the characters were my contemporaries, because the books came out as I was growing up. I could feel an affinity with them and the situations in which they found themselves.

Fortunately, I had a father whose spare time was filled with walking, cycling, climbing and gymnastics. He would do cartwheels along the edge of our lawn to entertain my friends (with whom he was popular) and me. He took us on walks over the Wren's Nest, the northern tip of which was close to my home, on the outskirts of the village of Woodsetton near Dudley. The area is hilly, with gaunt rocky outcrops and many trees and bushes. It is one of the most famous geological sites in Britain because the rock found here, called Wenlock limestone, is rich in the remains of sea creatures that lived over four hundred million years ago in the Silurian period. My father would point out the entrances to the deep caverns and teach us about the fossils. Mr Saville took great interest in what I had to say about the Wren's Nest being a possible story location.

Mr Saville knew that children of a certain age loved secret clubs and codes. Naturally, like many youngsters up and down the land, we created our own club in imitation of the Lone Piners. My father allowed my friends and me to use his garage as headquarters for our club. We thoroughly enjoyed our private meetings when goodies for our snack were provided by my mother. I remember that we had posters and our club rules were attached to the inside of the garage door. Our club also had its own code, just like the one that Peter and Dickie made up one wet afternoon when they were confined to Witchend with colds. We spent much time tracking our neighbours who seemed to take it all in good part, as our methods, I believe, were not particularly effective. I recall that we used to tread on each other, which gave rise to noises of protest. We were disappointed at the lack of sinister strangers.

I told my father about a book that I had read, which was set in a real place in Shropshire. When I mentioned the Long Mynd he said that he knew it well and that he had cycled and walked there. I asked whether he would show it to me and he agreed to do this as we had a car. One summer day, I was taken there by my parents. From my youngest days, my father had taken me on walks and I loved the feel of the springy turf beneath my feet and the warm brush of heather around my ankles. I recognised the rolling gentle grandeur that was the Long Mynd from the vivid descriptions in the story. I liked the vast openness and the quiet that was only broken by the calling of birds above and beneath me the murmur from hidden insects. After having a picnic and generally exploring I pleaded with my father to look for Witchend before returning home. We did this but we never found it. We must have passed the road leading to Priors Holt without realising its significance.

Over the years there were to be many visits, usually during summer weekends when the hills would be bathed in sunlight. The season that I liked best was when they were covered with mauve heather of varying shades. Years later, in what was to be the first home of my own, our bedroom was decorated in the colours of the Mynd, so that this part of Shropshire was always with me. On one occasion we were caught in the mist which rolled silently and swiftly around us. I stood in the cold eerie blanket and knew how dangerous it would be if I strayed from the car, and felt sympathy for Dickie and Mary alone in a Mynd mist. It was a relief when it lifted just as quickly as it had come. My father had taught me to have respect for the weather, particularly when I was on mountains and hills. I knew that his advice was sound because he had climbed mountains throughout England and Wales.

Even at an early age the real locations of the Lone Pine books were almost more important to me than the stories. Without using complicated words, Mr Saville brought those places to life in a way that instilled in his young readers a longing to find them. Cleverly, the characters give us information which could have proved tedious if spelt out in the narrative, and Bill Ward, a sailor with whom the Mortons share a compartment on their train journey to Onnybrook, gives a simple history lesson when he tells the Mortons (and the readers) about the country around their new home.

It was, as Bill had said, a long, smooth, rolling mountain … The slopes were bare of trees, and so suddenly did the mountain seem to grow out of the plain that it seemed as if they might lean from the windows and touch it. As they watched, the sun slipped down behind it, and a great shadow was flung across the country to the train. The slopes that had looked so smooth and inviting were now dark and mysterious as black clouds came rolling up from the south-west.

The magic of Witchend begins with the journey there. Trains play an important part in the Lone Pine books and, of course, in my childhood days they were what, to me, were proper trains—large, noisy and smoky. 'They changed trains at Shrewsbury' are the first words of the Lone Pine series and introduce us to the Mortons' train journey to Onnybrook. It is during this ride that the Mortons first glimpse the Long Mynd from the window of the train. At Onnybrook, Old John, the driver of a decrepit car, is waiting to take them on the final stage of their journey. The heavily laden car has to wait at the level crossing gates, but soon they are on their way.

The road crossed a brown, rushing stream and then turned up a long hill between woods … The climbing road twisted and turned for another mile before the trees thinned out, and they rushed out to the crest of a long hill. Ahead was rolling country with their road threading its way like a ribbon into the distance …

Old John turns sharp right into a lane flanked by trees. They pass through a wood and as the lane comes to an end, he stops the car and Witchend is before them.

As the Lone Pine series progressed, the Mortons' journeys to Witchend were to become so familiar that I felt that I had known Witchend long before I ever found it. On page one of the book, we meet what Mr Morton describes as 'those awful twins' and at the right age have we not all longed to emulate them in their infuriating behaviour? Mr Saville knew how to make his readers laugh: for example in the famous bog scene when Mary says to Peter, 'And if you don't like it I'll jump in, too, and then we'll both smell …' As I once told Mr Saville, this sort of humour appeals to young minds and is, to them, just as important as the story. We also learn quickly how supportive the twins are to each other and that they work with David as a team in a way that Peter as an only child cannot understand. This is brought home to her when she is tactlessly critical of Mackie becoming tired whilst exploring the Long Mynd and the twins refuse to go on without him. Peter soon realises that Mackie, the faithful black Scottie on whose collar Mary often ties a bow, is a cherished member of the Morton family. Peter learns a lot about team spirit from her friendship with the Mortons. We are soon acquainted with her generous heart when the twins do all that they can to stop Mrs Thurston from looking at the lone pine and Peter whispers, 'Those two are *grand*, David.' David shows wisdom beyond his years when Peter takes him swimming for the first time in the Hatchholt reservoir and, although he is the stronger of the two, he lets Peter win their race.

All the time I was reading the books, the Mortons, Tom, Peter and the other characters were stepping out of the pages and becoming real people and lifelong friends to eager readers like myself. When Mrs Morton first meets Peter she says, 'Now I've met her I'm going to treat her as part of the family ... I always wanted two boys and two girls.' I asked Mr Saville whether any of his characters were based on real people and he assured me that they were not. I always felt that he had based the Mortons and Peter on his own family and, on my pressing him, he did once tell me that he knew of someone who was very like Peter. When I said that surely he must have used some of his family's experiences in his description of the Mortons and Peter, he said that maybe unintentionally he had done this. I believe that a good writer does his best work with places and people with which he is familiar, and this must surely have been so in Mr Saville's case.

It was many years before I finally saw Witchend by which time I was with Brian and no longer a child. We only found it because Mr Saville wrote out the directions for us ... 'I know every step of your journey with your fiancé. You were within a mile of "Witchend" when you saw the signpost to "Priors Holt" because this old house is Witchend.'

It was a warm summer day when we drove along the narrow lane for the first time to Witchend. We passed Hamperley Farm which is Ingles Farm in the series: 'Ingles' farm was not very big, but the farmhouse of red brick was well set back from the road with a big lawn on the right and cowsheds on the left.' We saw the gate on which the twins stood when they visited the farm for the first time.

> When they got to the gate a jolly looking man was in the yard harnessing a big horse to a farm cart. He had half a cigarette behind one ear, a check cap on his head, and was wearing a brown overall. He was whistling as he worked.
>
> David knew from experience that the twins were best able to manage new introductions.

Below and opposite: Old photographs of Hamperley Farm—Ingles Farm in the Lone Pine series

Strangers were always surprised at them and to-day they were idiotically excited.

Without a word to each other they went to the gate, climbed up two rungs and leaned on the top bar watching.

At the end of the lane we parked the car but I could not see all the house that Mr Saville had named Witchend because it was partially obscured by bushes. I was aware of the sound of water as I walked up to the gate leading to the house and, leaning on this, saw Witchend. I was looking at it at a slight angle because the house is to the right of the gate. It appeared symmetrically built with windows either side of a doorway which was shielded by an attractive gable porch. There were shallow stone steps leading to the front door and curtains at the white-painted window frames. To the left of the house was a low barn. There was no garden, but some sparse short grass grew between stones. As I looked at the mellow house, nestling snug and serene against the security of the Long Mynd, I knew that in Mr Saville's heart it had always belonged to him, although he had never been able to purchase it (he told me that this was a great regret to him, but that the farmer who owned it wished to keep it and to give it to his son as a wedding present). Through his Lone Pine series he gave it to so many thousands of readers worldwide.

This was an emotional moment. This house had meant so much to me since I was a little girl and it was just like the picture that I had held in my mind for so long. However many times I would visit Witchend, this first time is the one that I will always remember. (An old photograph of the house, taken by Len Timbrell, appears on the back cover of this book.)

On another visit to Witchend some time later, we were dismayed to see it empty and

neglected and in a poor state of repair. As we leaned on the gate and looked at the house, it did not take us long to realise that it was uninhabited.

Cautiously, we pushed open the gate and walked slowly towards the house over rough ground where all traces of what could have been a garden had long since gone. We tried unsuccessfully to peer through the ill-fitting windows which were nearest to us and then proceeded to walk around the outside of the house. All was quiet on this warm summer day apart from the tinkling of the nearby stream.

I tried the door and to my surprise it moved slightly. With further encouragement it grated along the floor until it was open wide enough for us to enter. After hesitating only a moment we were inside Witchend.

In *Mystery at Witchend* we meet Agnes Braid, who is to be the Mortons' housekeeper. She is described as a 'tall, thin, forbidding-looking woman' who 'did not seem a friendly sort of person'. Initially the twins christen her 'Sparrow's Legs', which, I am sure, was to them an apt description and in no way meant unkindly. After an uncomfortable beginning Agnes becomes part of the household, much more than the hired help, and soon a real friend. It is not too long before the twins, great favourites with everyone, particularly in the early books, become 'my two precious rascals'.

Downstairs, I looked at a sorry, forgotten room that would have been the kitchen where Agnes keeps a cheerful fire burning in the kitchen range and a table full of good things for the Mortons' first meal in Witchend. The sun shone palely through the dirty windows revealing a ubiquitous film of dust. I imagined where the oak chest would have stood under the window and the home-made hearth rug, bright with colour beneath the black coat of a sleeping Scottie dog. This room, that I had read about so often, only needed the Mortons and their friends here to bring it to life again.

Our feet made a hollow sound as we carefully walked up the steep uncarpeted staircase which led to an uneven passage with creaking floorboards, which I recall did have at least one odd step. I found what must have been the room that David shared with Dickie. It was small, but I knew that David had pushed his bed under the window of this room. We opened the doors of the other rooms trying to guess which one had been assigned to Agnes as each was small. As we gingerly retraced our steps down the narrow stairs, I could almost hear a greeting from a grandfather clock whose loud tick told of the ever-passing time. If I had listened carefully I was sure that I might have heard the sound of a hymn being intoned by Agnes as she laboured in her scullery, to signify that all was well. She would sing 'Brief Life Is Here Our Portion', and more often than not 'Rock Of Ages, Cleft For Me'. This latter hymn we sing regularly in church, and I never sing it without being transported to Witchend and the family of which I feel I shall always be part.

We explored everywhere although I doubted whether it was safe to do so, but I could not afford to lose this unexpected opportunity to inspect Witchend, with which I felt so familiar and with which I had shared adventures over so many years.

I feel that the description of the house that Mr Saville gives, particularly in *Mystery at Witchend*, was similar to what we had just seen. He could have been inside the house or he may just have had an accurate imagination. I don't remember him ever telling me if he

This shows the side of the house and the barn which (in the fictional world) would be converted into a home for Mr Sterling and Peter many years later.

Mr and Mrs Saville were concerned about the dilapidated state of Witchend at this time and this photograph clearly shows the ill-fitting window. It had become famous following the publication of Mystery at Witchend *in 1943.*

had seen the interior, but I know that every time they visited Shropshire the first thing Mr and Mrs Saville did was to look at Witchend.

The house now stood lonely and forlorn, but it was easy to see that it could have been a happy family home many years ago. Before we came downstairs I looked into what could have been Mary's bedroom, and I remembered that in *Wings Over Witchend* Peter says her prayers before blowing out a candle and climbing into bed, where Agnes has thoughtfully placed a hot water bottle. The room is warmed by an oil stove. This was so like my childhood days when I had said my prayers and had had a crock hot water bottle. My home had electricity, so had no need for candles except when there were power cuts, but my mother had a supply of old ones that were placed in holders and when lit had their own peculiar smell. We had miniature candles on our Christmas tree, as did all of my friends, long before the days of fairy lights. *Wings Over Witchend* was first published in 1956, which was twenty years prior to the time of our visit, but we saw no sign of modernisation. The story gives a beautiful word picture of the Mortons' holiday home. I believe that this story is an important one for David and Peter. Their special friendship is apparent when Peter confides in Mrs Morton that 'David is wonderful and he looks after me.'

While it was obvious that the property had been vacant for a long time, there was no sign of damp. We went outside feeling quite subdued at all that we had seen. After securing the door as far as practicable, we retreated to the gate where Peter had tethered Sally to its post the first time she had visited the Mortons.

Although we scanned the hillside for the Lone Pine tree, we did not locate it, but Mr Saville assured us that there was one and that he would show us when we visited Shropshire to see him. Many years later he was to keep this promise (as I tell in Chapter V 'Holidays'), but Brian and I should have found it ourselves, as its location is accurately shown on the endpapers of *Mystery at Witchend*. We did, however, see where Mary's duck Jemima 'quacked rather gloomily'.

Before we left I had my photograph taken before the front door and imagined that I was the Lady of Witchend. I then took a photograph of Brian as he sat on the gate.

Mr Saville had seen Shropshire in all its seasons which was why he could make differing weather patterns an integral part of a story in such a natural way. It is easy to imagine the Mortons' first memorable journey to Witchend as they embark upon the final leg in old John's decrepit car, when 'the rain was still pouring down and it was dark and gloomy under the trees'. What a contrast to the fateful day when Hatchholt reservoir was blown up at the climax of *Mystery at Witchend*: 'The sun was fierce and down here, at the bottom of the steep-sided valley, there were no welcome breezes to dispel the drowsy heat.' You can almost feel the oppression of the stifling hot day for Tom and the twins toiling up the valley.

Food is always important to young people and to no-one more than Dickie. His pronouncement, 'This is Lone-Pine Camp, and we'll be the Lone-Pine Club … Now let's have something to eat …' suggests these two ideas were equally important. Picnics and feasts become a tradition of Lone Pine meetings throughout the stories, and the party at the end of this first book sets an important precedent. Considering that Mr Saville made these occasions so realistic that you almost want to savour the offerings yourself, it was a surprise to me when he said that he did not like picnics, nor did he approve of the habit of walking along pavements and similar places eating snacks. I recall that Mr Saville once sent me a photograph which showed his family's Christmas dinner table before the meal was served, impeccably set, and himself dressed accordingly for the festive occasion. It brought to my mind the party, when Mr Sterling is 'looking with distaste at the charred potato between his fingers' and I felt that there was something of Mr Saville in Mr Sterling. The more that I got to know him the more I recognised traits of his in some of the characters.

In *Mystery at Witchend*, it is wartime and Mrs Morton reminds the children of how this will affect their new life in the country … 'On Thursdays we shall have to fetch groceries from the farm because they don't like bringing them any further now that petrol's getting scarce. And on Fridays I believe we have to get the joint from Onnybrook, and that sounds like a job for the bicycles.'

David is glad to have his bicycle and relieved that it has travelled safely when he collects it from Onnybrook station. Bicycles were a necessity for children of those times, particularly for those like me living in the country where there were no bus services, and a long journey to school. Mine was strong and sturdy with a saddlebag, as well as a basket fitted at the front, which would have been useful for transporting Mackie. It served me well for many years and I was almost inseparable from it. I remember telling Mr Saville of the time when I skidded on the road and fell heavily while riding my bicycle to school one icy morning. To this day I can remember the feeling of sliding helplessly on the ice. There were not many cars in those days and I escaped with a few scratches and bruises.

Once when I explained to Mr Saville that it was often inconsequential comments that I remembered most from a book, he asked me what I meant. I thought for a moment and then gave an example from *Mystery at Witchend*. When Dickie asks why Peter was given the name Petronella, Mr Sterling replies, 'I believe I saw it on the back of a boat on Cromer beach on our honeymoon.' Mr Saville laughed when I told him that, whilst on holiday in Cromer, I could not help looking at the names on the boats, but I never found one called Petronella. Another instance was when Peter describes how, on reaching home after being out in the mist, 'Daddy put me to bed and brought me some bread and milk … he thinks bread and milk cures everything …' I also commented on the empathy of adults and particularly Mrs Morton who is not curious about the Lone Pine Club. The book states 'It was annoying in a way, but she was a well-trained mother!'

A good dustwrapper can be an invitation to open a book, and the drawing of Peter and David looking down on Witchend, while the owl glides silently by, is perfect for this first story. When I told Mr Saville that I felt that Bertram Prance's illustration of his most famous characters was just as it should be, he never contradicted me, so I knew that he was happy with this dustwrapper. On the spine, Peter is seen climbing the Lone Pine tree and although

Level crossing at Marshbrook—Onnybrook in the Lone Pine series. 'At last they were ready to start, but got no further than the level-crossing gates. A brown-faced signalman leaning from his window smiled at them through the rain, and Richard called out: "May I come and pull one of those levers one day?" but he couldn't hear the answer as a goods train clanked by.'

The second edition dustwrapper of Mystery at Witchend: *illustration by Bertram Prance*

she is an adolescent her two fair plaits do not look out of place. In those times, most young girls had long plaits. There is no comparison between these early drawings and those on the last books in the Lone Pine series with their modern, unrecognisable faces staring out of the covers. The astronomical prices of these hard-to-find books is something that would greatly concern Mr Saville. Although he understood my wish to collect the original hardback books complete with dustwrappers, for him it was more important for a young reader to be able to afford to buy the book and he was therefore a great advocate of paperbacks. He hated the way in which his stories were abridged, but accepted this to keep his stories in print. In April 1972 Mr Saville wrote in a letter, 'Each of the new editions has a note from me that the story has been abridged but the adventure is the same.'

Mr Saville was patriotic, and on the dustwrapper were printed the words, 'The boys and girls involved in these surprising adventures have always been the envy of every reader because they were able to help their country at a time of peril.' When Mr Ingles meets the twins for the first time he is whistling, badly, 'There'll always be an England' and when he pauses they take up the refrain by singing, 'There'll always be a Nengland.' We were proud when Sir Edmund Hilary conquered Everest and waved our flags enthusiastically when the Queen was crowned. Looking back fifty years, I can understand that it may be hard for young people today who read a Lone Pine book to realise that the life depicted was what it was really like, but it was, and I am so glad that I was part of it. Although Mr Saville did not realise it at the time, *Mystery at Witchend* was to be the commencement of a series which was to bring him worldwide acclaim.

Chapter III

The Gay Dolphin Adventure

'… for I say it's a magic little town that casts a spell over everyone who comes in under the old gateways and climbs its cobbled streets.' These words, spoken by Miss Ballinger to Jon and Penny during the train ride to their new home in Rye, explain in a brief description what this town meant to Mr Saville. I always felt that *The Gay Dolphin Adventure* did more to promote Rye as a tourist attraction than any guidebook ever could. Before reading this book, I had never heard of Rye and I was almost disappointed when my father pointed out on a map its location, tucked away far to the south of where I lived. It looked so small and insignificant, but I knew from Miss Ballinger's words that it was something special.

The story starts at a railway station, and the description of the beams of sunlight at Charing Cross is so vivid that, reading it, I could almost detect that grimy smell that was present at all stations in the days of steam, when the beams themselves would be thick with dust particles. On this occasion, 'a particularly broad beam caught and then held two hatless heads—one red and the other yellow.' This is our introduction to Jon and Penny, to me the most endearing characters in the Lone Pine series and of all Malcolm Saville's books.

Like many young people brought up together, cousins Jon and Penny have a closeness similar to that of brother and sister. Their comfortable inclination for each other's company is paramount throughout this story. On the first page there is an example of the friendly banter between the cousins, with whom readers were to become so familiar, and it sits easily on these two people whose young lives have been intertwined for so many years. They complement each other well, Jon with his quiet intelligence and Penny with her eager, friendly exuberance. Jon views the world through spectacles and has thick fair hair, which Penny once rudely tells him looks like 'a haystack after a hurricane'* and, although Jon is clever, he is not quite clever enough to realise that Penny 'would have walked through fire for him'. When they are in harmony with each other, he often calls her 'Newpenny' due to the colour of her hair, and Jon's father's description of her is 'a red-headed baggage'. Mr Saville was amused when I once told him that his weakness for redheads resulted in them having major parts in his books, but he was pleased when I said that, for me, Penny is his most interesting character. Penny muses to herself that as everyone says that Jon is clever and that she is a scatterbrain, she has to accept this, but nothing can dampen her affectionate, impetuous nature that allows her to make friends easily, in a way that brainy Jon never can. She admits that she is the sort of girl who is always losing things, and, as the book says, '… life, if she had permitted it, could easily be one long and desperate hunt for the things which detached themselves from Penny.' I have a great deal of sympathy for her; children often find themselves in these situations, and Mr Saville was clever enough to create characters with whom his readers might have an affinity. When *The Gay Dolphin Adventure* was published in 1945, many children were experiencing the after-effects of the war. In those times most children lived in secure family homes with parents and a close-knit community

---

* in *Treasure at Amorys*; see also page 90.

of grandparents, aunts, uncles and cousins. Some children had to face life without a father, just as Jon did when his father had not returned home from Normandy 'and they had a medal instead'. When I asked Mr Saville what made him write in the original enthralling way that he did, he shrugged and, with that special smile of his, said that he wrote the books that he would have liked to have read when he was young.

By the time I had finished reading *The Gay Dolphin Adventure*, I had fallen in love with Rye, but, although neither of my parents had ever visited the town, my annual pleadings for a holiday there went unanswered in spite of my euphoric descriptions. On overhearing me talking about this book to my cousins, AA checked its title with me. I didn't think about this again until I opened my next birthday gift from her. It was an ornament of a dolphin which was certainly happy. At that time I collected ornaments of animals. After many years where most of them have gone is a mystery, but I still have my own gay dolphin.

I can see now that it was quite fitting that my first visit to Rye should have been on my honeymoon, the year before I met Mr Saville in person. I sat in the car in quiet excitement as we drove through the Landgate and negotiated the twists and turns until we arrived at our destination: the famous Mermaid Inn, the original of the Gay Dolphin. We drove in under the archway just as Fred does on his return from Hastings with Jon and Penny. Eagerly I looked around this hotel which had meant so much to me for so long and, as we were taken upstairs and along narrow corridors, I almost had to pinch myself to appreciate that all of this was real. I remember opening the old-fashioned window of our room and gazing out into Mermaid Street where the buildings opposite seemed so close that I could almost touch them. Although we looked at many of the windows in the hotel we never found one with 'God Save England and ye Towne of Rye' scratched on it with a diamond, as Jon and Penny do. Like Penny, we got lost in the maze of passages and there was a staircase that could have led to her bedroom and the secret room that Jon and Penny have for their own. My regret at never having a secret room of my own has always been tempered with the joy of being able to share in Jon and Penny's and, through Mr Saville's words, even being able to share the excitement of the secret passage with 'a breath of dank, cold air—a smell of fungus and wet wood and decay.'

Although we knew that we were in the building that was the Gay Dolphin, we were keen to find its real location, which was not in the same place as the Mermaid. It was not long before we were outside and making our way towards Watchbell Street. Held tightly in my hand were the photographs that Mr Saville had given to us as our wedding present. In the accompanying letter he had remarked that, although they were getting a little faded, he thought that I might like to have some. He was right. They were all superb and I chose four before returning the others to Mr Saville with my grateful thanks for his generosity. He told

The four old black-and-white photographs shown opposite and on the following page were given to me by Mr Saville as a wedding present. The captions in quotation marks are his own words written on the reverse of the photographs. Opposite, top: '"Traders Street" Rye taken from almost outside the "Dolphin"'. Opposite, bottom: 'Street scene Rye Bottom of Mermaid Street'. This is where the Mermaid is—the original of the Gay Dolphin.

me that they were taken after the war when he had made friends with a young Hungarian photographer whilst he was in publishing. This brave Hungarian had escaped to England and was carrying out underground work for the Government. One day Mr Saville had shown him round Hastings, Winchelsea and Rye, and he had taken a selection of photographs which he had given to Mr Saville. It was with anticipation that, like Jon and Penny, we walked along the cobbles of Watchbell Street towards the swinging sign on a building on the right at the end of the street. It was the Hope Anchor and we knew that we were now gazing at the site of the Gay Dolphin.

> The Gay Dolphin hotel was at the far right-hand end of Trader's Street, which finished abruptly at this wall. A flight of shallow steps called Trader's Passage led down by the side of the hotel to the street by the river far below at the foot of the cliff. With your back to the wall you looked down the street and could watch, as Penny said, the cars and the people coming up to the Dolphin. You could watch the artists pitch their easels, too (for there are always artists in Rye), and the scarlet geraniums in the gay window-boxes of the other little houses in the street and the cats treading their delicate way over the cobbles.
>
> And when you turned round and looked the other way the view took your breath away. To the left which was the east, stretched the vast flat plain of the Marsh—on some days so crystal clear and on others hazy and mysterious—which was green inland, but brown—almost golden—in the sunshine where the sands of Camber merged in the shingle wastes round Dungeness. Straight in front the muddy river Rother ran across the green levels to the huddle of roofs known as Rye Harbour and then to the sea. To the west, Rye's little sister town of Winchelsea drowsed on a tree-covered hill, and beyond that—beyond the sweep of Rye Bay—rose the Fairlight Hills guarding Hastings from the east.
>
> The Elusive Grasshopper

We walked a few steps further, as do Jon and Penny, and looked over the wall at the end of the street and down to the muddy river. Further away, across the Marsh was Camber Castle and the sea in the distance, and we knew then that we really were in Jon and Penny's Rye.

Mr Saville told me that he had once stayed with his wife for a few days at the Hope Anchor in 1940. He said that throughout his life returning to Rye, to him, meant coming home. I had my photograph taken as I sat on Penny's wall and it became a favourite place for me and Brian. I looked down what is Trader's Street in the book and what Mr Saville believed to be the most perfect street in England. The real name of this street has (I quote Mr Saville from *Portrait of Rye*) 'the melodious name of Watchbell Street'.

Opposite: Photographs from the set given to me by Mr Saville as a wedding present. Top: 'Street scene Rye. The Land Gate.' Bottom: 'The Old Mill Winchelsea'. This has to be one of my most treasured possessions as the mill looked exactly like this—as you can see from my own photograph of it on p43.

Watchbell Street—Penny's wall, in Rye. (This photograph was taken for Mr Saville at his request.)

The street is named after the alarm bell used to warn the citizens that once again the French had been sighted in the Channel. It is easy to imagine how it would ring out across the huddled streets and round the church in time of danger and it saw plenty of that.

Portrait of Rye

From the abrupt end of the road it was easy to imagine the area far below covered with sea, and see why it was such a perfect place to observe unwelcome visitors. I gazed down at what I knew to be Trader's Passage leading down to the river, but that was to be explored tomorrow. In *The Gay Dolphin Adventure*, after Jon, Penny and the Mortons went down the secret passage from Jon and Penny's room in the Gay Dolphin for the first time, Jon explains, 'You see that the way we've come was the smugglers' secret way up into the town. That's why the Dolphin was marked on the map, and that's why the steps are called "Trader's Passage". Smugglers used to be called Free Traders. I bet our secret passage runs under the steps all the way.'

We walked along Lion Street and gazed at the impressive building, almost like a cathedral, the parish church of St Mary, so mighty that it dominates the town. We looked up at the unusual clock which was made in 1560 and knew that between the Quarter Boys the words, 'For our time is a very shadow that passeth away' were engraved on it. We waited patiently to see the Quarter Boys strike before going into the church. Our entrance was much more dignified than that of the Warrenders on Jon and Penny's first Sunday in Rye.

It was fortunate that the Gay Dolphin was near the church, but it was a silent and breathless trio that hurried into the big porch just as the two golden cherubs by the unusual clock overhead struck the first stroke of eleven. Jon ran his fingers round the inside of his collar and Penny felt that her face was as red as her hair as they slipped into a pew just as the choir entered.

The Gay Dolphin Adventure

We appreciated this beautiful building, particularly the soaring arches rising in lofty splendour. I tried to imagine where the Warrenders would have sat, and then, like Jon, could not take my eyes away from the majestic eighteen-foot pendulum. However, I could understand 'some mathematical problems connected with the swing' that he is trying to work out being banished abruptly from his thoughts when he realises 'in a wild panic' that he has lost the treasure clue. I was relieved that I did not have to share Jon's agonies.

Our visit was in December, which was mild and warm, and we mingled with the crowds in the town alight with Christmas decorations and the narrow streets thronged with people. Our exploration took us to a small crowded bookshop where we squeezed in, and where Mr Saville had told us he often stood in summer months watching the children picking up his books, discussing them and him, never knowing who was listening to them. I found his books, but on looking over my shoulder, saw only Brian gazing down at what I held. Brian was happy for this to be a Lone Pine honeymoon, and my enthusiasm on our explorations seemed to have infected him as well, as he was more than happy to pose for a photograph in the Gun garden looking for flying saucers.

Reluctant though we were to leave Rye, we wanted to visit Camber Castle and soon realised that the distances that Jon and Penny walk are quite great. We were pleased to have our car to assist us. We were disappointed to find that the castle, with its gently scalloped walls sitting isolated in its sea of green, was fenced, so that we could not climb to Jon and Penny's vantage point, look down and maybe see a large bulky-bodied artist, unsuitably attired in a check costume, being bettered by a black Scottie dog. We did, however, walk around the perimeter and were aware of the vast openness of the marshland that was so unlike anywhere else that I had ever been. I spotted the wall that faced south and imagined that just behind there was where Jon and Penny had their picnic and discussed the clue. For me, the most exciting part of this castle's history was that it had been the meeting place of the Warrenders and the Mortons.

As they lie in the hot sun Penny describes her feelings to Jon:

'There's the sea about a thousand miles away and the wind all the time, and the sheep and the bees and that noise of insects something like the noise in a shell.'
'Midsummer hum they call it,' Jon murmured.
'Of course it's silly and babyish,' Penny whispered, 'but somebody told me when I was little that only those who can see fairies hear this music.'

The Gay Dolphin Adventure

They are in complete accord with each other. I realised that I was standing where Miss Ballinger was painting when she is baited by Dickie, Mary and Mackie. As I shivered slightly in the fast-dying December day, I knew that I would have to come in the summer to sense the aroma of summer magic. Whilst walking round I was reminded of a brilliant interchange between Jon and Penny during their search for earthen vessels.

Penny looked at him solemnly. 'Oh, Jon!' she said softly, 'you've no idea how I *admire* you when you speak like that!'
'Like what?' he said suspiciously.

'Like—"it is safe to assume that the clue suggests,"' and she laughed and fled from him round the keep.

The Gay Dolphin Adventure

Whilst Jon is making notes, Penny asks, 'Am I looking too absolutely heavenly?'
The quote continues:

While he had been talking she had reached round and picked a small bunch of lilac scabious and was now strewing her face with the flowers.
'You'll always look more beautiful with your face covered, darling!' Jon retorted.

The Gay Dolphin Adventure

Is this not just the sort of conversation that children have with their contemporaries?

We walked, just as Jon and Penny do, along the soft white sands of Camber, which, like the Marsh, were wide and seemed to go on forever. We trailed seaweed in the light breeze and tried to guess where Jon was lying when Penny encourages a crab to attach itself to her cousin's toe without success. I fully appreciated this humour as a young reader and still do.

Before returning to Rye we paid a brief visit to Rye Harbour, as, like the Lone Piners, we had looked in this direction from the vantage point of Penny's wall. We found that it had a surprising variety of water craft, many of which were pulled up onto the mud. As the terrain looked so uninviting we contented ourselves with looking at the more sophisticated yachts at rest at their moorings and I had my photograph taken beside a particularly fine one. It was a peaceful place, with the silence only broken by the occasional tap of a burgee as it clinked against its mast.

Mr Saville's descriptions are always part of the story and never a lengthy paragraph to be skimped over to get to the more exciting dialogue. He is particularly good at describing the wind on the green and white marshes, and the dark dykes that appear so suddenly—where you need to watch your footing if you do not want to have wet feet.

We looked towards Winchelsea and knew that this would be the next place we would visit. Mr Saville always said that it was different from Rye and I wanted to see what he meant. And besides, there was Jon's mill to be found. Indeed, although Rye and Winchelsea tend to be mentioned in the same breath, and both stand on hills, were deserted by the sea and are Cinque Ports, they are as different as any two towns can be: Rye with its hotchpotch maze of streets and some buildings seemingly perched so precariously close to the cliff edge that I wonder they do not fall off—Winchelsea, all serenity and space with wide grass-verged streets and the whole town built in squares by order of Edward I.

On leaving Rye for Winchelsea we realised that we were on the road that Jon and Penny take when Jon leaves for the meeting at 'the old mill at six' and wants a quicker journey than that by road. He remarks to Penny, 'I could just hop over this black fence …'

'"And fall in that ditch," Penny interrupted with relish.' We drove slowly up the steep hill into Winchelsea and realised what Mr Saville meant. It was mellow and peaceful on this our first visit and we hardly saw anyone, but did go into a brightly lit shop named Manna

Plat where we purchased extra Christmas gifts for each other. There were no steep cobbled streets but elegant symmetrical squares dominated by a large church. As we walked around the quiet town it was hard to realise that Winchelsea was once a leading port. In 1250, a tempest had broken and a huge sea had destroyed half the houses and silted up the harbour. In 1287, another storm had obliterated the remains of the old port. After many years of silting, Winchelsea and Rye stand quiet and serene and it is easy to forget their turbulent history. We gazed across to Rye from the look-out where Penny unexpectedly says to Jon 'I want to get home.'

> '… I suddenly remembered home … Your home, Jon, and mine, too. The Dolphin, I mean, and the way the cats sit in the sunshine on the wall at the end of Trader's Street, and the way the cobbles hurt your feet through sandals—don't you dare laugh at me, Jon. If you do I'll never forgive you …'
>
> The Elusive Grasshopper

We were not returning to Rye yet because we were going to find Jon's mill. This proved to be easy, as it stood proud and tall as in the old photograph that Mr Saville had given us. It was exactly like the description in the book.

> Jon followed the directions and soon found that the town finished as abruptly to the north as it did to the south, although on this side the slope of the hill was more gradual. He went through a gate into an elm-fringed field, climbed a stile and found himself looking over flat country which stretched away into the blue distance of the Sussex Weald. The field before him fell away sharply in one place, and at the topmost ridge of the hill stood the gaunt, black ruin of a mighty windmill. There were no sails on this mill, and from where he was standing the sky showed through the timbers of the roof. This was certainly an old mill, if not *the* old mill …
>
> The Gay Dolphin Adventure

Walking up 'the rotting steps' just as Jon did

I climbed its steps carefully, just as Jon does. I had not expected to be able to listen to Slinky talking to Val although I would have liked to have done so, but as I stood on the steps and gazed around the peaceful, deserted countryside, I realised why Mr Saville had chosen this setting for a secret meeting. It was hard to imagine that this was the mill that Mr Saville had made famous and was known to so many children all over the world. I am so pleased now that I have this precious old photograph (see p38) together with ones that we took ourselves, as sadly the mill was blown down in a gale in the late 1980s.

Mr Saville took a great interest in the mill's restoration and The Gay Dolphin Adventure *made it famous. He visited it throughout the year as it was close to his Winchelsea home and he particularly liked to see the lambs in springtime. He was concerned when he knew that I had climbed the old steps as they were in a poor state of repair, but he understood that I wanted to climb them. Below: Writing by Malcolm Saville on the back of the photograph*

"Jon's mill". Winchelsea now repaired by the National Trust 1980

I am thankful that Mr Saville was never to know of its demise. He did, however, send me a photograph, dated 1980 (reproduced above), of the mill showing scaffolding around it, when renovations were being carried out by the National Trust. Although many of his letters to me were concerning the work that I was doing for him, often he would add little asides and descriptions that he knew I would enjoy, such as when he mentioned the bright May day of 1976 where 'the new lambs are in fine fettle round Jon's mill'.

Driving along the Levels to Winchelsea beach, we saw many bungalows, but, of course, knew that we could not find Miss Ballinger's home as this had been burned in the fire that occurs at the end of *The Gay Dolphin Adventure*. We walked along the sturdy wall and enjoyed the breezy openness and a perfect cloudless sky. Feeling hungry, we went to the Ship Inn in search of food. This was empty of customers, but the proprietor made some sandwiches for us. He told us that, although he had only been there in residence for a few months, he had known the area a long time. He asked whether we knew that the sea had once broken through the shingle wall many years ago. We nodded and he bade us sit down as he said that he had something to show us. He came back with a small pile of faded photographs showing a row of homes being swamped by the sea when it broke through, and the original Ship Inn which was also washed away at that time. This certainly enabled us to look for Miss Ballinger's bungalow and it seemed incredible to us that these properties could ever have been built there so at the mercy of an angry sea. As soon as we returned home we informed Mr Saville of our find. He wrote, 'I've never been in the new "Ship Inn" but the photograph you saw was, I think, the row of Coastguard Cottages which existed long before the first bungalow was built. I spent several summer holidays as a *very* young schoolboy in one of these cottages.' He had not seen these photographs and was pleased that we had found such a surprise for him that was part of *The Gay Dolphin* story. The unseasonal warm December days were short and, as I looked at the twinkling lights now beginning to show on Rye's hill, I knew that I wanted to go home to what I would always think of as the Gay Dolphin.

All holidays come to an end, but not, in this case, before we had found a telephone box. My coins dropped noisily and I pressed button 'A' and was soon speaking to Mr Saville at his home in Winchelsea. Excitedly, I told him of the wonderful places that he had described which, with the help of his marvellous photographs, we had now discovered for ourselves. How perfect it had all been and how could I ever thank him enough for giving me so much? He laughed and said that that was easy. He invited us to visit him in the summer and to show him the photographs we had taken. Of course I promised that we would, and we did, as described in Chapter I.

In his books Mr Saville has a variety of interesting villains, none more so than the gloriously named and attired Miss Ballinger and my own favourite, Mr Grandon, aptly named 'Slinky' by Penny. I have a particular fondness for Slinky, especially when his sensitive nature shows through and he explains to Penny and the twins that since he was two years old he has been strangely moved by roads that led to the sea, and that his mother was with him the first time he saw the sea and he remembers its smell. I, too, am a sea person and have a particularly childish thrill every time I see the sea, especially on the occasion of the first seaside holiday in any year. After Penny sees Slinky for the first time outside Hastings station getting into a taxi with Miss Ballinger, she shrewdly describes him to Jon:

> 'Anyway, he had very black sloping eyebrows, if you know what I mean, and a very small sloping black moustache thing on his lip ... I tell you what I think he is, Jon ... I think he's in a band somewhere and I don't think he's English either ... I tell you another thing, Jon. I think that if he hadn't been carrying her bags he'd have been waving his arms about. That's the sort of man he was,' she finished triumphantly.
>
> The Gay Dolphin Adventure

As he gives a little bow to Jon and Penny when they are introduced by Mrs Warrender, Penny was probably right. The Lone Pine books containing Slinky and Miss Ballinger are bettered by their presence, and also that of attractive Val who lets us know that Jon and David are growing up even though they are, as yet, unaware of this.

At Mr Saville's request I contacted many of his fans over the years and the general consensus of opinion was that *The Gay Dolphin Adventure* was the favourite Lone Pine story. I am in agreement with this. Maybe the warmth of this story is due in part to its publication seeming quite a family affair, with the endpapers drawn by David Saville and the dedication simply 'For My Wife'. Bertram Prance's dustwrapper, showing the Warrenders and the Mortons beside a fisherman's hut, safely marooned on a hill beyond Winchelsea beach, immediately captures the interest of the young reader and is an invitation to open the book. The sombre darkness of the scene, the bleakness of the windswept sky scurrying over an angry sea, which has submerged the Levels, made me shiver with anticipation. I have always felt that this is the most atmospheric of all the Lone Pine dustwrappers. I often wonder whether Bertram Prance had read the story.

Forty years ago I saw this book on a dilapidated shelf outside a second-hand bookshop in Southbourne. My fastidious father sniffed disdainfully when I said that I wanted it and urged me to walk past the shop. I remember my reluctance as we continued and then I halted, and said that I really *did* want this book. I have never forgotten that hot summer day when I asserted my independence and emerged triumphant from the shop clutching my purchase. I still treasure it to this day and, although rather battered now, it is still intact.

In a letter received from Mr Saville prior to our visit, he had showed concern. 'I hope you won't be disappointed with Rye. It's almost at its best in winter when it's not full of tourists.' Rye was perfect in winter, just as it was to be when bathed in summer sunshine. It cast a spell that will remain forever.

This is my own gay dolphin given to me by AA over fifty years ago.

Chapter IV

Jane's Country Year

'I can't remember whether you ever read *Jane's Country Year* but if you did not, I'm sure you would like it.' These are the unassuming words that Mr Saville wrote to me in January 1975. This was his favourite book of all the ones that he wrote and in his quiet way he was immensely proud of it.

The book tells the story of ten-year-old Jane, who lives in London. Her life is changed when she becomes ill after getting wet one day on her way back from school. She spends time in hospital before returning home, where she is compelled to stay many hours in bed. Although Jane improves, she does not completely recover and her doctor speaks these fateful words: 'A year in the country is what this young lady needs and what she must have. Fresh air, good food, no school till after Easter and plenty of running wild.' It is arranged that Jane will have a year with her Aunt Kate and Uncle William at Moor End Farm.

Jane's Country Year describes all the things that she sees and learns in each particular month of her happy life on the farm as she returns to good health. The book is half story and half nature guide, and is written with loving detail. Enthusiasm pervades all of Mr Saville's books and into this story he also put his heart. Its front cover is shown on the front of this book.

'*The ducklings were allowed to run free on the lawn. They grew quickly.*'
(*Illustration from* Jane's Country Year)

Jane learns many things about the basics of farm and country life, such as the importance of closing farm gates and of having respect for all living things. She sees robins making a nest (which in all my years I have never done), and the small mound of fresh earth which is the work of a busy mole as he searches for worms under the surface of the ground. She sees her first hedgehog, whose form of protection is to roll itself into a ball, and learns how it hibernates during the winter and only wakes in the warmth of spring. She takes an interest in the birds that she sees, which include the swift which can fly faster than any other British bird and is unusual as it rarely lands on the ground and catches flies and insects whilst in the air. As the months go by, Jane also learns about wild flowers and trees and the importance of weather to the success or failure of the farmer's crop, as well as how to recognise many birds by their plumage and their call. But we are also always made to remember that she is a little girl who wants to be the first to run over fresh snow and is deliciously frightened of the old witch.

At the end of each chapter is a section called 'What Jane Saw' where Mr Saville adds nature notes and also describes his own feelings about each month. In May, he writes:

> May is the month of flowers and bird song. The happy month. The 'merry, merry month', when everything is growing fast and every lane and field and hedge is bursting with new life. In May we are on the edge of summer and perhaps there is no other month in the year when there is so much to see in the country.

In the notes Mr Saville often gives more detailed background information about the sights Jane has seen. The chapter for the midsummer month of July, for example, describes how the sheep are sheared:

> The men who did the clipping sat on one end of a form and another man brought a sheep which they dragged on to the form on its back. Then the man with the clippers started clipping at the wool very quickly until the wool, which is called a fleece, was pulled off like an overcoat.

In 'What Jane Saw', Mr Saville adds:

> A female lamb is called a ewe lamb and the male a ram or tup. Lambs are weaned from their mothers at about five months and are then called hoggs—a tup hogg or a ewe hogg—until their first shearing at fourteen to sixteen months old.

When Jane has been at Moor End Farm for a few days she goes out exploring, taking Sally, her uncle and aunt's golden cocker spaniel, with her for company. They climb a little knoll which is crowned by three mighty trees, and she sits on a tree stump with Sally leaning against her knee while they both regain their breath. This is where she meets Richard Herrick, a boy of about her own age, and his father, who is the local rector. After an introduction, the rector says to Jane, 'We must get to know each other and you must come to the rectory and

'Five girls and two boys were standing on the bottom rung of the gate. "Happy birthday, Janey!" they called.' (Illustration from Jane's Country Year)

'Jane had a turn on the binder.' (Illustration from Jane's Country Year)

see the rest of the family whenever you want to.' Jane's growing friendship with Richard runs throughout the book. In August, George the farm worker informs Jane that August Monday is an important day as there is the Flower Show and cricket. What he does not tell her is that there are also sports, and it is only when Richard says he has put her down for three races that she learns of this. She does not do very well in the 100 yards sprint nor in the egg and spoon race. However, Richard does all that he can to encourage her to win the 220 yards race and she knows that she will do anything he asks of her and will never let him down. The readers are willing Jane to win and almost racing alongside her in an effort of even greater encouragement. Mr Saville, in his own clever way, builds up the tension even though we feel that he will surely let her win.

The chill of the month of November seeps through the pages with these words:

> The window was open a little and as the sun crept up the fiery sky Jane smelled the lovely scent of bonfire smoke. She remembered her uncle lighting the fire two evenings ago and it had burned slowly ever since. When she got back from school yesterday she had run out into the garden and watched the thin plume of blue smoke rising into the misty dusk and wondered how anything as damp as this mass of rubbish could burn so steadily. Then she put her hands into the smoke and felt the warmth of the fire underneath but when she got back to the kitchen Mrs Watson wrinkled her nose with disgust and told her that her hair would smell of bonfire for days.

From 'What Jane Saw' in November we learn:

November is often a damp and dreary month and although the days are short there is still plenty to see in the countryside for those who take the trouble.

Jane had a lesson in Astronomy—which is the name given to the study of the heavens—from Richard this month. She saw the *Pole Star* or *North Star* and the *Great Bear* or *Plough* and anyone can find and recognize these on a clear night. The Pole Star is always in the north.

The story ends with the joy of Christmas time with church on Christmas morning and the crib telling its wonderful story, before a turkey lunch and the excitement of presents. Richard's present to Jane is exactly right and something that she will treasure forever. 'He had drawn and coloured for her two maps—the first of Moor End farmhouse and garden and the other of the country round about—and Jane could see at once that they must have taken him weeks to finish. There had never been a present like this!'

Jane is happy to return home with her parents and her gift of Sheila, the puppy that she has chosen from Sally's litter, as a constant reminder of her year in the country. She is content in the knowledge that she will come back to the farm and to a warm and loving welcome from her aunt and uncle, Richard, and the many friends that she has made.

Jane's Country Year has a timeless appeal for anyone with an interest in natural history and country ways. It is a celebration of a way of life now largely gone—methods of farming,

'The trees were roaring and shaking in the wind as Jane was blown down the hill.'
(Illustration from Jane's Country Year*)*

for instance, having hugely changed—but also describes pleasures that are unaltered today, such as finding the first celandines or hearing church bells. Mr Saville wrote this book to impart his love of nature's cycle and in recognition of the growing number of children who did not live in the country, who had never seen a sheep or a cow, nor peered inquisitively beneath the hedgerows searching for wild flowers. For many years Mr Saville had been increasingly concerned at the swathes of countryside lost forever in the name of progress. Running parallel with the enchanting story of Jane is the knowledge imparted by Mr Saville from his own years of observation of the countryside and reading about its history and folklore. All of Mr Saville's books can be educational but *Jane's Country Year* is especially packed with interesting details and every reader will learn something from it. I did not know, for example, that the rowan tree was planted to guard against witchcraft, nor did I know that it is said that the ancient Druids particularly worshipped mistletoe.

When I was out with Mr Saville, it was usually because we were going to visit a particular location, but he always made me aware of the flora and fauna around us by pointing out a bird that he recognised or a small, brave wild flower peeping from between stones in a barren terrain. He would insist that I remember these walks because, he said, one day the countryside might not be there. I could hardly envisage then what he was saying. Now, so many years later, I see that this is coming true.

Mr Saville's words bring thoughts to his older readers like me who will be pleased with the opportunity to rekindle memories.

I was brought up in the country amidst a cluster of houses surrounded by cornfields and a smallholding where I watched a family of pigs in their sty. From my bedroom window I saw horses galloping freely in their large field.

My mother's friend was a farmer's wife and when I was young, I spent happy holidays on this farm. What I recall most is watching the sheep being sheared, just as Jane did, and I remember that their thin little bodies were blotched red where the clippers had caught them. I also recall roller skating around the large table in the kitchen where the metal wheels made a noise on the stone floor. I keep up the family tradition of the yearly picking of blackberries, and choose a sunny afternoon when the air is warm and mellow, just before autumn comes. There is a quiet satisfaction in picking this fruit, which we savour eating all the year round.

Also from those days, I recall my mother mixing a smelly meal for our fowls and trudging with her through all weathers to where they were housed, when we were greeted excitedly by them. My earliest memories are of being in my outdoor playpen, which was their wired-in enclosure, wriggling into the dust just as the chickens did. Like Jane's adopted ducks, they had names and personalities. Captain, of whom my father was inordinately proud, would help him round up our small fowl family after their hour of daily freedom when they were allowed to roam in our rear garden. Captain was also the one always deferred to by his companions. Bumblefoot of the sweet disposition was lame, and went to my mother for protection and to ensure that she never went hungry in the scramble at the food trough. Country girls accept that chickens are not pets but are there to feed us. I do not recall it being a problem when we ate them and my father commented on the tenderness of the texture and the succulent taste.

Jane's Country Year was first published in 1946, when Mr Saville with his family lived at Westend Farmhouse, Wheatonhampstead, St Albans. This was rented from a farmer, Robert Dickinson, and they lived there for several years. The endpapers at the beginning of the book which show a plan of Moor End Farm are based on Westend Farmhouse. When I asked him whether living there helped him with this story, he said that it did.

Throughout the book there are many illustrations by Bernard Bowerman. I particularly like the one of the picnic for Jane's birthday which is all warmth and summer sunshine. In sharp contrast to this is the cosy scene with the Christmas tree, and people sitting in the glow of the firelight away from winter's chill.

The Dedication is 'For Jane Norris (the Jane I know)'. I asked Mr Saville about this real Jane and whether she had played an important part in the writing of the story. He said that she had and that she had been ill when she was a young girl and had had to stay in hospital and was off school for a long time. Jane's father had known Mr Saville since school days and Mr Saville saw Jane in her formative years, as the two families were friends. Mr Saville had an avuncular affection for her and from what he told me I am sure she was very much like her namesake.

She is possibly not the only real character in the book. I have always felt that Mr Saville put a facsimile of himself into many of his stories and in *Jane's Country Year* this person is perhaps the local rector, Mr Herrick. The patience which Mr Herrick shows when describing country life to Jane mirrors Mr Saville's kindly nature when he gave similar explanations to me. He tells Jane, for example, that hundreds of years ago churches were built on a hill where possible, as they were God's house and must stand above everything else in a village. This was just the sort of thing Mr Saville might have said.

The copy of *Jane's Country Year* that I have is a second enlarged edition dated 1947. A reprint only twelve months after it was first published shows the book's popularity and how well it had been received.

At the end of the book, all the goodbyes have been said and Uncle William is ready to drive Jane with her puppy Sheila and her parents to the train station. As the car starts, Jane turns to look through the rear window; she knows that her country year is over. I asked Mr Saville whether he meant Jane to return to the farm and if that was why Jane's father decides that he would like to be a farmer. He was pleased when I mentioned this as he said it is what he would wish to happen.

The book ends with these words:

They were moving now. The house was behind them. Smaller, smaller. A dip in the road as it crossed the common and Moor End had vanished.
    Jane brushed her fingers across her eyes and then turned to smile at her mother.

Mr Saville put all of himself into his writing and never more so than in this book when he revelled in the joy and excitement of the unfolding of the seasons which he loved so well. *Jane's Country Year* is original in its construction and a classic in its own right. It will leave a lasting impression on all who read it.

Chapter V

Holidays

Everyone who becomes a Lone Piner (which is what Mr Saville hoped all his readers would be) will think about visiting the places that he talked about. People who live in the south of England will want to go to Rye. People who, like me, live in the central part of the country, will, I am sure, badger their parents to take them to Shropshire as I did. Over the years I was to become familiar with the Long Mynd and the surrounding country, first with my parents and then with Brian. I learned to love its gentle rolling grandeur and could understand Peter's unhappiness when she discovers that she and her father are to leave Hatchholt to live in Hereford with Uncle Micah. Dickie also becomes homesick, particularly during the summer term at school and wishes that he could be at Witchend.

> To Dickie, away on the Dorset coast, the term had not been so good. He detested cricket and, although nobody knew it, the summer term made him home-sick. Not badly, because Dickie was really a tough little boy, but just enough to nag at him sometimes, particularly when he woke early and thought not only of his home in Hertfordshire, but of Witchend and the stream that came chattering so happily down the valley, and of Mary and Mackie and David and Peter and the others.
>
> *The Neglected Mountain*

Not everyone in the books enjoys their home surroundings. Jenny is frightened of the gaunt mass that is the Stiperstones and even Peter finds it eerie. The gypsies explain to Peter that 'There is much that is bad on that mountain' and they shun it. As I tend to be more of Jenny's nature, I also shudder at the sight of this place and find it menacing.

In every foreword to the Lone Pine books it is clearly stated which locations are real places that can be visited and which are imaginary; however, Mr Saville also sometimes used real places disguised under a different name, and he did not always make it clear where these could be found. When I first decided to visit as many of the real places as I could, I was considerably older than the average Lone Pine reader, being in my early twenties, but that did not stop me. In the course of time, Brian and I had many of what we were to call Lone Pine holidays and outings. This chapter describes some that we enjoyed and that Mr Saville particularly took pleasure in hearing about.

As I have said, real locations are often given imaginary names and features in the stories; these can be found in the endpapers of the books. Wherever Brian and I went we took the relevant story and used these endpapers as our initial map. It was fun finding the locations that we were told were real places, but even more rewarding to find the ones that had been given a different name even if they were often only thinly disguised. Mr Saville said that if I wanted a treasure hunt, he would give me one; and, as all the clues were in the books, he would not tell me where the real locations were until after I returned home. However much I cajoled, he would not be moved from this and he knew that as he had

The photographs on the front of this postcard were taken by Mr Saville.

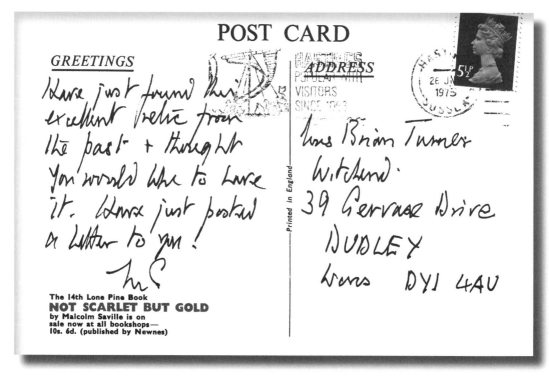

thrown down the gauntlet, I would pick it up. He made me work hard whilst on holiday!

My visits to the Stiperstones had always been in summer, although a true Lone Piner should have seen it with rain and mist. I knew, however, that this would be dangerous, and I always wanted to enjoy my days out in Lone Pine country. The last time that I was at the summit of this mountain was on an idyllic summer day. I embarked on the steep climb which was initially through sparse heather, and as the tracks became more rugged the Devil's Chair came into view.* There were the grim outcrops of rock evilly beckoning as, in almost frightened fascination, I drew closer to them. Standing on the top, feeling the hard stones through my soft summer shoes, I surveyed the harsh world around me and knew that Mr Saville had probably stood and walked in the place where I was.

Brian and I sat, breathing heavily, until we were able to appreciate our surroundings. We then lay back on the uncomfortable terrain, letting the hot sun beat down on us. I was aware of the stillness, as there was no wind, and the gaudy blue sky seemed close enough to reach up and touch. I closed my eyes. All was quiet until I heard a rustling before me. When I looked up, coming towards me was a little dog, so much like Mackie that I thought at first that it must be he. As he came closer I saw that it was not Mackie. He seemed all alone, and after sniffing my hand he ran off and I wondered whether I should see him again. We were reluctant to leave this wild place but finally started our descent where we met a few other people picking bilberries. Like the Lone Piners we joined them, staining our hands, and tasting the sweet fruit which had grown and ripened on these slopes, just as it would have done when Mr Saville had been there. Coming out of the heather and running towards me in recognition, was the little dog. I was pleased to see him reunited with his owner and scampering through the heather chasing butterflies, just as Mackie would have done.

As we had not taken provisions on our explorations, we were as hungry as Dickie would have been, but after a short search we soon found a patch of grass, partially secluded by bushes. We ate our sandwiches with relish as we gazed at the endless rolling hills stretching out before us until they kissed the brilliant azure sky. The few people that we had encountered had drifted away. As I turned to look at the rugged mountain hard against my back, I mused that maybe Mr Saville had once visited this tiny clearing, and perhaps had been given inspiration for a Lone Pine story.

We arrived at Barton Beach, with its post office and general store, a tiny village cringing below the menacing mountain—from which it takes its real name, Stiperstones village—and so important in Jenny's world.

'The mountain beats them. It's—it's too clever for them. It's too cruel for them. It wants to be left alone and maybe when it is left alone everything is all right round here … And maybe it's because those of us who live here know that's what the mountain wants that we try to keep away from it. I thought of a name for it the other day. It isn't that all this country is lonely like the Long Mynd. It's neglected. I call it the neglected mountain …'

The Neglected Mountain

*See the photographs opposite and on the back cover of this book.

Of course, I had to go inside the shop and experience its claustrophobic atmosphere. It was not Jenny with her welcoming smile nor her indomitable stepmother who inquired as to my wants, so I came outside into the sunshine, disappointed.

> Barton was looking its rather shabby best on the same morning that Harry Sentence arrived in Bringewood Chase. There was nothing picturesque about Barton's only street. There was a gloomy little church, an inn and one shop over which lived a fifteen-year-old girl called Jenny Harman. Her father owned the shop, which was also the post office … Mr Harman's shop sold almost everything. It was festooned with goods hanging from the ceiling and with cards of other goods such as packets of aspirin, tonic powders for dogs and cats, and cheap ball-point pens all hanging from strings and wires which criss-crossed the shop from unexpected directions and were a constant danger to taller customers. The door was up two steps and was fitted with an old bell on a spring that jangled a warning when a customer arrived. There was a stale-smelling telephone box at the back of the shop, a small counter behind a metal grille where post office business was conducted, and other counters piled with weekly papers, sweets, cigarettes and packeted food.
>
> The Secret of the Gorge

Barton Beach 'General HARMAN Stores' with adjoining inn

We did not look for Seven Gates Farm as Mr Saville had told me many years ago that it did not exist. It was one of the few of his locations that was purely imaginary. The idea had germinated when he had seen a property with a number of gates not in Shropshire but far away to the south. The winding road, leading round the base of the Stiperstones and always

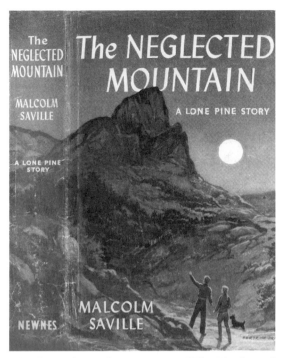

The first edition dustwrapper of The Neglected Mountain: *illustration by Bertram Prance*

dominated by them, had been travelled many times by Mr Saville. I always had an air of expectancy when I knew that I was retracing his steps.

It was easy for us to make day trips to Shropshire, but once, to save the travel back and forth, we hired a caravan at Hopton Castle. This was not one of the modern luxurious homes on wheels that many people have today, but a most basic small van sited in a corner of a farmer's field. Provisions were obtained from the farmer's wife on a daily basis which reminded us of similar visits paid by the Mortons to Ingles Farm. We visited Clun, one of the 'quietest places under the sun', as A E Housman describes it.

It certainly lived up to this reputation because it was a most peaceful place. We stood in the recesses of the unusual bridge

This is how Ingles Farm (Hamperley) looks today.

and, like Dickie, threw bits of paper into the river below, and watched them emerge from the other side of the bridge. Whilst on the bridge we saw a sight that the Lone Piners missed: a young girl with her pet goose waddling along after her. We looked at the houses in the main street and found the one which we were certain was the model for Keep View with a central front door which had coloured glass in it (Keep View is the small guest house kept by Agnes' sister where the Lone Piners stay in *The Secret of Grey Walls*):

> Keep View was a very ordinary and rather ugly house. It was not old, but there are tens of thousands of boarding houses like it all over the country, particularly at the seaside. The stairs were steep and led straight down into the hall, which smelt of furniture polish and linoleum. There was some coloured glass in the front door, and the dining-room on the left, and what Agnes called 'the lounge' on the right.

We walked up the hill to the sturdy remains of Clun Castle, which becomes HQ3. Time seemed to have stood still and I could imagine Mr Saville there, deciding that this was where Jon and Penny would be enrolled as members of the Lone Pine Club. We strolled around the small town and I remembered that Mr Saville told me that he had once found a café in Clun called The Gay Dolphin where 'the woman had so named it for all the right reasons'.

We were much younger then, and walked extensively. On our search over the hills, we believed that we had found the original of the Plough and Harrow, where Mr Cantor takes the twins and Mackie for lunch. It was certainly old enough: 'From the outside it looked as if it was falling to pieces and the old signboard creaked eerily in the wind as they stood wondering whether anyone had ever ventured over the threshold before.' When we told Mr Saville, he said that it sounded as if we had found the right place, but that after so many years it was hard for him to remember. This came as quite a shock until I recalled that he had written *The Secret of Grey Walls* over thirty years previously. With Mr Saville having so many books to his credit, perhaps I should not have expected him to keep in mind everything that he had once written. It is a sobering thought for me to realise today that it is over thirty years since I explored this countryside and I doubt that I would now be able to find that old inn. Later we walked along Offa's Dyke, which we found most impressive especially when we thought of the primitive tools that would have been used when it 'was built by an army of slaves over a thousand years ago'. Although we looked carefully, there were no sheep with AD painted on their sides to be seen, alive or dead, nor did we find any flint arrowheads, but we did discover lonely buildings which could have been Grey Walls or the farm Bury Fields. We bore in mind the description in *The Secret of Grey Walls* of the house of the title when trying to find it:

> … there was no sign of life, but the walls were too high for them to see over into the garden or grounds. The windows in the upper floors seemed to be uncurtained and stared at them with blank eyes. The chimney stacks might have been made for show. The great double gates with the little sliding wicket were closed …

The gaily coloured dustwrapper of *The Secret of the Gorge* belies the sombre setting of this story, which is in and around Leintwardine. This is:

> … on the borders of the counties of Shropshire and Hereford, where the river Teme is joined by its tributary the Clun. A few miles from the village the lovely river runs unexpectedly into a limestone gorge overshadowed by trees and strong-smelling elders, thick with creamy blossom in the summer, and heavy with purple fruit a few months later. Through this gorge the river runs smooth, fast and deep for half a mile until it swirls under an old bow bridge.

We entered the gorge, which was wild and secluded, and found it incredibly hard work struggling through the thick undergrowth, but we did manage to look for cave entrances amongst the limestone cliffs. We examined at close quarters the great water pipes from Elan Valley which crossed the river. They brought back vivid memories of a previous adventure that we had had when we had climbed onto an inspection bridge crossing the River Severn to look at the same pipeline, not realising that we were on closed circuit television. It was not long before a warden had arrived in his jeep demanding to know what we were doing. We had to convince him that we were not members of the Irish Republican Army (who were very active at that time), before we withdrew somewhat sheepishly but on friendly terms. I much prefer the shallow waters under the bridge at Leintwardine which is the setting for the fictitious Bringewood Chase. Sometimes we had a meal close by in what could have been the original of the Evening Star, as it was far too pleasant to be the Two Bells.

In *The Neglected Mountain* Mr Morton splits the Lone Piners up into pairs and sends them on different journeys to Bishop's Castle, where they will all meet to go to the fair. These are the orders that he gives to his twins: 'Walk down to Onnybrook at once … and catch the 11.50 bus to Ludlow. At the top of Broad Street, on the left-hand side just below the Butter Cross, is a café. At any time after 12.45 go in and ask for Mrs Martin and you will receive something to your advantage.' (This is a meal of their choice which has been prepaid by their father.)

> Macbeth liked buses and was no trouble on Mary's lap, so the journey, on the route they knew so well, was uneventful. They never tired of Ludlow, which their father had told them was one of the most unspoiled towns in England …

We visited the castle at Ludlow and gazed at the river winding far below. We looked around the town where there were a number of bookshops, the contents of which we appreciated. Like the twins, we saw Broad Street and the Butter Cross. We had tea in a nearby café, so I suppose we also had something to our advantage, but not unfortunately paid for by Mr Morton. We explored the very different Bishop's Castle, which at that time was the smallest borough in England. Here we looked for the Rose and Crown where Jenny has a marmalade roll for dessert when she and Tom are taken out to lunch by Mr Ingles.

Our Lone Pine travels took us further afield than Shropshire, and on our first visit to

Whitby, one of the settings in *Mystery Mine*, we stayed high up on West Cliff near the Whale Bone archway, where we could look down the steep zigzag road which is incongruously named Khyber Pass. Mr Saville would have appreciated the siting of the restaurant halfway down this hill, and the Lone Piners, particularly Dickie, would have enjoyed its generous fare. On our second visit we felt in harmony with the fishing community, as we rented a small cottage on the harbour side and were always aware of the cry of the gulls and the smell of the fish.

Looking around the jumble of Whitby's quaint narrow streets, we found some that were unattractive enough to have been the original of Prospect Way.

> It is oddly named because it is not a way to anywhere, being but forty yards long. There is only one way in and no other way out. If anyone is foolish enough to linger in Prospect Way it must be admitted that there is no prospect to see, for the roofs of the houses block a view of the harbour and the East Cliff on the other side of the river. Prospect Way is a squalid and depressing backwater …

Soon we were out in the open again. We walked alongside the harbour before crossing the swing bridge to the other side of the River Esk. We found the start of the old stone steps which wind up until they reach the edge of the cliff, and we thought of the dedicated Christians many years ago toiling up these steps on their way to worship. It is so different today with mainly holiday makers in varying degrees of breathlessness moving upwards. Automatically,

Whitby Steps: '[Penny] saw the long, long flight of worn, stone steps winding up towards the church on the edge of the cliff.'

I began counting the steps; there are one hundred and ninety-nine and I thought of Penny's desperate race up these, until, as she nears the top, she meets Jon coming down.

> She raced over the bridge, turned to the left along a narrow street of old houses and then, at the end, saw the long, long flight of worn, stone steps winding up towards the church on the edge of the cliff. There were plenty of people using the steps but she was nearly at the top when she saw Jon coming down. Her heart seemed to jump into her throat and then banged away so furiously that she stopped and leaned against the iron handrail, waiting for him to come to her.

It is in the moments following this meeting that they begin to realise how much they mean to each other as Jon leads her to one of the seats near the edge of the cliff.

> Then he took her firmly by the hand—the hand with the bruised, grazed knuckles, but she hardly noticed the pain—led her up the steps and then across the churchyard to one of the seats on the edge of the cliff.
> 'Now tell me everything,' he said, still holding her hand as they sat down.
> She told him. What had happened only an hour or so ago didn't seem important now, but it was still vivid and she didn't waste any words. He hardly interrupted, but when she admitted her panic when she banged on the locked door, he loosened the grip of his fingers and looked at her hand. When he saw the bruises and the blood he did something he had never done before. Without any shyness he lifted her hand and kissed it gently. She looked at him in amazement and felt herself blushing as he then tucked his hand into her arm and giving her an odd shaky sort of smile said 'Go on, Penny. Don't leave out anything.'

I like to think that we sat on that same seat. I have always felt that *Mystery Mine* was a particularly important book for Jon and Penny. It is also the first recorded time that Penny visits Hatchholt, although I am sure that she and Jon would have done so during their exciting winter holiday at Clun. At the time of this visit Peter's maturity shows over Penny's unreasonable reaction to David and Jon's visit to the moors without them. We walked around the Abbey ruins and thought of the story of the bells that refused to leave Whitby. As Jon explains to David:

> 'There's a good story about the abbey. Sort of story that Jenny would like. When the abbey was suppressed—Henry VIII I suppose, but I'm not sure—it was dismantled. The beautiful bells were sold and ordered to be taken to London.'

(Jon supposes that the bells had to be taken down the hundred and ninety-nine steps to the harbour for their journey.)

> 'Anyway, the story goes that the bells were got safely aboard the ship, and all the people of Whitby came out of their houses and lined the harbour with awful wailings

and lamentation. The sails were unfurled and the anchor weighed as the tide ebbed. The little ship moved slowly out of the harbour and then refused to carry its sacred burden further. Although it was a summer evening and nearly dead calm the ship sank slowly and quietly beneath the gentle waves. And out there within sight of where we're standing now, the bells remain at the bottom of the sea. Sometimes, David, those bells rung by invisible hands are heard by the superstitious, or by those who can hear what others can't …'

I felt exhilarated by the bracing air of the nearby moors. We found the Roman Road; we did not so much walk on it as jump from one worn stone to another, being particularly careful not to suffer Harriet's fate:

Philip Sharman puffed at his pipe.
'It's more or less in its original state, Harriet. Most of the stones must be part of the old paving although I agree that the road would have to be more level for the legions to march along it.'

Mary and Harriet follow him as he steps on to the road and that's when 'Harriet slipped on one of the stones and fell heavily.' Peter and Sharman examine her foot. 'Bad luck,' Sharman said. 'You've sprained it, Harriet, but I'm sure you haven't broken anything.'

The road stretched away before us like a mouthful of teeth with lots of gaps. I closed my eyes and was transported back to many years ago; I could almost hear the rhythmic marching of the legions proudly carrying their golden eagles aloft. History had always been a favourite subject at school for me and I was also an avid reader. I soon discovered the Romans, who were vividly brought to life for me in a story by Rosemary Sutcliff called *The Eagle of the Ninth*. Anyone who enjoys Mr Saville's books will like this story, which was broadcast on *Children's Hour* when I was young, as others may remember.

Like the 'Doctor' in the chapter of *Mystery Mine* entitled 'Goathland', we took a scenic ride on the North Yorkshire Moors Railway. As he would have done, we sat on hard seats, but the views made up for any discomfort. When we were well into our journey the train slowed down and finally stopped. None of the passengers seemed unduly perturbed at first, but after about ten minutes many became restive, and it was then that someone walked alongside and informed us that an engine some way along the track had broken down and we would have to wait until this had been removed. We followed the lead of other people and made an undignified jump onto the hard ground below, quite enjoying the tension. It was about an hour before we were told we could reboard and continue our journey and when we did eventually arrive at our destination of Grosmont, it was to much cheering. When I told Mr Saville about this he said that we were proper Lone Piners, as adventures seemed to happen to us.

I showed our holiday photographs to Mr Saville, which were taken in 1972, the first time we stayed in Yorkshire. He told me that he was particularly interested in the ones of Whitby as he had almost forgotten what it looked like. This reminded me that *Mystery Mine* was first printed in 1959 and that Mr Saville would have visited Yorkshire some time prior to this date. I told him a return visit was due to refresh his memory and that I knew the ideal guidebook for his use. It was called *Mystery Mine*!

It was only after we returned from our holiday in Yorkshire that Mr Saville told me that Goathland was the setting for Spaunton. What had completely thrown me off the scent was his use of Goathland as it really was, which had made me look elsewhere for his imaginary setting of Spaunton. He was quite gleeful that I had not worked this out and suggested that I revisit Yorkshire now that my test papers had been marked and I knew the correct answers! Mr Saville often sent me newspaper cuttings concerning places that we had both visited and which he knew would interest me. On one occasion, many years after our Yorkshire holiday, I sent him a like cutting. This was his reply: 'Thank you for letting me see the cutting about Goathland. As you know I found this little village most attractive and indeed we stayed there for a few days.' One of the great joys of a long friendship was having so many parts of our lives intertwined. I had loved Whitby from the moment I walked around the narrow old streets that I had first met in *Mystery Mine*, and I never forgot that it was Mr Saville who introduced me to yet another delightful part of my country.

I had never heard of Walberswick and Southwold until I read *Sea Witch Comes Home*. We stayed in Southwold with its immaculately kept houses and brilliant white lighthouse, which is sited at the edge of one of the many greens. It is fortunate that someone had the foresight to build this some distance from the sea, because the coastline is crumbling away. As part of the fun of our holidays was retracing Lone Pine steps, we first went to Gun Hill, just as Paul and David do, and looked at the six cannons before choosing one on which to be photographed. We gazed at the coastguards' precariously positioned lookout before walking along the High Street where Paul and David play hide and seek with Molly. We searched for the café to which she is lured and the boys forced to give her tea and toast with marmalade. As we ambled along by the sea enjoying a gentle breeze, I made a mental note to remember to ask Mr Saville how he found such fascinating places for his readers to visit. Ferry Road plays an important part in the story as the link between Southwold and Walberswick, and was also the only way to reach Yoxleys, (the house where Richard Channing is kept a prisoner by Simon Donald after his return from Holland). We often walked along the sandy road and sat in this delightful area where hundreds of pale yellow wild lupins were growing. We will always associate these flowers with this holiday, as we have never found them growing anywhere else.

It appeared that the ferry boat to Walberswick was always on the opposite side of the river to where we were and did not run to any timetable, but rather to the haphazard schedule of the ferryman, who did not seem particularly interested in his job. The boat itself was hardly more than a small dinghy and not nearly grand enough to be known as the ferry. I was rather dubious about it, particularly when we could feel the strong current of water pulling against the boat, and was relieved when the journey to the other side was over. Walberswick is a small place and almost immediately we were looking at what would have been the Miller's Cottage. The Channings' house, 'Heron's Lodge', stood 'fifty yards back from Walberswick's only street. It was the third house on the left as you entered the village from Blythburgh, which was indeed the only way by which anything on wheels could get to them ...' Coming from the ferry we counted backwards and immediately found our Heron's Lodge. It did have a weather vane, but not of a heron. We wandered around the outside, but no-one seemed to be about. Peeping through the windows, we saw signs that the owners were well equipped for living at the seaside, so maybe the Channings still lived there! We visited Walberswick on several subsequent occasions, but declined the ferry and went round by car. Of course we wanted to visit Rose's old red brick water mill that is so important in this story. We set out confidently along one of the many tracks until we were impeded from further progress by a deep dyke. Undeterred, we retraced our steps and tried again, but were always thwarted by dark black water edged with rushes and, as I stood in frustration at our inability to reach the mill, I was aware of the wild loneliness of this land. I knew that, unlike Rose, I would not wish to travel this way alone. After many attempts we were close enough to see that the sweeps of the mill had gone, but that it was still a veritable landmark in this flat marshy wilderness; we took a photograph of this solitary sentinel.

> There were two ways of getting to the old red brick water mill which, for as long as she could remember, had been one of her most secret and exciting places ...
>
> The quickest way was along the track below the great bank of sand and shingle which kept the sea from flooding the marshes. For ten minutes Rose walked south along the top of the dunes with the beach and the sea on her left. Ahead of her the gentle bow of Sole Bay curved round to the crumbling cliffs of the forgotten port of Dunwich. On her right, the wind was rustling the rushes fringing the dykes, and nearly half a mile away she saw the familiar shape of the old mill standing on a little green island in the midst of the dykes. Soon she scrambled down the bank onto the path thick with mauve sea-asters, and then crossed a narrow footbridge over a wide ditch and stepped up to the track along the top of a causeway. Within a few minutes she was again aware of the loneliness and solitude of the marsh ...
>
> There were no sweeps now on the mill which had been built in its unusual position to pump water from a wide ditch up to the higher level of a much bigger dyke which eventually found its way into the river ...

Blythburgh church is so magnificent that it is almost too big to be called a church. Because the church was built on ground higher than the surrounding country it is used, in *Sea Witch Comes Home*, by people who have been evacuated due to the Sole Bay disaster. As the twins walk down the steps of the porch into the church they are struck by its beauty.

> It was very big and warm too. Round an enormous iron stove a dozen or so toddlers were sitting on blankets spread on the stone floor listening to a woman reading them a story. Several old ladies were knitting in one of the pews and some school children were being taken round the big church by the vicar. Above the roar of the wind round the great belfry, they heard his voice as he showed them the broken brickwork of the floor by the font and the remains of an iron staple driven into one of the big stone

pillars. He was explaining that Cromwell's soldiers were believed to have stabled their horses in the church during the Civil War and the pounding of their hooves broke up the floor.

In its cool interior we saw the damage that had been perpetrated by Cromwell's soldiers. It seemed dreadful that they should have violated a sacred building in this way. We looked at the font near where Mary sees Simon Donald, and investigated until we found where he could have hidden the stolen picture in the 'big wooden box'. We almost felt sorry for him for the time that he spends being tormented by the twins. We looked at the list of curates who had served in the church and saw one of these had the fabulous name Flowerdew. When I asked Mr Saville whether this was where he had obtained his idea for the name of the character in *Rye Royal*, he said that it probably was. Apparently he often stored such items for future use in his books.

Blythburgh Church. Mr Saville particularly liked this photograph and took it with him on his many talks. He pointed out to the children to whom he was talking that I was holding my 'guide book', a copy of Sea Witch Comes Home *that is clearly visible on this photograph.*

Exploring all around Sole Bay, we found it hard to believe that Dunwich had been a great port and that this desolate area was once a thriving community. We visited Aldeburgh and Orford 'where a boat called Sea Witch was sunk at her moorings'. Having once lived by the sea, I knew only too well that one day's gentle lapping waves could be the next day's surging white-crested angry ones. It was easy to envisage how a little boat could have sunk.

Looking back, I consider it to have been a great advantage to have been a child in the days when most families, including mine, did not have television sets. My parents were avid readers, not only of library books but of their own collections, housed in bookcases in the recesses of our home. My young fingers would reach for these adult books, which I was not given to read, but rather told about instead. There was a varied collection. My mother liked gentle stories that to me sounded sad or soppy; I was more attracted to my father's choices. These included cowboy stories, many books on mountaineering, which was his great passion, and medical and geography books. What we also had in abundance were detective stories by Agatha Christie and a shelf devoted to a gentleman with the intriguing name of Sir Arthur Conan Doyle.

My father told me this man's most famous story was about a gigantic hound which was the curse of the Baskerville family who lived in an isolated house in the heart of Dartmoor. My mother reprimanded my father sharply, saying that this was not a story to be telling an impressionable young girl, and tried to turn my attention towards her books. It was to no avail, and the little that my father had told me continued to haunt me until my sweet and unsuspecting AA asked me what I wanted for my birthday. Immediately I said *The Hound of the Baskervilles*. In those days there were many bookshops; we had a fine one in Dudley called Hudsons where this book was ordered for me. After looking at its cover, my aunt checked with my mother whether she should purchase it, as she thought that it looked dreadful. On their enquiries I assured her that, yes, it was the book that I wanted, and it was not long before it was in my possession. The dustwrapper showed a terrified man running for his life, followed by a hideous hound with gleaming evil teeth in its open jaw from which a fluorescent glow issued that encompassed its head and staring eyes. My mother had been right when she thought that this was not a suitable book for a young girl and, although I never admitted it, I had many a sleepless night when I imagined that I could hear the agonies of Dartmoor ponies being sucked into the bog of the terrible Grimpen Mire. It was the words that described the hound which set upon Sir Henry Baskerville that haunt me to this day: 'A hound it was, an enormous coal black hound, but not such a hound as mortal eyes have ever seen. Fire burst from its open mouth, its eyes glowed with a smouldering glare, its muzzle and hackles and dewlap were outlined in flickering flame.' As I lay in my bed 'transfixed with terror' I thought that Jenny would agree that such words would curdle the blood.

I was given a copy of *Saucers Over the Moor* as soon as it was published in 1955, and it was almost with fascinated horror that I realised that its setting was that of *The Hound of the Baskervilles*. The Lone Piners' new friend Dan travels home from work in Plymouth on a train which crosses the moor; it is a journey of which he never tires.

> It was a grand evening but pleasantly cool as the sturdy little engine hauled its two coaches higher and higher into the heart of the Moor. Dan leaned from the window as he always did in spring and summer and watched the familiar landmarks. He knew every rushing stream now and every patch of bright green high on the brown hillsides—patches which marked the treachery of dangerous bogs. He knew the shapes of the weather-beaten slabs of granite on the tops of the tors, as the hills are called on the Moor.
>
> *Saucers Over the Moor*

It was approximately twenty years after reading these books that I was to visit Dartmoor for the first time, during a holiday when we stayed with Brian's cousin who lived in Exmouth. By this time I had explained to Mr Saville the impact that Sir Arthur Conan Doyle had had on me. He seemed greatly interested as well as amused by this, and confirmed that many of the real places in both books were the same and were still there to be found. I almost detected a secret that he was keeping from me, but he assured me that he would want to know every single thing about this holiday of mine. I was instructed to look carefully at his endpaper map in *Saucers Over the Moor* and use it as my guide. It seemed almost an afterthought when he added that I could take *The Hound of the Baskervilles* as well, but suggested that I might be happier concentrating on saucers rather than large dogs!

We drove out of Exmouth towards Exeter and were soon on the road to Ashburton. We passed through this town's narrow streets but, although we stopped and looked around, did not find 'a dark little shop in a back street' with a sign of 'CYCLE REPAIRS GEO. HONEYSETT Prop.' advertising it. We continued on our way with me balancing *Saucers Over the Moor* opened at the map, and a superb road atlas which had been presented to my father-in-law by the firm where he worked. This dear man, with whom I forged a strong bond of trust and understanding, would be so pleased that this gift to him was used by us all those years later, and indeed is still in use today. The edition that we had was dated 1957 and, as *Saucers Over the Moor* had been written just two years earlier, I felt sure that they would be compatible.

Just as the Lone Piners did, we went through Holne, and then the car climbed onto the moorland road which was as described by Mr Saville, lonely and wild enough for all sorts of exciting events to happen. I pleaded with Brian to drive slowly as I wanted to look at everything as well as follow the maps. As we descended the steep hill to Dartmeet, I thought sympathetically of Peter rushing down on a bicycle with faulty brakes. Dartmeet was a most attractive place, and we decided to stop and have our picnic there.

> The water was clear and fast running, sparkling and singing round the polished brown boulders and pebbles.
>
> 'I'm going to paddle,' Peter said suddenly. 'You can go away if you don't want to be seen with me. Come to think of it, this is something I've wanted to do all day … Here. Look after my shoes.'
>
> She squealed as the water, cold still from the bubbling springs high in the lonely moor, washed over her feet. David pretended that to paddle was childish, but it wasn't long before he joined her.
>
> *Saucers Over the Moor*

The water looked inviting, but when I tested it with my finger, it was surprisingly cold and only James, my young son who was with us, was enthusiastic about paddling. I decided that I could hardly let him go in alone and it was not long before we were all paddling. After the first shock, we enjoyed the rush of water over our toes. We then sat on some of the many boulders strewn in the water. On looking about I was only slightly disappointed that there was not anyone with a stall selling fizzy drinks and ice cream.

Continuing on our way it was not long before we came to the Hexworthy turn. I knew that King's Holt (where the Lone Piners stay for their holiday on Dartmoor) had to be between there and Two Bridges. This is clearly marked in the endpapers of *Saucers Over the Moor*. On my father-in-law's map a building called Prince Hall was shown which appeared to me to be exactly where King's Holt should be. I shouted to Brian to stop as we passed what looked like a secluded private road. It looked as if there had been a gate at some time across the entrance of the drive, which was not in a particularly good condition and was bordered on either side with a single row of trees. It seemed a long walk before we came to the house, which looked quite sad and deserted. We hesitated, but as we could not see anyone about, we decided to walk around.

When Dan's mother tells him that King's Holt has been let furnished, Dan says: 'I know that place. Didn't I tell you I'd found an owl's nest there? It's a big house. Lot of stables and old sheds at the back. There's a rough drive leads up to the house from the road and it's the loneliest place I've ever seen ...' Dan visits the house in the evenings to look for the owls who were nesting in the loft over the stables.

> King's Holt was built of the grey granite of the moor with a pillared porch in the centre facing the drive. Brown paint was peeling from the front door and the closed windows stared like lidded eyes at the spinney of whispering pines. Grass was growing in what once must have been a well-kept drive and swallows were busy about their nests under the gutters. Not all the windows were shuttered and Dan could see furniture in one of the big rooms downstairs. It had two storeys and two wings like the upper and lower strokes of a short letter E jutting out of the back.
>
> Saucers Over the Moor

Cautiously, we peeped through windows, where the rooms appeared to be furnished with what would once have been elegance, but the inside now looked old and faded, in fact, just as Mr Saville described it:

> The furniture was old-fashioned and shabby but what there was was comfortable. To the right of the stone-flagged hall was a sitting-room. Above the marble mantelpiece in here was a stuffed fox in a glass case at which Mackie barked madly, and some very curious pictures on the walls. The room smelled damp and stuffy. On the other side was a dining-room with the table laid for a meal, and next door was an enormous kitchen also with a stone floor and a fire burning in an old-fashioned range. Beyond this was a vast scullery with a door leading into the yard.
>
> Saucers Over the Moor

It was almost as if the owner had secured the house and then left. We spent some time there knowing that we had found King's Holt. On walking back down the driveway the sun shone through the trees and, where it was blocked out, caused lined shadows on the drive. I remembered Mr Saville's words when Dickie and Mary walk to the end of the drive to meet Dan: 'The sun was high now and the twins carefully stepped over each of the black barred shadows of the pine trees thrown across the drive.' Not wanting this special moment to end, we walked slowly back down the drive stepping over the tree shadows just as the twins had done, and wondering about the tales that this house no doubt had to tell. On taking a last look down the drive before leaving, something bothered me that I felt I should remember, but, however hard I thought, nothing came to mind.

Driving slowly over the moor, we were watchful of the sturdy ponies that did not seem to see danger in their close proximity to the moving cars. I thought what a harsh life they had, and how bleak and cold it would be here in winter. We stopped, and I realised with apprehension how easily they could endure a torturous end in a bog. I shuddered at these thoughts, all the more dreadful because I knew that these events really still happened, and firmly shut them out of my mind. On our return home I saw my treasured copy of *The Hound of the Baskervilles* and then I knew what I was trying to remember. I turned the pages with excitement to find the description of Baskerville Hall, when Sir Henry visits his ancestral home for the first time. These were the words that I had been trying to remember: 'Through the gateway we passed into the avenue, where the wheels were again hushed amid the leaves, and the old trees shot their branches in a sombre tunnel over our heads. Baskerville shuddered as he looked up the long, dark drive to where the house glimmered like a ghost at the further end.' The words of *The Hound of the Baskervilles* were as familiar to me as those in *Saucers Over the Moor* and this description of the driveway to the house was so similar that I felt that King's Holt and Baskerville Hall could be one and the same. At the first opportunity I asked Mr Saville this intriguing question and he told me that this was possible, and he liked to think that it was so. Sir Arthur Conan Doyle is reputed to have stayed at Rowe's Duchy Hotel in Princetown while exploring Dartmoor and working on his new story. It is almost certain that he would have been aware of Prince Hall and may even have been invited there during his stay in Devon.

Mr Saville's advice had been that the way to see the real Dartmoor was to leave the car. Whilst walking, we were careful to keep to well-trodden tracks, as I realised with a shock that, should we venture into bog land, there was no-one around to help us. It was easy to feel the desolation all around us, and the underlying sombreness of this harsh granite world was starkly apparent. We spent many hours on the moor soaking up its mystery, but I was always aware of its dangers, so we moved on to Princetown to lift our spirits! Mr Saville describes this as an 'ugly little town' and even on the warm day of our visit the large, gloomy grey building that was the prison would have struck foreboding into anyone who was to become one of its inmates. Whoever chose this site could hardly have bettered it as a place to inspire wrongdoers to repent of their sins. We regarded it with awe and, in spite of a notice warning that it was not to be photographed, felt we could not leave without some memento so a young James was strategically positioned for this honour. We walked along the wide main street of Princetown hoping to find the Moorland Pixie, as we could have done justice to one of Mrs Sturt's meals. She must have disliked the Midlands exceedingly to come and live in this place, whatever hard times she had previously experienced.

Enjoying some lighter moments during our time exploring Dartmoor, we visited Widecombe in the Moor and, whilst driving there, sang 'Uncle Tom Cobley'. We strolled along the rows of wares put out in the sunshine to tempt tourists and, of course, we bought a tea towel with all the verses of the famous song printed on it. We sat at an outdoor table and had tea and scones with jam and cream, which made our fingers sticky, and watched visitors being lured to the trinkets and relieved of their money. Of all the places that we saw, this was the only one with many people, notwithstanding it having only a song to recommend it. We bought wooden mementoes of Dartmoor ponies that were so lifelike they could have been carved by Colonel Longden. Dan is first shown one of these carvings by his mother:

> … she took from the mantelpiece a block of wood about half the size and thickness of a brick. 'See Dan. There's a carving on the front of a Dartmoor pony and very good it is. The colonel does these himself and told me that wood carving is his hobby.' The little model was certainly an attractive novelty, and although he was not an expert Dan could see that the pony, in relief, had been carved with skill and knowledge of the subject. He ran his fingers over the outline sympathetically and admired the proud carriage of the pony's head.
>
> *Where's My Girl?*

Two family holidays were in the delightful seaside town of Paignton, when Dartmoor was again high on our list for exploration. We used a different route which took us through the interesting town of Totnes, with its narrow shop-lined streets thronging with people and completely unsuitable for cars. As we continued our journey we saw the impressive building that was Buckfast Abbey. This reminded me of Jon and Penny travelling with Penny's parents and stopping at Guildford, where a new cathedral is being built. Mrs Warrender says: 'It's grand to think we can still build cathedrals.' That made me realise how often Mr Saville brought churches into his stories. I felt that they were a subtle reminder to us never to forget why they were built and that we belonged to a Christian country.

It was not long before we were on the familiar road taking us once more onto the moor. We drove carefully down the steep hill before crossing the bridge at Dartmeet and continued, but this time we turned with expectation where the road sign pointed to Hexworthy. Before proceeding I glanced at the road in front of me and was almost disappointed that I did not see David and Peter each transporting a complaining twin on the carrier of each bicycle whilst Mackie, sitting serenely in his basket, '… sniffed the moorland air appreciatively'. As always my icons of information were with me—*Saucers Over the Moor* and my father-in-law's faithful atlas where the word 'Inn' was clearly marked. The endpapers of *Saucers Over the Moor* were so detailed that they adequately served as our guide. We crossed Huccaby Bridge, just as the Lone Piners did many years before, and continued over the moorland, enjoying being on a road that we had not traversed before. All the time I was gazing at the landscape that had been Mr Saville's world while he wrote *Saucers Over the Moor*. Even in summer, the moorland looked breathtakingly dramatic with its granite crags and tors creating a bleak panorama. Soon we were in Hexworthy looking at the White Lion. We went into the inn, following in the footsteps of David and Peter when they make their enquiries as to whether Mr Green was a resident. I liked to think that I was where Mr Saville had been and wondered whether he had modelled the man with the sandy hair on one of the residents. It was an interesting old inn, like many of its time.

Out in the sunshine again we set off on foot to find the Swincombe Brook. The further away from Hexworthy that we walked, the more aware of our surroundings we became. Often we were able to hear the tinkle of water that we could not always see and, once again,

I reflected that the walks the Lone Piners do are quite lengthy. It was a day without a cloud in the sky. We felt that we could walk far without any inclement weather descending upon us. Perseverance had its reward when we came to the Swincombe Brook where the water sparkled in the sunlight, '… the track ran down the other side of the hill into a small wood beyond which they could see the Swincombe Brook sparkling in the afternoon sunshine.' David and Peter with the twins continue walking. 'Fifty yards away the Swincombe was splashing over a shallow fall into a pool …' We sat and rested and trailed our fingers in the water of the Swincombe Brook. The only sounds were those of nature and we never saw a helicopter flying overhead. I thought how this brook might become a raging torrent in winter, and even on that summer day I was aware of the melancholy wildness of this moorland country, where the twins and Mackie have their fun with Mr Green. In this relevant chapter of *Saucers Over the Moor* we have the twins in action at their best. When I first read it I was willing Mackie to drive Mr Green into the pool which, of course, he does, and which, I am sure, gives great satisfaction to readers. Mr Saville cleverly allows his characters to have such small moments of retribution without them coming to any actual harm. As an aside, I have always enjoyed the twins' dialogue, which usually commences with 'My name is Mary Morton. This is my brother, Richard. We're twins.' Dickie is rarely called Richard apart from introductions and at times of big decisions. I was surprised when Mr Saville told me that he understood that some readers, probably the older ones, found the twins irritating and that he did himself. He said that he could never let the twins grow up because readers wanted them to stay as they were with this, now famous, banter of words that they shared in such a special way. I told him that I did not find them irritating but great fun and that I agreed with the readers who wanted them to stay just as they were. I knew that he was pleased with what I had said and he assured me that they would not grow up.

On another day we parked the car at Two Bridges where the Dart is more a stream than a river and where we could walk over the boulders, playing a game of trying not to get our feet wet. On this excursion we wanted to see the stunted oaks of the strangely named Wistman's Wood. Jon gives us Dan's description of it as 'dwarf oak trees all bent one way by the wind'. We found the terrain incredibly hard and soon became out of breath, but it was worth the effort. Like Peter and Jenny we almost felt the need to speak in whispers as it was like an alien world. Dartmoor itself was hard and menacing, but here was something different. Peter hates the trees and I agreed with her and thought, 'Gosh! Mr Saville does bring us to some awful places', as I struggled to get a grip on the moss which seemed to cover everything. At David's suggestion, Peter and Jenny explore Wistman's Wood.

> They found themselves speaking in whispers as they came to the wood. There was no mistaking it for neither of the girls had seen anything like it before. The stunted oaks were not only growing out of the clitter [sic] of loose rocks but their branches sprawled out across the boulders, and rocks and trees alike were covered with a thick, grey moss.
>
> *Where's My Girl?*

It was good to return to Two Bridges and the normality of the bright water as it danced on its journey to the sea. On our way home I looked across the moor and was able to see Prince Hall in the distance, although partially obscured by trees. I found it sad that this house, that had been part of such a thrilling tale, should seem so deserted and, as I searched my mind for the right word, it came to me—forlorn.

Like Tom and Jenny, we enjoyed Plymouth when we had a holiday there. We often sat high on The Hoe and ate ices just as they do. Like them, we looked at the interesting area from where the Pilgrim Fathers had set sail for America, and where we embarked on a variety of boat trips. Like Dan, we explored Brixham and watched the boats arriving in its attractive harbour, but we never saw one named *Lucky Girl*. However, we did appreciate looking at the replica of the *Golden Hind* which was moored there.

I almost felt that I had known all of these places long before I ever found them, and I suppose I had. It was Mr Saville's writings that made me familiar with them. All became places that I wanted to visit, some that I knew would give great pleasure and others that I would look at with veneration. My Lone Pine holidays were some of the best that I have ever had, and, of course they were all described to Mr Saville as I relived them after I returned home. He wanted to know everywhere that I had found and often praised my abilities as a sleuth. He showed a boyish triumph when I had not been successful and like a school teacher would say, 'Go and visit it again and you will find it.' This was something that we were often able to do as we had more than one holiday in many of the locations.

I often detected a wistfulness in him when I described our travels and realised almost with incredulity that he would have liked to have shared these times with us and to have retraced his own steps. I did say that perhaps I would do better with a guide and offered him the job but, although he was pleased to receive the invitation, it was hardly practical. I knew that everywhere we explored he was with us in spirit. He seemed to derive almost as much pleasure from our holidays as we did and was always eager to have copies of the photographs that we took, many of which he had pinned up in his room where he did his writing.

The climax of all our location visiting was the time when we combined it with a visit to Mr and Mrs Saville. Their favourite holidays were when they came to Shropshire and stayed at Cwm Head House with their long-time friend Mrs Tyley. In the summer of 1975, we were delighted to receive an invitation to spend a day with them. Mr Saville sent us instructions of exactly where to go: 'The house where we always stay, and which I first knew in 1936, is Cwm Head House next door to a slovenly farm of the same name, which can be reached up a track up a field (possible for car) just before you come to Cwm Head Church, about 100 yards further than the Priors Holt sign post.' When we arrived, we found Cwm Head House was an attractive building with a well-tended garden and there were our dear friends coming to meet us. The four of us were soon chattering and laughing together on this bright summer day.

We sat together in the garden and just knew how good it was to be together again. We looked at each other's photographs of our various travels. Mrs Saville also requested copies of some of ours to keep with their collection, which they had built up over the years, of pictures we had sent to them. Many were of our Lone Pine holidays, which they found particularly interesting and which brought forth their own reminiscences of holidays, to which we were only too eager to listen. Mrs Tyley was a delightful lady and did all she could to make us welcome in her beautiful home, as she led us inside to her elegant dining room where we shared a superb lunch. I looked at our host and hostess and was gratified to see how well they looked, but, as they said, the Shropshire air always made them feel good and it was like their second home.

After lunch we pored over the maps that Mr Saville spread across the table and he pointed out all the Lone Pine locations to us. This had been intended to precede a tour, but in reality we all found it hard to stop talking and just enjoyed being together. The following few moments are as clear in my mind as on that day we shared in Shropshire. I sat with my hands clenched tightly onto the chair and looked up at the man standing before me. Mr Saville observed me with a half-amused, half-quizzical smile. In that instant our lovely

The garden of Cwm Head House, Shropshire, the holiday destination that Mr and Mrs Saville loved and which Mrs Saville called 'this complete oasis of peace'

surroundings were charged with tension and I was hardly aware of Mrs Saville's pleasant voice as she talked to Brian. I gazed in supplication at my mentor, but he did not make it easy for me, and made me ask for what he knew I wanted to know. Almost in a whisper I reminded him of the times that he had promised to show me the Lone Pine tree and I asked—was there really a Lone Pine tree, just as he had always said? Time hung as we looked at each other, and then I relaxed as he smiled and said that of course there was. As I stood up in eager expectation, our host announced that we were going to find the Lone Pine tree. That was when Mrs Saville gave me a quick smile of sympathy and quietly said that she would stay at Cwm Head House. Mr Saville drove us down the rough track and on to the road. I hardly noticed passing Ingles Farm, and then Witchend was before us. It did cross my mind that whenever we were out with Mr Saville, he automatically used his car. We looked at Witchend and, although the Lone Pine tree had made the Lone Pine series famous, it was only then that I realised that it was this house and not the tree that was more important to Mr and Mrs Saville. As we climbed upwards in single file along a narrow rough track the land became steeper with clumps of heather and bracken and I was aware of the silence being broken only by the sounds of nature. Higher up there were bushes and trees and when Mr Saville pointed his hand, I knew that the moment had come that I had been waiting for, it seemed, all of my life. I looked at the trees above me and I knew that, without him, I would never have located the Lone Pine tree because it was not alone any more, but was surrounded by others. I realised just how lucky I was to have Mr Saville as my guide to savour this moment.

Returning to Cwm Head House, we all took photographs as mementoes, which I am so glad to have, before having tea and then leaving with reluctance. Mrs Tyley was included in our farewells and, on our thanking her for the day's hospitality, she issued an invitation for us to visit at any time we wished, as all of Mr and Mrs Saville's friends were welcome at her home. Reluctantly we drove down the track to the road, twisting our heads and waving, until Mr and Mrs Saville were out of sight, knowing that we had shared a perfect day to treasure.

The most exciting part of all of these holidays was walking where Mr Saville had walked and knowing that I was seeking what he wanted Lone Piners to find. The memory of those holidays will remain with me and I will always be grateful that Mr Saville allowed me to share his enchanted world.

Witchend—'Under the roof in front two gabled windows jutted, while at the back the hill came so close that it looked as if the house was leaning against it.'

Chapter VI

Quizzes

Mr Saville was always keen to find ways both to encourage children to read his books and to maintain their interest so that they would be eager to read more. The first Newsletter appeared in the summer of 1971, and Mr Saville aimed to produce four a year in spring, summer, autumn and winter. They gave information about the books that were in print and reminded readers that these could be borrowed from public libraries. Mr Saville suggested that his books made good presents and often an appropriate flier would be enclosed with the Newsletter. He included excerpts of letters from his readers and always added his home address so that he might be contacted. Regular recipients of the Newsletter were kept on a mailing list. When a child wrote to Mr Saville for the first time, a copy of the latest Newsletter would be enclosed with his reply to the child. These Newsletters were produced for approximately ten years and the last one that he addressed to me is dated autumn 1981. He always appeared to me to have his own personal crusade to give children a good start in life, by introducing them to his books at a young age, and showing them the delights of exciting stories. We discussed possible ways to diversify and I was asked to think of ideas. Of course, I promised that I would, but it was not I who provided an answer, but Mr Saville himself.

Letters from Mr Saville were always welcome and eagerly awaited by me. One, arriving in July 1972, started in the usual way by thanking me for my last letter to him, being apologetic and stating: 'This is an unworthy answer as I am very hard pressed.' I found this amusing as his letters were invariably lengthy and full of news. I soon came to the paragraph that was to draw me even closer into his life by allowing me into the private world that he shared with his readers. This is what he wrote: 'Would you like to devise a Lone Pine Quiz as a competition in the next Newsletter out in October? I should like you to do this and think it would be popular. The questions can cover the series but remember that the average age of readership is 12 and there are more girl readers than boys. The purpose, of course, is to tempt the fans to read all the books. [Keep] some questions easy like—What does this mean? nt 8 April 7. I'll announce that we'll take age into consideration and offer ten book prizes—5 for boys and 5 for girls. What do you think of it? I hope you'll agree. You and your husband can get busy.' Reading these words took my breath away, but, as Mr Saville knew it would be, my reply in the affirmative was sent by return of post and I was soon working hard.

Using Mr Saville's guidelines, I set to work on what was to be the first of many Quizzes that I planned and brought to fruition. These were prepared on my old manual typewriter, with the top copy for Mr Saville and a carbon copy for myself. I still have a number of these, albeit much faded now. It soon became apparent that with such a wealth of possibilities, the important (and hardest) thing would be for me to discard ideas, or the Quiz would become too lengthy and daunting. I had the comforting knowledge that what was omitted on one occasion could always be used at a later date, as, during our initial discussion, it had been agreed that, should this first Quiz prove successful, I would be asked to do others. Of course setting the Quiz meant re-reading the series, which was always a treat. I started by choosing

THE LONE PINE QUIZ

Please use a ball point pen for your answers and name and address and write as clearly as you can. There is at least one question about each of the nineteen Lone Pine books, but five of them refer to the same book twice.

Name ....
           (Block Capitals)
Address ....
....
....................Age ....

Your answer to each question <u>must</u> include the name of the Lone Pine Book
(Example: Question 1 below)

Question   Answer

1. Why was the holly tree unusual?   It had yellow not red berries.
                                                      (Not Scarlet But Gold)

2. Who got lost in the fog on the Mynd?   ....
                                                      ....

3. Where did Harriet Brown hide the   ....
    diamond necklace?   ....

4. Who dreamt about the Mithraic Temple?   ....
                                                      ....

5. Who gives Jenny an old silver spoon?   ....
                                                      ....

6. Where did Jon give Penny a green   ....
    necklace?   ....

7. What was hidden in Offa's Dyke?   ....
                                                      ....

8. Where did Peter risk her life for   ....
    Mary's sake?   ....

9. What was hidden in the fish boxes?   ....
                                                      ....

10. What clues did Great Uncle Charles leave?   ....
                                                      ....

11. Who rode in the miner's cable car?   ....
                                                      ....

12. Who pilots the lone glider?   ....
                                                      ....

13. Who came from Germany to find hidden   ....
    back notes?   ....

14. Who goes to Zutten in Holland?   ....
                                                      ....

15. Who lives at The Moorland Pixie?   ....
                                                      ....

16. Which Lone Piner does Harriet first meet?   ....
                                                      ....

The quiz reproduced above and opposite was the first one that I set.

Question	Answer
17. What did The Grasshopper represent?	....
18. Who dopes the guard dogs?	....
19. Who gets hijacked in a lorry?	....
20. Where is the Elizabethan document hidden?	....
21. Where was uranium found?	....
22. Where did the Mortons first meet Jon and Penny?	....
23. Who made fake Victorian Jewellery?	....
24. Who carved Dartmoor Ponies?	....

MY FAVOURITE LONE PINE STORY   (Write your reasons in space below in not more than 150 words).

IF I WIN A PRIZE I SHOULD LIKE A COPY OF ....

one question from each book, trying to ensure that the questions were not so hard that younger readers would get discouraged, nor so easy that older readers would get them all right.

Mr Saville warned me that, as searching for the real locations was a popular pastime, I would have to make sure that any details about real-life locations used in the questions were correct—it would not be enough to take them from the books. He suggested that I check out as many locations as I could, and also asked for my help with a mixture of queries that he needed clarifying for his own use. Shropshire was easy to check, as I lived so close to that area. Besides, visiting Shropshire helped me to soak up the atmosphere that Mr Saville had made his own. When Mr Saville said he would like settings checked on locations further afield it seemed a perfect reason to have working holidays. He was clever to suggest Brian's involvement because Brian was the person who chauffeured me to the Lone Pine sites that had to be checked.

I dispatched my first attempt to Mr Saville and anxiously awaited the verdict which came later in July. I need not have worried as his letter began: 'Thank you very much. It's a super Quiz and I suggest we discuss it and work out the final details when we meet here in September. We shall have to print it on a separate sheet (same size as Newsletter), leaving space for answers on the right. Part of each answer must feature the name of the book and the judges (probably you) must take age into consideration. We shall have to fit one question to *Where's My Girl?* which will be out end of November and will leave room at the bottom of the sheet for 100 words on "My Favourite Lone Pine Adventure" on which final judgment will be made from those who have all answers correct.' Mr Saville wrote on 8 September 1972: 'I'll tell you how I'm going to put over the Quiz and announce it in the Newsletter when I see you, but I plan to give 5 L.P. books a month until the end of March to the 5 best entrants and see how it goes. If it's a success you can do another. We'll talk about the other questions too. A better one for WMG would be "Who carved model ponies as a hobby?"' It was not long before all was finalised.

I received a letter from Mr Saville on 29 September 1972 which read: 'Thank you for your nice letter and the Quiz which was very beautifully typed! This has gone off to be duplicated and I'll send you a few copies when it comes in. We may be disappointed in the result but I'm sure it's worth trying and I certainly couldn't tackle it without your help.' Later in the letter he continued: 'I liked the Quiz questions and answers and I'm genuinely grateful to you for taking this over. I only wish you lived near enough to do secretarial work for me because you would save me hours! I promise I'll ask for your help when I need it.' I am so glad that in the years to come he did ask for my help in many ways; he always knew I was happy to give it. He continued: 'We shan't be getting any quizzes back before the end of October but I'll send them to you weekly and you can adjudicate and classify the results for me, proportion of boys to girls, ages etc.'

Although Mr Saville wanted his readers to have fun with the Quiz, he also wanted it as a starting-off point to publicise *Where's My Girl?*, and was concerned to have it finalised before the book came out. All went well, and the question on his new book did seem to persuade children either to purchase it themselves or request it as a gift.

When the Quiz was sent out, I was delighted to be acknowledged as the person who had devised it, and so I entered an important new phase in my friendship with Mr Saville. For the first time, I was to come into close contact with his other readers who were so important to him, and learn at first hand how they felt about him, how much they enjoyed his books and, of course, when they did the Quiz, how knowledgeable they were. The essays on 'My Favourite Lone Pine Adventure' from the entrants made fascinating reading, were often humorous and usually very well thought out. I found a stark contrast between girls' entries and boys' entries. The girls' handwriting was always so much neater and easier to read, and the friendships between the characters were of great importance to them. The boys enjoyed the exciting and dangerous parts of the adventures, but all readers seemed to enjoy the twins' escapades. I saw every essay that Mr Saville received and then they were all returned to him with my comments. When I sent him the ones that I had selected for a prize, I had to explain to him how I had arrived at my decision.

For the most part, I was never surprised by the high number of correct answers, because it is much easier to assimilate and retain details from adventure stories such as these at a young age. I made out tables for Mr Saville of the number of entrants and of the five winners each month, which are printed overleaf. I would be interested to know if any of the names are familiar to today's readers of the Lone Pine series, and whether they remember submitting their entries. This chapter also includes copies of two other Quizzes which may be fun to do. Perhaps readers who entered the competitions all those years ago, when they were first made up, will recall the answers—but if they don't, they are printed at the back of this book.

Mr Saville was always looking ahead and putting himself in the place of his readers; in a letter dated 13 November 1972, he said: 'When you send me your 5 winners with their entries with the <u>wrong</u> answers marked in red you can send with [them] a list of the answers on which you made your judgment. I will return the entries to each winner, but <u>not</u> the answers which I want for my records.' I had not thought of returning the entries, but it did make sense and of course I realised that the children would want to know how their winning formula had been reached. I became fascinated with these children now that I was having an insight into their thoughts. When I mentioned this to Mr Saville he wrote, 'The point about the boys is that they don't read LP as avidly as girls nor write to me as freely. But their criticism is often shrewder.' I was surprised that any criticism was made, but knew that it was taken seriously as it was given with the open honesty of children. Young people were the pivot of Mr Saville's life and in consequence their refreshing comments meant far more to him than those of any adult critic. The entries continued to come, many obviously attempted over the Christmas holidays. I liked to think that this was due to the children having a Lone Pine book gift.

In January Mr Saville informed me that he was to go to Amalfi in Italy for two months, but this did not mean that the competition was on hold. He would not let that happen. To ensure that our smoothly running system did not grind to a halt while he was abroad he wrote, 'All my mail goes to my daughter, Mrs Richard Dowler, and I will ask her to forward all Quizzes to you. But please send me your 5 as usual for Jan and Feb and I will write the winner a note as usual and Rosemary will post them in England.' I liked receiving mail with Italian stamps and the Amalfi postmark became familiar to me. Upon receipt of Quiz entries

LONE PINE QUIZ 1972 - 1973

	NOVEMBER	DECEMBER	JANUARY	FEBRUARY	MARCH
No. of entries	Boys Girls Total	Boys Girls Total	Boys Girls Total	Boys Girls Total	Boys Girls Total
	6 7 13	3 3 6	3 7 10	5 4 9	6 8 14

Total number of entries 50   Boys 22   Girls 28   Ages from 8 to 16 (one 27)

Choice of Favourite Story

	Boys	Girls	Total		Boys	Girls	Total
Mystery At Witchend				The Secret Of The Gorge		1	1
Seven White Gates	3	2	5	Mystery Mine		2	2
The Gay Dolphin Adventure	4	5	9	Sea Witch Comes Home			
The Secret of Grey Walls	3	1	4	Not Scarlet But Gold		2	2
Lone Pine Five				Treasure At Amorys			
The Elusive Grasshopper	1		1	Man with Three Fingers	2	7	9
The Neglected Mountain	1	2	3	Rye Royal	1	3	4
Saucers Over The Moor	2	1	3	Strangers At Witchend			
Wings Over Witchend	3		3	Where's My Girl?	1	3	4
Lone Pine London	2		2				

Tables of the first Lone Pine Quiz entrants 1972–1973 (above) and of the monthly winners (below). Pat Young, age 12, won a consolation prize for the month of March.

LONE PINE QUIZ 1972 - 1973 (Monthly Winners)

	NOVEMBER	DECEMBER	JANUARY	FEBRUARY	MARCH
1st	Michael Shelton, Age 15	Raymond Crawford, Age 13	O. Martin Leach, Age 13	Sally Anne Pitts, Age 8	Vicki Grant, Age 12
2nd	Kevin Mason, Age 15	Nigel R. Taylor, Age 27	Cathy Daly, Age 13	Lynne Jones, Age 12	Catherine Lloyd, Age 12
3rd	Elizabeth Wray, Age 12½	N.S. Bailey, Age 12	Mandy Jameson, Age 12½	Andrew Etheridge, Age 13	Richard Staines, Age 13
4th	Mark Pryce, Age 12	Miss P.D. Gough, Age 14	Susan Long, Age 13	Stephen Wateridge, Age 12½	Kevin Smith, Age 11
5th	Susan Hill, Age 15	Bradley Garrood, Age 10	Duncan Etheridge, Age 12½	Ian Crook, Age 11	Joanna Chandler, Age 13

LONE PINE FUN QUIZ

This exciting Lone Pine Quiz has been devised by Vivien Turner, a Lone Pine fan. Have fun with your friends, testing your knowledge of the Lone Pine books and see who knows most. If you get stuck, you will find the answers on the back.

1) In SAUCERS OVER THE MOOR, who did the twins drive into the Swincombe Brook?

    Answer ....

2) In MAN WITH THREE FINGERS, who gave Tom the horseshoe scarf?

    Answer ....

3) In THE GAY DOLPHIN ADVENTURE, who did Penny want to fall into a ditch?

    Answer ....

4) In MYSTERY AT WITCHEND, who pulled the twin out of the bog?

    Answer ....

5) In THE SECRET OF THE GORGE, what was Mrs Quickseed's house full of?

    Answer ....

6) In THE NEGLECTED MOUNTAIN, what was the name of the Detective the Lone Piners met at the Fair?

    Answer ....

7) In SEVEN WHITE GATES, who helped Peter when she had a puncture?

    Answer ....

8) In MYSTERY AT WITCHEND, who gave the lonely owl hoot?

    Answer ....

9) In HOME TO WITCHEND, who had their portraits painted by "Pam"?

    Answer ....

10) In WINGS OVER WITCHEND, what was the forester's name who was knocked down by the twins on their sledges?

    Answer ....

11) In TREASURE AT AMORYS, who swam in the Military Canal?

    Answer ....

12) In WHERE'S MY GIRL?, what was hidden in the fishmonger's van?

    Answer ....

13) In RYE ROYAL, who celebrated Rye Fawkes Night?

    Answer ....

14) In NOT SCARLET BUT GOLD, who falls out of her hiding place in the wardrobe?

    Answer ....

15) In STRANGERS AT WITCHEND, who walked with Kevin over the Long Mynd from Witchend to Seven Gates Farm?

    Answer ....

16) In THE GAY DOLPHIN ADVENTURE, who seized the Ballinger's paint brush at Camber Castle?

    Answer ....

This was not a competition but was just for fun.

Mr Saville would always forward them to me for comments and marking, and then I would return them to him. When he was in Italy his daughter did indeed send the Quizzes to me, and after marking them I would forward them to his address in Amalfi.

Mr and Mrs Saville were often away from home, usually looking for places on which to base new stories. In a letter of 2 April 1973, Mr Saville wrote 'Did you notice—no, I'm sure you wouldn't—that the two girls who got 100% in this last batch lived near each other in N. London. I did, and I bet they go to the same school and may have collaborated! I've asked them if they know each other.' He was quite right—I had not noticed this. As I remarked to him, it was as well that I had him to keep an eye on me too! Mr Saville never told me whether he ever learned if these two girls knew each other.

All subsequent Quizzes also asked competitors to write an essay, usually of one hundred words. Themes could vary from favourite story, character, villain and even setting. Mr Saville cared passionately about his readers' opinions, as he always wanted to write what they wished to read. These essays gave the children an opportunity to voice their own impressions of his books. For Mr Saville this was probably the most interesting part of the Quizzes. Often the children would make comments and quote Mr Saville. He would add a note to me saying, 'Did I really say that?' Most of the time I would reply, 'Yes, you did!' He was amazed that he had written certain things that he had forgotten, and we found this amusing. Occasionally things were said that were a complete mystery to us! Mr Saville was once asked why the twins and Mackie ran away with Jenny. He wrote to this child and said correctly that the twins, Jenny and Mackie didn't run away in any of the Lone Pine stories. The child never said where this information came from.

Another child once wrote to Mr Saville stating that, in *The Secret of Grey Walls*, Peter doesn't seem a very nice person. He could not recall Peter saying anything unpleasant but I could assure him that this child was right, reminding him of when David expresses his doubts to Peter as to whether Jon would wish to become a Lone Piner: 'Peter whirled round and faced him with burning cheeks. "Yes," she said, "I see what you mean, David! You're ashamed of the Club and afraid Jon will laugh at you … Very well. You two had better go off together and be grown-up somewhere else. The twins and Tom and Jenny and me will make Penny a member …"'

Another occasion was when a child was concerned that Mackie was given chocolates, as these are not good for dogs. Mr Saville

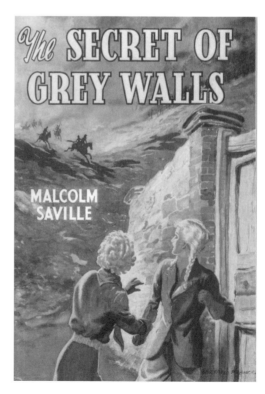

First edition dustwrapper of The Secret of Grey Walls: *illustration by Bertram Prance*

said he couldn't remember doing this. I assured him this had happened in *Lone Pine Five* when the twins and Mackie were in Smithson's caravan.

'… What about some eating [probably an error for eating some] chocolates, kid? Don't object to them, do you? We've got some tucked away somewhere that you won't see anywhere else.'

It was difficult to refuse an offer like this, and when Percy, with a sour smile, followed his father's lead and offered a carton full of the biggest and most exciting chocolates that the twins had ever seen they could not resist. Then, much to Percy's obvious annoyance, Mary picked out a specially succulent-looking beauty and gave it to Mackie. Unfortunately it had a caramel centre, and the little dog had the greatest difficulty in controlling it, particularly as Mary refused to put him on the floor.

First edition dustwrapper of Lone Pine Five: *illustration by Bertram Prance*

The Quizzes were issued and circulated at regular intervals and continued in popularity. I always had to make it clear that all the answers were to be found in the books. Mr Saville was certain that the Quizzes helped to quicken interest in his books and to boost sales. Not all of the Quizzes were used in the Newsletter. Mr Saville made many public appearances at book-signings, schools and talks generally, and Quizzes would be circulated at these events.

In the summer of 1978 I suggested a Quiz to help promote *Home to Witchend*. I was delighted to receive the following from him written on 10 July 1978: 'Thanks for your welcome P.C. and news. Yes—I would like to see your suggestions for a LP Quiz very much, thank you … I'm now making plans with Collins for the launch of *Home to Witchend* and have an idea that a Quiz might go out with the October Newsletter. I'll discuss this with them as soon as possible and let you know.' This letter had a PS dated 12 July 1978: 'Have seen Collins who are most enthusiastic over the Quiz. We may circulate it at Schools and Book fairs etc at end of Sept when *Home to Witchend* is published.' Mr Saville was keen that we did not make this competition too easy, and in November 1979 he said, 'I have only one suggestion for the Quiz and that is we should have about 4 or 5 more questions dealing with any of the 19 books that you like—19 questions for 19 books makes it a little easier for the competitor to [do] some guessing by elimination.' Mr Saville knew that I would do anything that I could to help this Quiz be a special one on the publication of the final Lone Pine story.

I realised the trust that Mr Saville placed in me in allowing me almost a free hand in compiling the Quizzes and judging the entries. He knew that I had enjoyed sharing these special years and that I would never let him down.

Home to Witchend Quiz

Here is the Quiz that I devised to help promote *Home to Witchend* when it was first published. There is at least one question about each of the 20 Lone Pine books, and each answer has to include the name of the relevant book.

Questions
1. Where is Peter's hired bicycle stolen?
2. Who tells the twins where 'Pam' lives?
3. Who finds Tenby Mews?
4. How many steps are there to the Abbey?
5. Who works for Charles at Seven Gates?
6. Where do the Channings live?
7. Who enjoys three platefuls of Peter's stew?
8. Who ride on the 'Ghost Train'?
9. Where is Penny's new home with her parents?
10. Which 'bad type' does Arlette see on the train?
11. Who blows the whistle and finds Reuben?
12. Who finds the 'dog' newspaper cuttings?
13. Where does Mrs Thurston live?
14. Where is the 'old mill' and who finds it?
15. What is the stone in Peter's engagement ring?
16. Who comes to England from Australia to find a diamond necklace?
17. What lone object does Dan see over Swincombe Tor?
18. What does Mr Morton promise to give David and Peter one day at their engagement party?
19. Where are the twins in danger when the hill bursts open?
20. Who carves Peter a Romany whistle?
21. What stand like sentinels at Rye station?
22. Who gets lost in a blizzard on the Long Mynd?
23. Who visit Wistman's Wood?
24. Where does Charlie put Kevin's glasses?
25. What is the name of Thomas Seymour's business partner?
26. With whom do some of the Lone Piners take up 'board residence' and where?
27. Who fires the hay in Charles' Dutch barn?
28. Who does Ned Stacey work for?
29. Where is Harriet Brown's letter hidden?
30. Who lets rooms in her home to Mrs Warrender at the Dolphin?

The essay for this quiz is 'My favourite Lone Pine villain'.

Fontana Paperbacks

14 St. James's Place London SW1A 1PS
Telephone 01-493 7070
Telegrams-Herakles London SW1
Telex-25611 Collins G

11th September, 1978

Mrs Vivien Turner,
Witchend,
39 Gervase Drive,
Dudley.
DY1 4AU

Dear Mrs Turner,

    Malcolm Saville has passed on to me your Lone Pine Quiz. He freely admits that you seem to know more about his characters than he does! We are delighted with it - thank you very much indeed.

    We are hoping to produce it in a slightly shortened form, and it will be printed, with acknowledgement, and sent out with Malcolm's next newsletter. We are also hoping to use it at Malcolm's many forthcoming public appearances in connection with the publication of Home to Witchend.

    Thanking you once again.

Yours sincerely,

Selina Bird
Children's Publicity Manager

Registered as Wm. Collins Sons & Co. Ltd. (Scotland)

Letter from Fontana Paperbacks, with a copy of my reply

Newsletter No. 25
Autumn 1981

9 Delves Way,
Ringmer, Lewes,
East Sussex. BN8 5JU

Dear Vivien

~~This is rather a special Newsletter, which is being sent only to those of my loyal readers who have already~~ taken the trouble to reserve it.

First I want to thank you for proving to me that there are still plenty of intelligent young people who are keen readers and who realize the importance of WORDS in a "picture age". I believe you to be one of these, and I hope that your parents and teachers agree that there really is something very special about books in the home as well as at school. I know that it is often less trouble to watch T.V. than to read a book, but apart from the fun and entertainment of an adventure story which you can read again, it is a fact that the habit of reading will help you at school, because books are the key to all learning and, in years to come, will enrich your life.

Now, because I know that you are interested, I give you the latest news of mine.

NOT THE END OF THE LONE PINE TRAIL

MYSTERY AT WITCHEND, the first of the Lone Pine adventures, was published in 1943 and until recently it has always been kept in print. Nineteen more stories have followed and the last, HOME TO WITCHEND, is still in Armada Paperbacks. But not for long. Sadly, only six books remain in print and when they have sold out, I cannot tell you when, and if, they will appear again. It is only right that you, as a loyal reader, should know that although over two million copies of these books have been sold over the years, Armada have decided that it is no longer possible to reprint any of these books in the future. Please understand that this sad situation is nothing to do with me. I can only make a living if readers BUY my books, but with the help of people like you - and particularly the support of the hundreds of members of my Lone Pine Club - I hope to find another Publisher to follow the Lone Pine trail. You can help by telling your friends about these stories and perhaps lending them your books - but be sure to get them back! Certainly ask for them in Public Libraries and shops, specially if your School has a Bookshop, and tell your School Librarian what is happening and ask for their help. Remember that I am always pleased to hear from you, and will reply to your letters. I hope you will fill up the Form at the end of this letter so that I have your name and address and can let you have further news of my books. Christmas is coming. Books make the best presents and the 6 Lone Pine Armadas still available are wonderful value. And remember that you may never have another chance of completing your set of these stories.

Those of you who have been taking the Newsletter regularly will remember that have always printed some extracts from some of my readers letters. This time I only want to share one with you. It is from an Irish girl of 13 whom I have never met. She writes:-

> "I really enjoyed reading Lone Pine stories and HOME TO WITCHEND was a beautiful ending to a beautiful series. All other series have no ending but yours had. It is unlikely that an ending to a series would be any good, but yours was a masterpiece in its own right. I am sure that these books will live on in the hearts of many..... Thank you, thank you for the Lone Pine and Marston Baines thrillers. Their memory will live in me and I will recommend them to my children"
>
> - Patricia Creedon - A Lone Piner for ever!

Newsletter Number 25—Autumn 1981 (front)

SO NOW FOR MARSTON BAINES

Years ago I realized that the time would come when Lone Pine readers like you and Patricia Creedon might wish to widen their reading by enjoying romantic and exciting stories featuring older characters. So I invented Marston Baines the Secret Service Agent, who is also an Author! His young friends - particularly his newphew Simon and his girl-friend Rosina are of undergraduate age, and they all have thrilling adventures in different European countries which I have visited. I'm sending you details of these stories. Some readers think that I am Marston Baines! I'm not. Just an author whol likes to explore other places but is always glad to come back to his Sussex home.

WORDS FOR OLDER READERS

You know by now that words are not only my business but my delight, and so I want to introduce you to a beautifully produced book of poetry and prose which I have collected during a lifetime of working for young people. It is called WORDS FOR ALL SEASONS. You might be able to look at it first in your School or Public Library, and I'm sure your Teacher will agree that it will be helpful to those of you taking English in you "O" or even "A" levels. I promise you that this is a very unusual book, and will make a splendid and original present for anyone of any age who is a keen reader.

And as I write these words I can share some good news with you. I have just heard that there is also to be a paperback edition of WORDS FOR ALL SEASONS so if you would like to know more about this, and when it will be published, just fill up the form at the end of this letter and send it to me with a stamp and I will add your name and address to my Mailing List.

OUT OF DOORS BOOKS

Most of you will remember that I have written several illustrated books about the Countryside and Seashore. You will find the titles on the pink Order Form which you can use if buying through the post. All six of these books are amazing value and make splendid presents. I will send further details with pleasure, or you can tell the Bookshop that they are published by Carousel.

With Best Wishes for happy reading, and don't forget to fill up the Form below and sent it to me with a stamp.

Address to Malcolm Saville, 9 Delves Way, Ringmer, Lewes, East Sussex. BN8 5JU

CUT ROUND THE LINE AND SEND COMPLETE

Please add my name to your Mailing List, so that you can send me news and details of your books.

PIN - NOT STICK stamp for 2nd Class Mail here

NAME : ....

ADDRESS : ....

....

..........Post Code..............

WRITE CAREFULLY IN BLOCK CAPITALS.

Age ....

Newsletter Number 25—Autumn 1981 (back)

Chapter VII

Index

My friendship with Mr Saville commenced in an entirely predictable way—a letter from an adoring fan to a famous author who wrote the most exciting books that she had ever read. Over many years the respect and admiration that I had for him was hardly to change, only to deepen. It was his friendship with me that changed in a way that I could never have envisaged when I wrote that first letter. To him, I was one of the hundreds of people who wrote him polite respectful letters and was pleased to have a reply by return. In the early years his books were the pivot of our letters and he was amused by my knowledge of his popular Lone Pine adventure stories. He would laugh when he asked a question at random and I could always quote the relevant passage from any of the Lone Pine books. As I grew older, subtle changes occurred in our correspondence; he would ask my advice on locations to be used, the characters that I liked to read about most and how the relationships between the various characters should develop—a constant source of concern to him.

For my thirteenth birthday I was given a copy of *Saucers Over the Moor*. To this day I can recall the moment that my impatient fingers wrestled with the string and then the brown paper that held my new treasure. I knew what the parcel contained. It was a gift from AA, who had that peculiar wisdom that some doting maiden aunts can have—she always bought me exactly what I asked for. At last I held it in my hands and gazed at the cover of the Dartmoor scene, before turning the stiff pages of my pristine copy—a book to be read and re-read and treasured forever. Then something jarred about the cover, and I noted with dismay that Jon's hair was black when I knew perfectly well that it should be yellow—it was described by Penny as looking like a 'straw rick after a hurricane'*. Bertram Prance repeated his error with *The Elusive Grasshopper* and Charles Wood continued it with *Lone Pine London*. The superb wrap-around dustwrapper of *Mystery Mine* also has Jon's hair dark, and Michael Whittlesea gives Tom blond hair when it should be black in *Man With Three Fingers*. It is not only colour of hair that is wrongly depicted. In *Seven*

First edition dustwrapper of Saucers Over the Moor: *illustration by Bertram Prance*

*in *The Elusive Grasshopper*; see also page 35.

First edition dustwrapper of Mystery Mine

White Gates there is a description of the Romany caravan where it states that the roof is green. On Charles Wood's happy cover of *The Secret of the Gorge*, the roof is coloured white.

I was shocked that such glaringly obvious errors could ever have been made, wondering how the author had allowed it to happen. Over the years I was to find many other mistakes in the text itself, such as Mary's eye colour, which varies in the different books. In *Mystery at Witchend* she has 'brown eyes'. In *Seven White Gates* they are 'wide, dark-blue eyes'. In *The Gay Dolphin Adventure* she has 'big violet eyes'. *The Secret of Grey Walls* describes her 'grey eyes'. In *Lone Pine Five* we read of her 'violet eyes—always attractively large …'

As I read the books, I started jotting down the discrepancies until I had a lengthy list. Then I wondered what I should do with it. It would take a lot of nerve for someone who was only just a teenager to point out these errors to a famous and extremely popular children's author. It was only as I grew older and had established a warm and trusting friendship with Mr Saville that I tentatively pointed out the obvious mistakes on the dustwrappers, just to test his reaction. The amazing answer from him was that he was such a busy person, with an incredibly full life and many writing projects on the anvil at the same time, that he had not even noticed them! Once he had given the final approval for publication, he took the view that other people would sort out any irregularities. I did wonder whether proof reading and continuity checks were ever carried out by anyone! I was more than a little relieved when he was grateful that I had pointed these matters out to him.

In a letter dated 29 September 1972, he ended, almost casually as if it were an afterthought, with this paragraph: 'Perhaps one of these days I'll ask you to do a card index of all the LP characters together with their ages, physical characteristics etc. Every character, child or adult would have to be mentioned together with a record of the careless slips of description made by the author and his various editors!' When he made this suggestion I jumped at the chance. What fan wouldn't? Besides, I loved reading his books better than those of any other author. This would assist with the production of the final Lone Pine book so that it would be just right. It would also help Mr Saville in compiling the Lone Pine Story, details of which I have discussed on page 22. I was now an integral part of Mr Saville's working life and what was to follow was eighteen months of dedicated work to give him orderly detailed documentation of the Lone Pine characters, their friends and enemies, and the Lone Pine homes, camps and locations for the stories. Animals were also included.

We wrote to each other on an almost daily basis, interspersed with phone calls, to discuss vital points. One problem I encountered with the work was how easily I allowed myself to be diverted by becoming engrossed in the story, rather than extracting the relevant details! Each person and location was allocated a piece of paper on which I would note the page number and detail to be written down. I would type out my draft which would then be submitted to Mr Saville for correction, amendments and improvement before typing out the final copy. It was then forwarded to his secretary for inclusion into a loose leaf binder. He had long since decided that cards would not be large enough.

I received a typed letter on 14 May 1973 which commenced: 'When we are talking about such vital subjects as LONE PINE, I do think it a very good idea to type our letters. I'm sure that you are too polite to tell me that my handwriting is very difficult to read, but I know that it is. Your typing is faultless but I do find your handwriting very difficult too, sometimes!' I found this most amusing, but, of course, I agreed to do this as it made sense. However, I did enjoy teasing him by suggesting that when giving me specific instructions maybe he should have them typed! He never did this, but it was not necessary. These were pre-computer days and most of the letters that I wrote to Mr Saville and received from him were handwritten. At first I had found his highly individual writing hard to decipher, but I soon became familiar with it. When I told him that I could read his writing far more easily than I could read my own it was a case of touché, but we did try to improve the legibility of our writing to each other—at least for a while, until haste and volume superseded clarity. We lived in a time when it was natural for us to communicate by letters and sometimes telephone. This is the way that we liked it and the Index proceeded in harmony.

Appropriately I started the Index with *Mystery at Witchend*, and I anxiously awaited the comments on what I had dispatched to Mr Saville. On 26 May 1973 he wrote: 'Thank you for your letter, which to my shame, I see was dated a week ago. Thank you too for the tremendous amount of work you seem to have done on "Witchend", but I am inclined to think that you are doing far too much. I don't mind the idea of typing the information on to sheets big enough to go into a loose leaf binder. What is important is the appearance and ages of the characters and how much I have varied them, through carelessness, and in what books. For our record we want basic facts, eg Height. Colour of hair. Eyes. Temperament and most noticeable characteristics and in what stories they appear. It would be helpful to know very briefly in what books I described Witchend, Seven Gates, Clun, Rye, Winchelsea and the page numbers in the Newnes editions up to *Rye Royal*, *Strangers* and *Where's My Girl?* which are Collins.' I agreed that we must use Newnes and the Collins 80p hardbacks as standard. He continued, 'And not just the Lone Piners. What is Mr Cantor like or Mr Morton for that matter? Would it not be a good idea to do Peter, Penny and David as specimens first and let me see them. Take the character rather than the book and work that way. And only relevant facts eg Peter, Characteristics. Courage—Sacrificing herself for Mary. *Neglected Mountain* page???'

Mr Saville was always helpful with many ideas of how to proceed with the Index. On 5 June 1973 he wrote, 'By all means continue to make what notes you wish in your own way but would it not be a good idea to establish a <u>formula</u> for the presentation of the facts you dig out? I feel that perhaps we must meet to discuss all this before you do too much work on it but I'm fairly sure that the formula first is essential so that you know what you need <u>not</u> look for.' On 15 October 1973 Mr Saville wrote, 'I hope you are [not] having too much trouble with the Index. I never wanted this to be a chore for you but if ever I wrote a history of Lone Pine called "The Lone Pine Story" it would be invaluable.' I hastened to assure him that it was certainly not a chore, but it was important that I did what he wanted. Mr Saville was constantly encouraging and always grateful for anything that I did for him. I wonder whether he ever understood what a great pleasure it was to be part of the exciting world of this remarkable person.

In a further letter of October 1973 he wrote, 'Your formula is fine. Yes, Mortons in all books. Your incorrect facts should I think be on the same page or reverse. I know I've changed the colour of Mary's eyes and Tom's hair and in such circumstances it would be helpful to have the book and chapter recorded. Page numbers would be hopeless because there are so many different editions. Where one—or two in the case of the twins—do something particularly brave or memorable it would be helpful to record it. eg Peter's action to save Mary in *Neglected Mountain* and where the twins were particularly brave in *Wings Over Witchend*. Facts like these which readers remember and refer to will be helpful. I don't remember that I've ever specifically mentioned a character's height although we know that Jon is the tallest. Why don't you do a specimen page and show me?' This letter ended with the line, 'Enjoy your holiday, you lucky girl!' (This referred to our pending holiday in Mallorca which would include researching the Marston Baines sites.)

As Mr Saville's favourite character was Jenny, I was particularly interested in what he had to say about what I compiled about her. He wrote on 8 November 1973, 'Firstly I do not think the length of each entry matters very much as long as you get in the relevant information as tersely as possible and I have therefore made some rough pencilled corrections to your specimen, Jenny Harman. On the whole I think this is excellent and you have included the sort of information which will be of great value to me, or indeed to anybody who is doing an intensive study of Lone Pine. I think it would be a good idea to give the title of the book instead of the number in the series, as I can never remember the order in which I wrote them!' To help him out I typed out a complete list of book titles chronologically with the appropriate numbers. On many of the dustwrappers the titles were listed according to where the stories were sited rather than when they were written.

On 3 December 1973 Mr Saville's letter started, 'My dear Vivien,' a sign that he was pleased with me. He stated, 'Thank you very much for your letter of 22nd November and for the revised details on Jenny Harman. These seem to be very good now, but I am returning them to you because I think it would be very much better if you keep them together until your collection is complete. But by all means send me each one as you do it, so that I may go through it and save you revision later.'

My notes, of course, included those about the property Witchend itself, nestling at the base of the Long Mynd and from which the Lone Pine series was to evolve. Nearby, elevated from the road, was Cwm Head House, where Mr Saville's family stayed in the war years of the early 1940s. Would the Lone Pine series ever have been written without this move to Shropshire? This was all to be discussed in The Lone Pine Story. We also discussed a Lone Pine Handbook and Diary, and together outlined the plot and characters who would appear in our joint idea for a new Lone Pine story. This was to go back in time to the early years and would be set in Shropshire. He would use the Index for all of these ventures.

Mr Saville once showed great concern that I had made a mistake in the Index and stressed the need to be careful that everything was accurate. I agreed with him and wanted to know what I had done wrong. He told me that I had said that Tom had appeared in *Mystery Mine* when he knew perfectly well that he had never gone to Yorkshire. I assured him that there was no cause for worry because Tom does appear in *Mystery Mine,* albeit only briefly. This is when Penny, in high dudgeon, visits Hatchholt with Peter, and together they go to see Tom at his uncle's farm. He was still not convinced, so I gave him the page number and suggested that he read it himself. He did this and apologised profusely and said that he was quite amazed that Tom had appeared in *Mystery Mine* as he had no recollection of having written that bit. I found this funny, but it did prove the point of the necessity of the Index. There were to be other similar distress calls, but I was always able to ease Mr Saville's mind, and eventually he accepted that if I had said that he had written something, then he had. In any event, the proof was always there in his books!

And so my work continued. Sometimes the pages were received with immediate approval, sometimes sent back for alterations, but gradually it all came together, and after eighteen months of hard but fascinating work it was completed. My reward came in a letter dated 21 March 1974. 'I have now got more time to write to you about your splendid Index but I find it very difficult to express my genuine thanks to you for such a painstaking work. It really is a remarkable effort and I do congratulate you. On looking through this I realise that you have told me countless facts about my own work, which I had forgotten as soon as the books were finished. I am particularly grateful to you for the clever way in which you have spotted errors, which, although basically my responsibility, had been missed by sub-editors, who ought to have known better than to let me get away with them. I shall get a special folder for your Index and I am sure that in the future I shall turn to it again and again.'

Mr Saville was fiercely possessive of his writing creations, and of none more than the Lone Pine characters. He guarded them with an almost jealous zeal. Knowing this, I realised how privileged I was to be allowed to work in such close proximity to his writing. I never

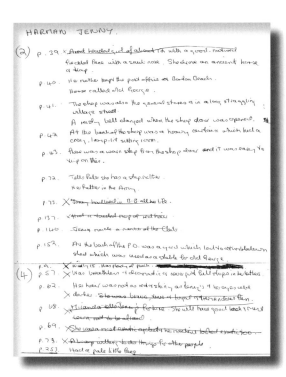

This page: my notes on Jenny taken from the Lone Pine books

forgot that they were his books nor that I was helping him in *his* work. Although many times he said I knew so much about his characters, they were *his* characters. I understood this and he knew that I understood this. It was one of the reasons why our friendship continued for the rest of his life.

Many times Mr Saville told me how invaluable the Index was to him and how much he would like me to work for him, and how sorry he was that I had not done this many years earlier. I did point out that as I was born in the year *Mystery at Witchend* was written, this would have been rather difficult, but that I had done all that I could to make up for being born too late! He used the Index when he gave talks and of course in the writing of Lone Pine 20 (*Home to Witchend*) with which I was honoured to be involved closely. He said the Index was always to hand as it was kept on his desk and he used it often.

HARMAN JENNY — over the series

Age ranges from 12 to 17

Hair Red

Eyes Grey

Has appeared in the following ~~Lone Pine Books~~

Seven White Gates
The Secret of Grey Walls
Lone Pine Five
The Neglected Mountain
Wings Over Witchend

The Secret of The Gorge
Not Scarlet but Gold
Man With Three Fingers
Strangers at Witchend
Where's My Girl?

Jenny makes her first appearance in Seven White Gates as a 12 year old. She had a good natured freckled face with a snub nose and a mop of tousled red hair.

Jenny is made a member of the Club at H.Q.2 in this book (p.140) Her Father ~~kept~~ helps the Post Office and General Store in ~~the long~~ the straggling village ~~street of~~ Barton Beach. ~~She had been~~ Born over the shop and ~~had~~ lived in Barton ~~Beach~~ all ~~of~~ her life. ~~Went to~~ School in Bishops Castle and until she met Peter had been lonely and ~~sometimes wished she had~~ longed for brothers or sisters.

Her own Mother had told her stories of the Stiperstones, round the fireside on a winter's evening, ~~and~~ She still feared the mountain but not as much after Miranda ~~had~~ the Gypsy told her fortune and said that she would have good luck but must learn not to be afraid.

Her Step-Mother was not always kind to her, particularly when her Father was away ~~in the army~~ in the war. ~~She adored her Father.~~ she adores Mr Harman ~~Her step-Mother~~ could never understand that Jenny needed friends of her own age.

~~She was~~ Jenny is small and neat and incurably romantic. She ~~had~~ has plenty of pluck and ~~was~~ is always willing to ~~do things for~~ other people. She ~~was~~ is brave, true and loyal and tremendous fun. She ~~had~~ has the feminine lust for bargain hunting, ~~although she hardly ever had any new clothes but was used to this.~~

Tom and Peter are the two most important people in Jenny's world and Tom is the staunchest and most wonderful friend she ~~had~~ has ever known. Ingles

Jenny ~~spent~~ spends most of her spare time reading the more colourful literature that ~~adorned~~ adorn the shelves of her Father's shop. She ~~lived~~ lives the stories, particularly the beautiful heroines ~~and~~ never tires of ~~repeating~~ quoting the stories to her Lone Pine friends.

Above and opposite: my original draft of Jenny with Mr Saville's amendments

As she grew older (15 yrs, book 11) she wore her hair in a pony
tail and thought of being a nurse as she enjoyed looking after
anyone hurt or ill. She was usually scatterbrained but on
occasions could be very definite and could hold her own with
most people.

She was an erratic cyclist and had an erratic machine and
particularly disliked cycling in thunderstorms.

She loved Shrewsbury but was not interested in poetry, and was
only interested in history about people, but she hated museums.

She was a poor swimmer but did not mind as Tom was not interested either.

She was Possessive of her friends and was a little jealous of Harriet
when they first met (book 14) but they later became very good friends.

At 17 Jenny was very modern and loved pop music, and was devoted to
Mrs. Ingles and was never happier than when she was on the Farm.
(book 15) She realises how much Tom means to her before he realises
she is the girl for him, and she learns patience and understanding
and really grows up and the happiest moment in her life is when Tom
tells her she will one day be a farmer's wife.

Jenny still has difficulties with her step-mother (book 19) although
they both love Mr. Harman and realise he would be much happier if they
could be friends. They have a very important discussion (p.159)
when Jenny realises she has sometimes been horrid and Mrs. Harman
realises she has never tried to win Jenny's love and they both decide
to start again. It is a wonderful day for Jenny when her step-
mother accepts Tom.

Jenny's bedroom was small with an old wardrobe in the corner and a
chair by the bed and the wallpaper had large red roses which Jenny often
counted. She often stayed in bed and was late for breakfast as she
loved reading books.

Jenny shows courage in book 4, p.234 when she goes alone to Denton's Farm.
    "   "   book 9, p 228 when she climbs the Fire Tower.
    "   "   book 16 Chapter 10 when Tom is missing and she
                      grows up.

Harman Jenny

Errors

Book 15 p.9. Is stated as being 17 years old which would mean
              she was older than Peter. (see p. 11).

Some Discrepancies in the Lone Pine Series

In *Mystery at Witchend* Mrs Morton says that Peter can sleep at Witchend. In *Seven White Gates* it states that Peter stays at Witchend at Christmas. In *The Neglected Mountain* Mrs Morton says there is not room for Peter to sleep at Witchend. In *Wings Over Witchend* Peter stays at Witchend.

In *The Gay Dolphin Adventure* Miss Ballinger smokes cigarettes and in *Treasure at Amorys* it states that she hates tobacco.

In *Seven White Gates* it states that Tom is a few weeks younger than David. In *The Secret of Grey Walls* he is six months younger than David. In *Wings Over Witchend* and *The Secret of the Gorge* Tom and David are both sixteen. In *Not Scarlet But Gold* Tom is nearly seventeen and David is sixteen. In *Man With Three Fingers*, *Strangers at Witchend* and *Where's My Girl?* it states that Tom is the oldest Lone Piner.

In *Seven White Gates* Reuben refers to David as Mr Reuben when he should have said Mr David.

In *Seven White Gates* Ward is the postman at Onnybrook. In *The Secret of Grey Walls* George is the postman and in *Wings Over Witchend* Charlie is the postman.

In *The Secret of Grey Walls* Mrs Smithson keeps the post office in Onnybrook. In *Wings Over Witchend* it is kept by Mrs Grimley.

In *Lone Pine Five* Barton Beach is approximately ten miles from Witchend. Later in the book when describing Mr Morton's journey to *Seven White Gates* he travels twenty-one miles.

In *Lone Pine Five* it states that Mary is usually the leader of the twins. In *The Secret of the Gorge* it states that Dickie is used to being the leader.

In *The Elusive Grasshopper* Jon's mother drives a car and in *Treasure at Amorys* it states that she does not drive and that her car is mostly used by Vasson.

In *Saucers Over the Moor* Penny's father's name is Jack and in *Where's My Girl?* it becomes George.

In *Saucers Over the Moor* a paragraph starts with David speaking and ends, without any reference to a change, with Jon speaking.

In *Saucers Over the Moor* a letter to Penny from her father states: 'We know how often you like to go to Witchend in Shropshire ...' Mr Saville does not bring the Warrenders to Witchend until *Home to Witchend*.

In *Saucers Over the Moor* it states that Dan Sturt's father died when he was fourteen. On the following page it states that it was just before his sixteenth birthday that his father died.

In *Wings Over Witchend* Tom has dark hair. In *The Secret of the Gorge* Tom has black hair. In *Man With Three Fingers* and *Where's My Girl?* Tom has fair hair.

In *Lone Pine London* it states that Jon stayed with the Mortons in their London home once before and then later in the book it says that this is his first visit.

In *Sea Witch Comes Home* Detective George Summers is later in the book called Bill Summers.

In *Man With Three Fingers* Lieutenant Colonel Nicholas Panthill is later in the book called Lieutenant Colonel Charles Panthill.

Index notes for Description of Witchend

Witchend is an old farmhouse a few miles from Onnybrook and is at the bottom of the Witchend valley of the Long Mynd, built so close to the mountain that it looks as if it was leaning on it.

At the end of the lane which led only to the house is a white gate between a wall of loose stones. Beyond the gate is a gleam of water, and a long barn on the left of the house. Under the roof in front two gabled windows jut. A stream runs under the wall which disappears under the hedge at the bend of the lane.

The little brook runs down through the heather until it broadens into a pool before the front door of the house, dashes on again through a narrower channel under the stone wall and then slides down the side of the lane that leads to Ingles Farm. Jemima, Mary's duck, spends a lot of time in this pool.

The bicycles are kept in a shed round the corner of the house and the old barn is used as a garage.

There is a tank on the roof for water, which has to be pumped. Pipes have been run from a good spring upon the hill behind the house and the old range in the kitchen heats the water.

Dead wood from the wood has to be collected daily as the coal man only calls once a year.

Milk has to be fetched twice a day from Ingles.

It is a fascinating house—friendly downstairs and really lived in. The kitchen—where they have their meals—is the jolliest room and full of surprises. An oak chest under the window and a hearth rug made of scraps of coloured cloth sewn together, a copper warming pan which reflects the firelight from one wall, while on the other two peculiar pictures make this a fascinating room. An old calendar hangs above the mantelpiece which carries a row of blue tins labelled currants, rice, sugar, etc. The kitchen is a big room with a low beamed ceiling from which hangs a large oil lamp. The floor is of stone and along one wall is a big kitchen range with a cheerful fire.

A narrow uncarpeted staircase leads from the kitchen and another door opens into a scullery which has a sink and a copper and a bath. In another corner is a grandfather clock with a loud tick and a pendulum. Upstairs is a muddle. From the top of the stairs nothing is straight. There is a loose board on the landing that creaks violently and the passage has two turns and three odd steps. Some of the windows are almost on floor level and the boys' room has a door into Mr and Mrs Morton's room.

David's bedroom at Witchend is small and he shares it with his brother Dickie. It has a long sloping floor and a little dormer window looking out over the stream to the edge of the wood. Since the first night he has pushed his bed right under the window so that he seems to be sleeping almost on the mountain itself.

There is a big room full of lumber at one end of the landing and Agnes' room isn't much more than a cupboard.

There is no electricity laid on and they have lamps and candles.

Downstairs there is a long low room with a wood fire and the front door has a latch.

Mr Morton had installed a tiny bathroom (*Wings Over Witchend*).

In *Strangers at Witchend* the house is now on the telephone, and Mr Morton has had a long barn converted into two bedrooms, living room, kitchen and bathroom for Peter and Mr Sterling for as long as they want it for their home.

David John Morton

Age ranges over the series from 15 to nearly 18
Hair: Brown
Eyes: Dark

He appears in all the books.

David is fairly solidly built and has a pleasant open-air look about him. He has a snub nose, brown hair, dark eyes and very white, even teeth in a tanned face. He has a decisive voice and is one half inch taller than Peter.

He is steady, fearless and always to be relied upon and is a born leader. He is a Scout and good at managing things. He is undemonstrative, but would never desert a friend if he could help it. David does not talk unnecessarily.

He snores and is not good at getting up in the morning. He enjoys camping and prefers a sleeping bag to a bed.

David is the Captain of the Lone Pine Club which he founded with Peter; they are the sort of friends who do not need to talk much to understand each other. He is crazy about cricket, and, although Peter is a good swimmer, David is better. He is not like the twins to look at. The twins are often tolerated by the other club members for David's sake. He can never understand Jenny and at first did not really like her.

He is not particularly clever but is above average at school work and games.

When David is sixteen (*The Neglected Mountain*) he begins to realise what a grand girl Peter is and that she is the most sensible girl he has ever known. Unlike her, he does not like Alsatians.

Although David has learned to love London since moving to Brownlow Square, he is never happier than when he is at his parents' holiday home Witchend.

In *Not Scarlet But Gold* David suggests that Harriet be the last Lone Piner as nine friends who promise to be true to each other is enough, and this is agreed.

Although only sixteen, David, after misunderstandings with Peter, realises that he cares very much about her, and tells her that there has never been any other girl for him, but that he has been foolish not to tell her. He informs her that he has been jealous of John Smith.

> Suddenly she was being kissed and when she recovered her breath and said, 'David! You've never done that before,' he kissed her again.
>
> 'That's a pity,' he laughed. 'I grew up yesterday, Peter. There's never been any girl but you but I've been a fool not to tell you—and all this just because my letter never reached you …'
>
> *Not Scarlet But Gold*

'There was nothing new in what they said to each other. Nothing new in the way in which they mended a quarrel and nothing new in the promises they made.'
Not Scarlet But Gold

At nearly eighteen, David has just left school and has just passed his driving test (*Man With Three Fingers*).

In *Rye Royal* he lives and works in London. He tells Peter that he is hoping to be a junior partner near Onnybrook when he is through his articles so that he will never have to ask her to leave the Shropshire Hills, now that they know that their lives will always be spent together.

David shows courage in:
The Secret of the Gorge When he fights Sydney Blandish who attacks the Lone Piners' camp. (Chapter—'The Attack on the Camp')
Not Scarlet But Gold When he defends Peter against John and Jem at Mrs Clark's cottage. (Chapter—'She Knows Too Much')

Errors
The Secret of Grey Walls p138 Last line first paragraph. Should read 'Is it a good idea?'
Lone Pine Five p234 States that Peter is a better swimmer than David. (See *Mystery at Witchend* p129 'Peter swam very well indeed, but David was better'.)
Saucers Over the Moor p82 States that David has grey eyes. (See *The Gay Dolphin Adventure* p125 'dark eyes'.)
  p172 Starts with David speaking and ends without reference with Jon speaking.
The Secret of the Gorge p155 David says that Peter is a better swimmer than himself. (See *Mystery at Witchend* p129.)
  p191 David says he knows that Peter is a better swimmer than himself. (See *Mystery at Witchend* p129.)
Sea Witch Comes Home p20 States that he has grey eyes. (See *The Gay Dolphin Adventure* p125.)
  p24 States that he does not like London. In *Lone Pine London* p54 he says that he does like London.
Not Scarlet But Gold p29 States that he has grey eyes. (See *The Gay Dolphin Adventure* p125.)
Treasure at Amorys p66 States that he is obviously the twins' brother. (In *The Gay Dolphin Adventure* p202 Val says 'You're not much like the twins, are you?')
Rye Royal p191 Third paragraph from end of book—line four. David tells Peter that the 'others' would like her to join the club. It should read Jon and Penny would like to join the club.

Petronella Sterling (Peter)

Age ranges over the series from 14 to 17
Hair: Blonde
Eyes: Blue
She appears in the following:

Mystery at Witchend	The Secret of the Gorge
Seven White Gates	Mystery Mine
The Secret of Grey Walls	Not Scarlet But Gold
Lone Pine Five	Man With Three Fingers
The Neglected Mountain	Rye Royal
Saucers Over the Moor	Strangers at Witchend
Wings Over Witchend	Where's My Girl?

Peter first appears in *Mystery at Witchend*.

She is tall and slim with long fair plaits which she refuses to cut off. She has a brown laughing face, a jolly grin and blue eyes. She does not resemble the Sterlings to look at but is like her mother whom she can only just remember. She is quiet, steady and fearless and has not an enemy in the world. She is not good at pretending and is entirely natural. She is seldom demonstrative but is warm-hearted and can be very friendly and charming. She only wants to live in her Shropshire hills, never enjoys crowds and is not very keen on school. She is a boarder at Castle School in Shrewsbury, has been since she was ten years old, and is in Pollards House. She is always excited at the end of any term, when she becomes pale and unable to eat. She wins the Upper School Essay Prize for her subject 'Winter on the Hills' and her prize was her favourite book *Bevis* written by Richard Jefferies. Peter usually wears old brown jodhpurs and a bright blue open-necked shirt. Soon after meeting David she tells him that for the last ten years she has lived with her father—the last five at Hatchholt close to the top of the Mynd where her father is in charge of the reservoir. She lives with her father, her Welsh mountain pony, Sally, and a goat, Hepsy.

From the beginning, David knows that they will be great friends but realises that Peter is very strong-willed. She suggests that they form a secret club and that she be camp cook. She is elected vice-captain. At first she finds it hard to accept leadership from David or anyone else and has a lot to learn about team work.

During the first year of their meeting, Peter teaches David to ride Sally, something she has never done before. She soon realises that she will never fail David when he asks her to do something and she will also do anything for the twins.

When Peter meets Reuben, Miranda and Fenella for the first time, Miranda tells Peter her fortune, which comes true in *Not Scarlet But Gold*. She tells her that she will have many adventures before obtaining her heart's desire (*Seven White Gates*). Peter meets Jenny and suggests that she be made a member of the club. She also now realises that she is beginning to rely on David's decisions in all their adventures.

Peter has a rare understanding and great sympathy for all living things, particularly animals. She is not scared of any dog and can do anything with them. She is a good whistler, would never panic or lose her head or scream, and is not easily scared. She likes weak tea but hates very hot drinks. She is a good runner and David finds it difficult to catch her. She does not like cricket but is a good rider. She is a good swimmer, but David is better, although he lets her beat him when they race the first time they swim together in Hatchholt reservoir.

Peter suggests in a letter to David that Jon and Penny be made members of the club before she meets them (*The Gay Dolphin Adventure*).

After spending two weeks in London with the Mortons, she realises that she hates it and feels too dressed up and respectable. She longs for Shropshire where she always sleeps with her bedroom window open (*Lone Pine Five*).

At sixteen Peter is a very pretty girl and wears her plaits coiled round her head (*The Secret of the Gorge*). Later she wears her fair hair in a bun (*Mystery Mine*).

As Peter grows older, she has her hair cut to her shoulders and it looks like a golden shower and is even prettier. She is not very happy when her father tells her that they must leave Hatchholt as his work there is over, and he is too old to be high up in the hills alone while she remains at school (*Not Scarlet But Gold*). Peter realises that when she is older she will not be interested in any man more than David. She also knows that she is important to him too. There have always been close bonds between them, and when they are in great danger, she tells him that she has always loved him from the day they met on the Mynd. David tells Peter that he has been a fool not to tell her that she has always been the only girl for him.

When she is nearly seventeen, Peter leaves school and starts work in a big riding school in Ludlow, which is what she has always wanted to do. She now knows that one day she will spend her life with David and is very happy, particularly as she and her father will now live at Witchend, in the barn converted for them by Mr Morton. Mr Morton has asked Mr Sterling to look after the house while his family is in London, and to treat it as home for as long as he and Peter wish. They are to pay a small rent for this. A telephone has been installed (*Man With Three Fingers*).

At seventeen (*Rye Royal*) Peter is almost as tall as Jon and serenely beautiful. She tells David that she will go anywhere in the world with him and be thankful that he asked her.

Peter's bedroom at Hatchholt is tiny and has a dormer window jutting from the roof and facing down the valley. Her bedroom window is always open. There is a slanting roof by the bed and a door with an old-fashioned latch.

Peter shows courage in:

Seven White Gates Chapter 'The Caravan'—when she saves Fenella's life by stopping the runaway caravan.

The Secret of Grey Walls Chapter 'The Girls to the Rescue'—when confronted by a large Alsatian dog.

The Neglected Mountain Chapter 'The Cave'—when she risks her life to save Mary in the cave in Greystone Dingle.

Not Scarlet But Gold Chapter 'Peter and David'—when they are trapped in the cave with John.

Where's My Girl? Chapter 'Our Girls'—when she is kidnapped with Jenny in the fish shop in Plymouth.

Errors

The Secret of Grey Walls p11 States that Mrs Sterling died when Peter was born. (See *Mystery at Witchend* p85: Peter tells David that she can only just remember her mother.)

Saucers Over the Moor p90 Hated very hot drinks. In *Secret of Grey Walls* p82 she enjoys a flask of scalding coffee.

Wings Over Witchend p11 She is not very keen on school. In *Secret of Grey Walls* p11 she likes school.

The Secret of the Gorge p54 States that Peter wears her hair in coiled plaits. On the dustwrapper her hair is in conventional plaits.

Not Scarlet But Gold p27 States that Peter cannot remember her mother. (See *Mystery at Witchend* p85.)

This page and opposite: my original draft of Penny with Mr Saville's amendments

```
PENELOPE WARRENDER (PENNY)

Age ranges over the series from 15 to 17

Hair   Red

Eyes   Grey

Has appeared in the following:

The Gay Dolphin Adventure      Lone Pine London
The Secret of Grey Walls       Mystery Mine
The Elusive Grasshopper        Treasure At Amorys
Saucers Over The Moor          Rye Royal

Penny first appears in The Gay Dolphin Adventure.  She is 15 years old
with naturally curly red hair which is her special pride.  She has wide-
set grey eyes and a tip-tilted freckled nose.  She has an awful temper
but is a rare fighter for her friends and for what she believes to be
right.  She was affectionate and loyal; impetuous and independent and in
many ways old for her years.  — At the Gay Dolphin in Rye

Penny's Father worked for the Government in India and Penny hardly ever
saw her parents and always lived with her cousin Jon and his Mother in
the holidays.  She had worshiped Jon's Father who had been killed in the
war and her Aunt Margaret was like a second Mother to her.  Apart from
schoolmistresses her Father was the only person to call her Penelope as he
did not like abbreviations, particularly when the name was nice.  Her
cousin Jon called her "Newpenny" when he was pleased with her because of
the colour of her hair.  Penny had helped Jon with all sorts of crazes,
the strongest of which was collecting train numbers and she was always
happy to do as he wished as he had never let her down when she needed him
and for many years her faith in him had remained unshaken.  Although she
often teases and infuriates Jon she would follow him to the end of the
world.

Penny only wore a hat at school and looked best in her emerald green
linen frock with a scarlet belt and sandals.  She hated wearing gloves but
loves the necklace of green beads that Jon gave her while they were on
holiday in Paris. (Elmineshopper)

Penny was made a member of the Lone Pine Club at H.Q.3 - Clun Castle - in
The Secret Of Grey Walls (p.102).  She was a much better whistler than Jon
and could soon imitate the peewit call.

She hated the explaining part of an adventure but loved danger.  She was
impulsive, moody, quick to love and hate but liked excitement and an
adventure.
```

who called her a red headed jaguar

p27 States that she knows no home but Hatchholt. (See *Mystery at Witchend* p85 Peter says that for the last ten years she has lived with her father—the last five at Hatchholt.)

p29 States that she can swim better than David. (See *Mystery at Witchend* p129 'Peter swam very well indeed, but David was better'.)

Rye Royal p124 States that Peter can swim better than David (see *Mystery at Witchend* p129.)

p191 Third paragraph from end of book—line four. This should read that Jon and Penny would like to join the club and not Peter.

Home to Penny is The Gay Dolphin Hotel and the Marsh which she describes as "green and white". She loves Rye and nearby Hastings.

For many years Penny had kept a daily diary which was very private but most of the contents eventually found their way to her parents in India. She always responded well to people who were interested in her and preferred people to things.

[?which book] Penny's birthday is in July and Miss Ballinger once gave her a gift of a painting she had done of the "Dolphin".

Penny was not studious and the only thing she was good at at school was gym. Hates cycling and thunder and was secretly ashamed that she could not ride a bicycle without using her hands.

At 16 (The Elusive Grasshopper) Penny was a very attractive young lady even though she was still a scatterbrain. ~~She knew no morse and~~ her French was not good and although it annoyed Jon she relied very [where shown] successfully on sign language. ~~She still found it difficult to keep still and hated waiting for anything and was breathless and incoherent when excited.~~

Jon tells Penny ~~that~~ she is an awful writer and she always gets ~~angry~~ when he reminds her of the difference of a year in their ages. She was a good mimic and once tells Jon that only those who can see fairies can hear the music of Midsummer hum like they could but Jon was usually too practical to understand what she meant.

Penny had been on Sally's back occasionally but was not keen on riding. She was a good swimmer but never settled long enough to be good at any sport. At 16 (Mystery Mine) Penny was growing up and although she had once thought Jon was a substitute for a brother she realises that he is much more important than that now.

When Penny is in danger (Treasure At Amorys) she realises just how much Jon means to her and also her to him and she tells him that she knows he will always come when she needs him and that she only wants him.

At 17 (Rye Royal) Penny has now left school and is at Domestic Science College in Hastings.

Penny's room in the Hotel was tiny but gay with chintz. There were flowers on the window-ledge by the fluttering curtains and on the little dressing-table with its dainty frill. She had a hand-basin in her room which looked out into the little walled garden and on the other side of the wall were the shallow steps of Trader's Passage.

Penny shows courage in The Gay Dolphin Adventure when she is locked in the Ballinger's beach bungalow (Chapter Noah's Ark).

Saucers Over The Moon when she escapes down the improvised rope to rescue the other Lone Piners (Chapter Penny in Danger).

Treasure At Amorys when she is captured in The Smugglers Rest (Chapter Ballinger Again).

Chapter VIII

Lone Pine Wales

During the many discussions I had with Mr Saville, I would reiterate, as I had done so often, how much I loved the *early* Lone Pine books, and how I always felt that these were his greatest work. He said that he understood my feelings exactly and added that the later Lone Pine books were written much within the guidelines of Collins. They wanted mileage from a popular series, and for books that they produced to be modernised with less description and more action. I was most indignant when he told me of this, but, as he sadly made me realise, the only way to remain in print and continue the series was to bow to the pressure of the publishers. This is what happened, but for Mr Saville the gradual disillusionment never left him, and he felt that his precious Lone Piners were no longer completely in his hands, as they had been originally.

I learned of Mr Saville's possessiveness towards his characters when he asked me to take over the running of the Lone Pine Club for him and devise competitions and quizzes. In a letter to me of 30 April 1973 Mr Saville told me that one reader wrote to him informing him that he had not enough time to do competitions because he was too busy writing his own Lone Pine story. He enclosed a copy of a chapter for Mr Saville to read entitled, if I recall correctly, *Not Quite Jenny's Day*. Mr Saville sent this to me and I thought that he would explode with indignation that anyone would dare to write about one of *his* characters—and that that character should be his favourite, Jenny, only added insult to injury. He said that he wanted nothing more to do with this former fan, and from that day we never mentioned him. It took a long time on my part to soothe him, but I did receive confirmation of one important lesson, not that it was one that had ever been necessary for me. Mr Saville's characters belonged one hundred per cent to him and for anyone to dare forget that was to bring down his wrath upon their heads.

When equilibrium had been restored, I told Mr Saville of an idea that I thought would take his mind from the injustices that he was experiencing from many quarters of the writing world, and, after cautious interest and listening intently to what I had to say, I finally convinced him. We agreed to say nothing to anyone else for the present. I had persuaded Mr Saville to write another early Lone Pine story and I promised to be his personal assistant. I recall drawing attention to gaps in time, when it would be easy to slot in another story that would sit comfortably between the two books chronologically on either side of the new one. I knew that Mr Saville had an endless quest for territory that his sixth sense told him would provide scope for an adventure. I had to suggest somewhere that would harmonise with those early books.

In May 1973 Mr Saville had written to me '… and if I ever wrote another, Jon and Penny would have to play the leads.' These words pleased me greatly as the last Jon and Penny story had been *Rye Royal* in 1969. This had been followed by *Strangers at Witchend* in 1970 and *Where's My Girl?* in 1972. The years between 1973 and 1978, when *Home to Witchend* was published, were busy years for Mr Saville. *Diamond in the Sky*, which completed the

Buckingham series, was published in 1974, and *Marston—Master Spy*, which completed the Marston Baines series, in 1978. Other publications included *Eat What You Grow* in 1975 and *Portrait of Rye* in 1976.

Our discussions about this book were pushed in between Mr Saville's busy schedule of publishing other books in that five-year period, and in a letter of September 1978 I was to read these words: 'It is strange that I've never brought the Warrenders to Witchend.' It was indeed odd that, in a series spanning many years, this had been the case; that the cousins from Rye had never officially been brought to Witchend. This new book would go back in time to rectify the omission. At every opportunity I had done my utmost to take Mr Saville on a guilt trip for underexposure of Jon and Penny. When I had said that I was not really asking for preferential treatment for them the interjection came swiftly that I certainly was. Often I would feel that my entreaties fell on deaf ears, and then, with the surprise and power of a spring freshet, the visionary words came tumbling out. Of course he agreed with everything that I had said about Jon and Penny, and, yes, they must have a special story. It would contain the cousinly camaraderie that the reader first enjoys in *The Gay Dolphin Adventure* and rekindle the innocent friendships shared with the other Lone Piners in the early books. It was almost as if he wished to reassure me that Jon and Penny had not been forgotten. It was only then that I realised that all of Mr Saville's characters were of equal importance to him. He had the difficult task of gauging how much prominence each was to have in relation to what his readers wanted.

'"Look!" whispered Jon, staring at the envelope. "It's addressed to me! Do you think it's a trick?"'— illustration from The Gay Dolphin Adventure

I proposed a story about Jon and Penny coming to Shropshire, commencing at Witchend with a Club meeting, held as it should be in the shadows of the Lone Pine tree. They would then move to other locations with the Mortons and Peter. I indicated places where I knew that I could help him with minute detail, like Bridgnorth with its unusual cliff railway, its open-air market and the remains of a ruined castle.

Warming to my subject, I said—'Let them go to North Wales.' As a half-Welsh girl I had always thought that such a background was just right, considering Wales' proximity to Shropshire. Although many of the Shropshire stories were tantalisingly close to the Welsh borders, Mr Saville's Lone Piners had never stepped over the boundary into this country; but when I threw down the gauntlet, Mr Saville picked up the challenge. Travel could be by train; and I told him of the many holidays that I had spent in Fairbourne where there was a miniature railway, and where at its terminus you walked over the sand to a small ferry to be taken to the larger town of Barmouth. I knew that this would make Mr Saville think of *The Elusive Grasshopper* and *Sea Witch Comes Home*.

I talked about the magic of Criccieth, which I visited annually and, of all the places in the world, was the one to which I always longed to return, and I assured him that I knew almost every pebble on its beach. I

First edition dustwrapper of Rye Royal

described the ruined castle, high on its hill, dominating two beaches. I told him of the wild openness of the beach that stretched to Black Rock, which is volcanic and maybe the oldest rock in the world. I said that you could walk along this shingle and all that you would hear was the bleating of sheep and the murmur of the sea, or the crashing of the waves, depending on the season of the year. Mr Saville was particularly interested in the community hymn singing that was held every Sunday evening in the summer season, weather permitting. This took place on a grassy area between the lifeboat station and the sea and, of course, the hymns were a mixture of English and Welsh. My request for my favourite hymn 'Calon Lan' sung in Welsh had never been refused. The singing always ended with a proud rendering of 'Land of my Fathers' that sent a thrill through everyone whose heart belonged to Wales.

Through my eyes I showed him the vast expanse of Tremadog Bay where Criccieth sits, and how David Lloyd George was reputed to have said that this was the best view in Wales (he was right). His wife Maggie loved Criccieth and he was to build a home there for his family—Brynawelon—which overlooks the sea. I mentioned the statesman's boyhood home at nearby Llanystumdwy, in which village he was to spend the final years of his life at his home, Ty Newydd. He was buried close by on the banks of the Afon Dwyfor. I felt that there was every likelihood that Llanystumdwy would feature in this new story, as it is only one and a quarter miles from Criccieth. The small village of Tremadog is noted for being the

Criccieth promenade and Castle taken in August

birthplace of the legendary T E Lawrence (Lawrence of Arabia). Mr Saville agreed that I had given him plenty to think about.

Whatever ingredients Mr Saville decided that he wanted for this story, I assured him that he would find them in my favourite corner of Gwynedd. There was a peaceful lake tucked away amongst the mountains, the shores of which would be ideal for a Lone Pine camp. A few miles away is Stwlan Dam poised high above Blaenau Ffestiniog and I did not need to remind Mr Saville that he knew how to use these to great effect. One of the most superb miniature train rides was available for his use, the terminus of which would point him to a maze of underground passages in a slate mine which also had a story to tell. He said that I appeared to have thought of everything.

I assured Mr Saville that whatever the season in which he chose to set his story, I had witnessed it. I was familiar with mountains covered with glistening snow in winter, and hot summer days when sea and sky merged in a shimmering haze. In between these came vicious gales, when the wind would howl and moan around our holiday home and the water from heavy rain would make unwelcome lakes on the paths outside the front door. Mr Saville said that some of this sounded rather grim, but agreed that the Lone Piners would like it.

With what I thought was a clever ruse, I said that I had once read a book by a brilliant author who had explained perfectly what it was like to want to go to a place so much that a peculiar feeling overcame one. This was how I felt about Criccieth, and, when Mr Saville had seen it, I knew that he would feel the same as I did. I described how, when nearing our destination, after our first glimpse of the sea, I would be quiet and my heart

David Lloyd George's boyhood home, Llanystumdwy

would beat a little faster because I would know that after negotiating the next bend in the road I would see Criccieth for the first time in twelve months. I would feel the familiar thrill as I gazed upon the scene that meant so much to me. I once read that when, after an absence, David Lloyd George travelled along this same road with his family they would cheer on rounding the final corner at the sight of Criccieth. I then said I would read the words to Mr Saville from the book that I was talking about. I had his complete attention now as I quoted, '*To-morrow* I shall really go home. *To-morrow* I shall see Daddy. *To-morrow* I shall go up the valley again to lovely Hatchholt.' My listener was highly amused at my relating his own words from the beginning of *Seven White Gates* as an encouragement to write about somewhere new, but I assured him that Wales would be an ideal Lone Pine location.

I knew that people were important to Mr Saville, so I told him of real characters who lived in Criccieth. There were Alan and Mary, whose home we rented during the summer months, when they would live in a caravan at the rear of their Beach Café which was so busy during the holiday season. I mentioned how Mary in her spare moments would bake scrumptious apple pies and the best lemon meringues in the world. I felt clever also mentioning Jim, as I knew of Mr Saville's interest in the history of lifeboats. Jim, the Welsh wizard of the motor car, who was also a lifeboat man, had told me many stories of how he felt about irresponsible holidaymakers who would float out to sea on airbeds, putting lives at risk when they should have known better.

New ideas were listened to eagerly and I suggested a dramatic scene for Penny which would involve the Criccieth lifeboat. It was not unlikely that she would get into trouble on the coast, as these were hitherto uncharted waters for Lone Piners. I described how the lifeboat house was sited almost hidden at the foot of the steep narrow road that led up to the castle. I drew a word picture for Mr Saville of how, when needed, the lifeboat was towed by a tractor over the road, down the slipway and across the pebbles to the sea. This manoeuvre could be done with great speed and almost before the final maroon had died away. Mr Saville did think that Penny would like to be at the centre of such a cry for help. I reminded him of his own words which proved this point. 'Penny loved danger. She was impulsive, moody, quick to love and quick to hate, but she liked excitement and an adventure.'

'Dickie launched the eclair with great success.'—illustration from The Gay Dolphin Adventure *(which includes the three villains to have been in* Lone Pine Wales*)*

As Slinky liked the sea I suggested that he be given an airing. In addition, that there should be a visit from Arlette, as my one complaint was that Mr Saville hardly ever gave brunettes much word space. Mr Saville had once written to me, 'A girl of about 12 the other day wrote a nice letter and at the end said: What about a brunette for a heroine just for a change? You do like redheads and blondes, don't you? and that made me think and I told her I would do my best soon with a dark beauty with hair as black as a raven's wing.' I was smug when I realised that I had an unknown accomplice in the promotion of dark-haired girls, but I did accept that Mr Saville would never deviate from his penchant for redheads.

My enthusiasm for this project in introducing Mr Saville to a part of Wales that I loved so well had the desired effect, and he promised to think about this. It was not long before he said it was a good idea, and did I have any suggestions for a plot? I proposed something to do with a gold mine in Wales, because the wedding rings of our Royal family are traditionally made from Welsh gold. He thought that this was a good idea. I promised to keep this delicious secret and to help him all that I could to bring this book to fruition. As an afterthought I reminded him that all we knew about Charles and Trudie's wedding was that Peter had been bridesmaid. Maybe the wedding could be elaborated on and mentioned in the story. Why should not Trudie have a Welsh gold ring?

There was much to-ing and fro-ing of ideas for this book which would go back in time. There was always a cheerful or fun message at the end of letters such as, 'So be happy and have a wonderful time,' and 'Up the Lone Piners as Dickie would say.'

Inevitably, I bombarded Mr Saville with all sorts of ideas until he pleaded with me to

First edition dustwrapper of Lone Pine London

stop, but he did agree that I had given him plenty of suggestions about which to write. By now he was greatly excited and I made him laugh giving outrageous titles for the new book. If he ever decided on a title for this story he never told me but it was most likely to be Lone Pine Wales because of its similarity to *Lone Pine London* which had proved a popular title. This new story would probably be placed after *The Neglected Mountain* and before *Mystery Mine*. It gladdened my heart that I had cheered Mr Saville and encouraged him to be enthusiastic once more about the days of the early Lone Pine books, a time in his life when I felt that he was at the peak of his creativity. He told me that he had sent each chapter of *Mystery at Witchend*, as he wrote it, to his family for them to read, but of course he wrote his books for all children everywhere.

He took me, a child of the 1950s, into an enchanted world and gave me all those new places that in latter years I was to explore and enjoy in real life. I like to think that in encouraging him to write this book, which he admitted he had never thought of himself, I brought back the eagerness of writing he had in the days when he wrote exactly as inspired.

I knew that Mr Saville made preliminary notes for this story, as he discussed numerous ideas with me but sadly it was never written. Maybe lack of time and the demands of Collins were the reason that this book never came into being. He never lost his enthusiasm for writing this story but *Home to Witchend* had to come first. Other writing projects then seemed to take over and I was particularly disappointed about this. However, it made me glad that I was able to assist my friend and assure him that older readers wanted to stay in their time warp in the magical world of the early Lone Pine books. They had given me the best guide as to how to live my life.

Chapter IX

Home to Witchend

'Besides my family and my friends, I am obsessed with Children and Books.'

Mr Saville wrote this in a letter to me in September 1972. In these, his own words, he told me the secret of his success as a writer for children, and I was to see the truth of this statement during the years that we were in contact with each other. He also wrote, 'I love my work and know how lucky I am to have the appreciation of my readers—of all ages! I'm not sure whether I shall write more than 20 Lone Pine books but there is a wise saying that you should stop when you're reasonably sure that you've reached the best you can do.' These were indeed wise words and although I wanted Mr Saville to continue to write books for ever, it was with regret that I knew that this could not be.

Of all the books that Mr Saville had written, it was the Lone Pine series that had made him famous and was the most popular. It was probably for this reason that he pondered over what was to be the final story, because he knew that it had to be just right. There were so many loose ends to tie up, so many characters in the previous nineteen books. He had to decide who would be in this story and, of course, he had to decide its setting. We had many discussions about this, long before a single word was written, and had some differing views, particularly over the prominence that Jon and Penny should have.

When Mr Saville had first introduced his readers to these characters at Charing Cross railway station, he had no idea that he would still be writing about them over thirty years later. Their cousinly friendship had always been special, but now their creator had to decide whether it was to be put on a formal footing, and this worried him. In a letter to me he wrote:

> I've got myself into rather a mess with J and P because they are cousins and 'are supposed not to marry'. I must check on this as medical opinion may have changed and this could be 'an old wives tale'. What does Brian think? One ingenious suggestion is that Penny must marry Dan Sturt but what happens to poor old Jon? Is he sentenced to celibacy? This is rather tricky but if I was clever enough we might [start] this story with Jon seeing Sturt and Penny together and telling them he'll be their brother for ever at which Peter and the others can affirm that marriage is never the end of the story but only the beginning of another—specially for Lone Piners!—and that will keep the reader guessing—and me.

Although I assured him, as did Brian, that it was quite legal for first cousins to marry, I knew that he was unhappy about this. He then mentioned to me that maybe he would not have them in this story after all, but would instead have a letter written by them to David and Peter congratulating them on their engagement as a way of including Jon and Penny in the story without them actually appearing. I disagreed strongly with him over this idea.

I am certain that the success of my friendship with Mr Saville was that, to me, he was first and foremost my favourite author, who welcomed me into his life and work. Although our friendship was built on trust and loyalty, I was always the adoring fan happy to do his bidding without question, and delighted to be the one that he asked. This was one occasion, however, when I was aghast that he could even consider leaving Jon and Penny out of the story. He quickly assured me that it was not that he did not want them in, but that he just did not know what to do about concluding their relationship. For David and Peter it was easy, as the whole story was to be set around their engagement party, and I knew that he had similar plans for Tom and Jenny. I reminded Mr Saville of the closing paragraphs of *Treasure at Amorys* where he had made it abundantly clear that there was a budding romance between Jon and Penny.

> … As the car disappeared round the corner of the lane Penny turned blindly and ran back up the drive. Jon ran after her and they saw him give her a clumsy hug and then she grabbed his arm and led him round the side of the house.
> The Major cleared his throat.
> David put Mackie down.
> Dickie said, 'Well. What do you know? Who's going to get our breakfast now? And come to think of it we haven't been very long finding another treasure have we, twin?'
> 'No,' Mary replied thoughtfully. 'No, we haven't. Nor to have another love affair on our hands but I s'pose we've had this one nearly as long as David and Peter. We shall get used to it I s'pose.'

Mr Saville was hoist with his own petard. He knew that I would never let him retract one single incriminating word of his admission that Jon and Penny meant more to each other than their blood relationship. When he rather hesitantly asked what I thought of the idea of Penny having Dan Sturt as a boyfriend, I replied that I was firmly against it, as I felt instinctively that this would not be right, and that his readers would not be happy about it. I thought it was rather clever to make the point in this way as I knew that if he felt his readers would dislike something, he certainly would not do it. I strongly believed that Jon and Penny had to be together somehow, even if not officially. I suggested that maybe they could have a chapter to themselves set in Rye early on in the story, a device he had used with great success in previous books. As Rye shared nearly equal importance in the series as Shropshire and was home to Jon and Penny, it would be a natural way of explaining their future, quite separately from the rest of the story. When Mr Saville said that he liked this idea and would consider it, I knew that I had won. He knew that I would always champion Jon and Penny and, as I told him years later, the chapter that he wrote for them was perfect.

The story to end the series was to be set in Shropshire, around Witchend and also Barton Beach. It could be no other way, as the rolling grandeur of the Long Mynd and the sinister Stiperstones had been important presences throughout the series. Notes and jottings of a kaleidoscope of ideas started to drop through my letterbox. I realised that he must have used up an enormous amount of paper in his long writing career. It was quite normal for me to receive notes written on the back of old manuscripts as well as receiving letters on out-of-date notepaper. I was always amused at Mr Saville's continued thrift and, of course, always eager to read his ideas. Numerous plots were suggested, some to be discarded and others elaborated upon. There were to be many alterations before Mr Saville was finally satisfied with the ideas set out before him like a map. It was only then that he started to write. Always the professional, he felt it was extremely important that he gave the readers what they wanted.

The Gypsies, Reuben, Miranda and Fenella, were to be in this final story. Indeed, Fenella plays an important role by locating where Miss Ballinger lives:

'I am not frightened now I hear you. It is like a magic. Dickie, tell Mary that I have done what you ask. What you and Mary ask. I will always do what you ask. Any time you want I will do it for you … This is it … The house where the fat Pam lives is not far away … Some of our Romany friends have told me. It is called Appledore … Now I must go but I always do what you ask and I do not know what else to say—' and then surprisingly and not quite as loud, 'I love you both and Petronella very much.'

Home to Witchend

For a long time, since their introduction in *Seven White Gates,* the Gypsies had been an interesting and picturesque feature of the books, never playing a very major role but often

First edition dustwrapper of The Secret of the Gorge, *showing the Gypsy caravan*

Seven White Gates *dustwrappers by Bertram Prance (left) and Charles Wood*

giving important help when it is needed. Peter first meets them as she journeys to Seven Gates: 'Up the road from Shrewsbury came a gaily painted caravan.' As the caravan passes Peter, Reuben calls to her, 'Good luck, little *chi* …' This Romany word means child or girl. Through the Gypsies' friendship with Peter and later the other Lone Piners, the reader learns other Romany words like *errate* which Reuben explains to Peter means 'of the true gypsy blood'. Peter shares with her new friends a meal of *hotchi-witchi* which has been cooked on the Gypsy fire and is what we know as hedgehog. *Rawni*, the reader learns, means lady and Reuben uses it to address Mrs Morton when he greets her at Witchend. Mr Saville lets the reader know that these Gypsies are honourable and trustworthy and that different lifestyles and cultures are all acceptable in our world and should be treated with respect.

Before Peter leaves them Miranda offers to tell her fortune. Miranda then says that 'One day you will have your heart's desire, but there are many adventures to come first …' This is the promise which comes true in *Home to Witchend* on Peter's eighteenth birthday.

There had been so many fascinating characters in the series, many of whom had appeared only once. Mr Saville wanted to reintroduce a number of these. Mr Cantor and James Wilson were on this list and I knew that the villains would be Miss Ballinger, Slinky and Val. It could hardly have been otherwise, as this triumvirate had been as much a part of the series as the Lone Piners. I asked whether Arlette could be included as I was sure that she would give 'Ze luffley table' to David and Peter as a wedding gift. Mr Saville laughed at this and promised to let me have a list of the guests when he had decided on this and I had to be patient and accept this answer because I knew that he would tell me in his own time.

When Mr Saville first asked for my help on the twentieth Lone Pine book, particularly with regard to the plot, I thought hard about how to set about this. The answer was obvious: I would need to reread all of the Lone Pine stories set in Shropshire, not just to refresh my memory as to what had been written previously, but to get inside the books and renew the feel for them. Due to life's pressures, I had not read the Lone Pine books in recent years as regularly as I would have wished, but now I had the perfect reason to do so. This resulted in a stream of ideas being passed to Sussex and I often wondered whether I put forward too many suggestions. The reply, when I asked, was that I could never do that.

I received a letter that gladdened my heart with these words: 'I have a big file marked "LP20" which contains records of ideas received from readers over the years—and yours is the most important of these! … your splendid and invaluable Index will now come into its own.' I could not have read anything to please me more. The paragraph continued: 'I'm trying to re-read some of the Witchend stories, which is something I rarely do and have become rather intrigued with *Strangers at Witchend*. Next I shall read *Man With Three Fingers*.' I replied to this news that I was so pleased to learn that Mr Saville was reading such improving work in his spare time and glad that he was enjoying the stories. I felt a little self-satisfied that he also found it necessary to re-read the Shropshire stories before embarking on this most important book.

Mr Saville asked his readers in the Newsletter of spring 1973 what they would like him to write about in this final Lone Pine story:

Now suppose, just suppose, that I told you that the 20th Lone Pine Adventure was to be the last in the series which began in 1943? It has to end some time, and there are not many series of books for young people that have gone on for so many years. The Lone Piners have become part of my life, but I would like to know what you would like the last one to be about. Many readers have given me their views, but I do want ideas from as many of you as possible. I want to write what you would like to read now, and keep to read to your own children one day. Here are some of my ideas. What do you think of them?

The last L.P. must be set at Witchend where it all began. It must feature ALL the Lone Piners and the occasion might be a big party to celebrate the engagement of the three elder couples who must not be more than a year older than they were in the last book. Who else should be there? The parents, of course. James Wilson and his wife Judith? Arlette, the French girl from *The Elusive Grasshopper*? Mr Cantor? Rose and Paul Channing from *Sea Witch*? and what about the villains? Obviously the Ballinger, Valerie and 'Slinky'. Perhaps the twins could recognise one of them up to some villainy in the district? One very senior L.P. reader suggests that the Ballinger might now be concerned with the forgery of banknotes and I'm sure I could find her an old house in the Shropshire hills from where she could operate. Some readers have said that they would like to meet 'John Smith' the German boy from *Not Scarlet* again, and although there won't be room for everybody I would like to hear from all keen and loyal Lone Piners what sort of adventure they would like me to write for the last in the series.

New in paperback

The 20th Lone Pine Adventure

MALCOLM SAVILLE'S Thrilling LONE PINE ADVENTURES

LONE PINE adventures

The sign of the pine is the symbol of the LONE PINE CLUB, and reminds hundreds of thousands of boys and girls – and their parents – of the adventures described in Malcolm Saville's *Lone Pine* books. Each story is set in a real part of England, which can be, and often is, visited by *Lone Pine* readers.

This familiar sign stands not only for exciting adventure, but also for courage, loyalty, friendship and resourcefulness. The most important promise of the original Lone Piners was, "to be true to each other whatever happens", and so they have been. Today, boys and girls all over the world are founding their own Lone Pine Clubs, based on these qualities.

2 Million

Two million Lone Pine books have now been sold, and there are twenty different stories for you to collect. The first *Lone Pine* book was published more than thirty years ago, so this immensely successful series now delights and enthrals a third generation of young readers. The *Lone Pine* adventures are published in hardback by Collins and in paperback by Armada.

HOME TO WITCHEND

The elder Lone Piners have now left school and discover, in this fast-moving story, what they mean to each other. Set mostly against the background of their beloved 'silent hills', in this story the Lone Piners unexpectedly face some old enemies and meet many old friends. The twins, of course, become involved in a terrifying natural calamity, but they all have thrilling parts to play in a breathless adventure, culminating in a glorious, happy reunion – home at Witchend.

The Author

Malcolm Saville is a versatile and experienced writer. He is the author of more than eighty books – the first was *Mystery at Witchend*, the first *Lone Pine* adventure. At one time in his career he was editor of a children's weekly paper, and the books he now writes prove how much he enjoys writing for young people. He also delights in 'places', travels widely and explores the settings of all his stories, the most popular of which is undoubtably *Lone Pine*.

He welcomes letters from readers about his work and will answer yours if you write to him – c/o Armada Paperbacks, 14 St James's Place, London SW1A 1PS.

ALWAYS LOOK FOR THE SIGN OF THE PINE

Malcolm Saville's Lone Pine Adventures

1. **MYSTERY AT WITCHEND**
The exciting story of the founding of the Lone Pine Club, set in the wild highlands of Shropshire. The Mortons – David, and the twins, Dickie and Mary – Petronella (Peter) Sterling and Tom Ingles help their country in time of peril, in this, their first adventure.

2. **SEVEN WHITE GATES**
This thrilling story is set in the shadow of Shropshire's grim, haunted Stiperstones and the lonely farmhouse with seven gates. David, the twins, 'Peter' and Tom find a new member for their club – red-headed Jenny Harman.

3. **THE GAY DOLPHIN ADVENTURE**
In the romantic Sussex town of Rye, on the edge of Romney Marsh, David and the twins meet Jonathan and Penny Warrender, and help them in their hunt for smugglers' treasure from the famous old Gay Dolphin hotel.

4. **THE SECRET OF GREY WALLS**
Jon and Penny from Rye join the Lone Piners in Shropshire, where a new Lone Pine camp is established in the ruined castle of the little town of Clun. The Warrenders are enrolled as Lone Piners, and help to foil a gang of sheep stealers operating from the house with grey walls.

5. **LONE PINE FIVE**
In the fifth Lone Pine adventure, the Mortons, 'Peter', Tom and Jenny are involved in an exciting, dramatic hunt for Roman treasure in the Shropshire hills, and are endangered by an overflowing underground lake.

6. **THE ELUSIVE GRASSHOPER**
This thriller, dealing with modern smuggling, opens in Paris where Jon and Penny are finishing an 'educational holiday'. They return to Rye with the fascinating Arlette and, on the journey, recognise an old enemy. They send for the Mortons, who stay at the Gay Dolphin and help to solve the mystery of the antique shop known as 'The Grasshopper'.

7. **THE NEGLECTED MOUNTAIN**
This is Lone Piner Jenny Harman's name for the mysterious Stiperstones, in whose shadow she lives, and the setting for this exciting and unusual story. Her special friend Tom Ingles, the Mortons and 'Peter' become involved in a conspiracy concerning the drugging of guard dogs.

8. **SAUCERS OVER THE MOOR**
First seen over Rye by Jon and Penny, and again over Dartmoor, where the Warrenders meet the Mortons and 'Peter', these 'Unidentified Flying Objects' interest others more sinister than the Lone Piners. This gripping story is set against a background known to thousands of tourists.

9. **WINGS OVER WITCHEND**
Christmas tree thieves in the State Forest on the Long Mynd, a mysterious glider which only appears at night and a terrifying forest fire are dramatic features of this fast-moving Shropshire story. Macbeth, the twins' Scottie dog plays an important part.

10. **LONE PINE LONDON**
Jon and Penny Warrender visit the Mortons in London and become involved in a most unusual adventure concerning forged paintings. They meet again James Wilson, the journalist Who helped in the adventure of *The Elusive Grasshopper*, and the twins make a new friend, Harriet Sparrow.

11. **THE SECRET OF THE GORGE**
'Peter', David, Tom, Jenny and the twins hunt for the 'Whiteflower Diamonds' in this enthralling story set in Shropshire, with a thrilling climax in a deep gorge, through which the river Teme runs on its way to Ludlow.

12. **MYSTERY MINE**
A deserted mine on the North Yorkshire moors near Whitby is the setting for this unusual and topical adventure for Peter, the Warrenders, the Mortons and the twins' friend Harriet, a prospective member of the Lone Pine Club.

13. **SEA WITCH COMES HOME**
David Morton has no time to take anyone but the twins when he rushes off to his schoolfriend's home near Southwold in Suffolk, to help him solve an urgent, distressing family problem – the mystery of the missing *Sea Witch* and her master. The terrific climax is based on fact, when the sea breaks through the defences of East Anglia after a great storm, as they did in 1953.

14. **NOT SCARLET BUT GOLD**
The Mortons join the local Lone Piners in a search for treasure hidden by an enemy spy in the Shropshire hills in the last war. David and 'Peter' are trapped in an old mine and have to discover what they mean to each other.

15. **TREASURE AT AMORYS**
In this exciting Rye story, the Warrenders and the Mortons help to discover evidence of a Roman temple, when helping a lonely old man who befriended them, and the twins play a lively part in the foiling some old enemies.

16. **MAN WITH THREE FINGERS**
An old friend persuades Tom that lorry driving pays better than farming. But the lorry in which he makes a trial trip is hijacked, and the other Lone Piners fight to keep him out of trouble, and help a friend to find a treasure, in this exciting Shropshire story.

17. **RYE ROYAL**
During 'Peter's' first visit to Rye, she helps the Warrenders and Mortons to solve the mystery of a missing Elizabethan document, in a story featuring the famous Rye Fawkes bonfire celebrations.

18. **STRANGERS AT WITCHEND**
In this exciting story, Harriet Sparrow, the new Lone Piner, first visits Witchend. With the twins, she befriends a runaway boy and they all become involved in a desperate adventure which culminates in the burning of a lonely cottage on the summit of the Long Mynd.

19. **WHERE'S MY GIRL?**
The Mortons, 'Peter', Tom and Jenny are staying at a riding school guesthouse on Dartmoor. Strange goings-on arouse their suspicions and the Lone Piners are tumbled into exciting adventure. When 'Peter' and Jenny fail to return from a walk in Wistman's Wood, both David and Tom have reason to ask, "Where's my girl?"

Fliers like this were sent out at intervals

It was not long before he had a flow of readers' letters arriving at Chelsea Cottage. These were sent to me with the request that I would give my comments when I returned the letters. I found them fascinating reading. This was long before the book was published and on 30 April 1973 I received a letter which commenced:

Here is the first batch of letters about LP20 and I'm sure they will interest you. Basically, of course, I want guidance as to what will be the most acceptable plot—and I know you have ideas about that. Anyway will you go through these and give me your reactions and findings? The number who are passionately opposed to the closure of the series are few and many of the kids just repeat our ideas already given [in] the Newsletter. You will be pleased to see that a few suggest that the story should start in Rye with Jon and Penny and this may be an excellent, practical scheme. If you can give me some sort of breakdown on all these letters it will be very helpful. And your views too. In the end it is the author who must decide what he is going to write but there may well be some guidance for him in the views expressed by these young enthusiasts. You see that a few are much in favour of some retribution for the villains!

As someone who appreciated all weathers, he ended the letter, 'Lovely rain for the garden today'.

Reading Mr Saville's letters was almost like a diary of events, and decisions often changed. In May 1973 he wrote: 'We will have a Witchend party to celebrate David and Peter's engagement and we agree about the villains.' At that time neither of us knew that the party would be held in the barn at Seven Gates. He continued, 'It seems an excellent idea to start the story in Rye just before Jon and Penny go up to Witchend. I like this and think that it would still enable me to postpone the decision about cousins marrying. Quite a lot of children have written in the past saying what will Jon and Penny do because cousins can't marry.' Later in the letter I was pleased to read, 'You are right, of course, about the impossibility of bringing all the characters back again, and I should not attempt that, but a lot depends on the plot and action. Mr Cantor, YES. Arlette, yes. I may not be able to think much more about this until next year but I have arranged to talk to Collins about it all as soon as I have delivered the present story. It would certainly be nice to meet and talk all this over with you and I hope we shall later.' This letter ended with the PS, 'I am a bit worried about Uncle Micah, Mr Sterling, Jenny's parents, Charles and Trudie not to mention the Gypsies although they might be very useful to the plot! We shall see.'

I was always interested to hear all of Mr Saville's news and this snippet ended one letter: '… thank you, I'm feeling fine except that we are still suffering from "Gas Conversion" and have had no central heating for a week.' I gave the obvious sympathetic answer to this news and said that I hoped he was well wrapped up as he sat at his desk in Chelsea Cottage writing.

In April 1975 I was to learn Mr Saville's choice of a title for his story. He wrote, '… I think that when I have written LP20, which I shall call "Where It All Began", it will be published *only* in Armada first.' Naturally I was interested to know the title of the new book and wrote back that I thought it a good one, although to myself I did have reservations, as it did not mention Witchend.

In a later letter I read,

> I want to check with you firstly that Jon and Penny have never been to Witchend. I don't think they have been nearer than Clun and so we do have a specially good reason for bringing them up to the Big Party and bringing them into the story at Rye, say in Chapter III. Many readers agree with you that Rye must come into the story in some way and I agree too. We know that Mr and Mrs Warrender (Penny's parents) now really run the Dolphin and we might have some counterfeit notes passed there and a visit from the journalist Wilson who is investigating the passing of forged money in the Channel Ports. Anyway Jon at 18+ is still at Sussex University and could be home at [the] Dolphin in Christmas holidays when I think the story must start so that Peter's Party is Easter holidays when Witchend and Seven Gates would be very pleasant. I've already got up my sleeve a surprise engagement between Jenny and Tom who have kept it a secret until *after* Peter's big party! What do *you* think?

As was nearly always the case I replied that anything that he chose to write would be fine. Mr Saville also knew that it was right for Peter to be working in a stables in Ludlow and for romantic Jenny to work in a bookshop in Shrewsbury. When Penny embarked on her domestic science course, I could never quite see her as a cook, but to be helping at the reception desk in the Gay Dolphin and welcoming the guests was exactly right for her. Later in the same letter I read,

> All went well with my editor who, however, does not think 'Where It All Began' is a good title and wants <u>Witchend</u> in the title. I see what she means. What about 'Home at Witchend'? or 'Return to Witchend' or even 'Home is Witchend' because it will be Peter and David's home one day. On another point these two must get engaged *before* the big Party—in other words he must *ask her* before all the others are involved. Anyway I'll let you know how it progresses.

In 1977 I had noted that Mr Saville stuck an E before the Sussex of his address and when I mentioned this to him, this was his response: 'You query the address of *East* Sussex. We are still in the same place but the idiotic Authorities decided to divide Sussex into two—East and West. Aren't you now West Midlands instead of Worcestershire? Even so, some of my letters go to Winchester first. The P.O. doesn't believe Winchelsea is a real place.' I did find this amusing but entirely agreed with him and much preferred it when I lived in Worcestershire. It was quite a while before Mr Saville's notepaper was changed and told the world that he lived in East Sussex. He ended with the cheering words, 'All the best to you all. Hope to see you soon.'

The title of the book had now been decided and was to be *Home to Witchend*. I thought this was perfect. It was a long time since the story had started life as 'Where It All

Began', but I knew that Mr Saville was happy with the change when he agreed that the title should be *Home to Witchend*. In February 1978 I was delighted to read,

> I am able to give you some up to date news of the Lone Pine situation. Firstly, and most important, I am on the last chapters of the book now, but I have been so busy with other matters that I have rather fallen behind with my general work ... we are going away to a hotel in Eastbourne for a week from March 5th, and if I do nothing else I shall finish *Home to Witchend*. The plot in the later stages has been altered a little, so as to give Peter a little more prominence, but I cannot remember now whether I sent you a copy of the original plot. [He had done so] It would be very confusing for me to send the amendments, but what I am doing is to send David off on his own to see if he can discover where the Ballinger is hiding. He will be caught by one of the villains, imprisoned in the underground machine room at Appledore, and rescued next day by Peter on Sally, who goes off alone to find him. You may remember that the Ballinger has been deserted by Valerie and is left alone without her specs in the empty house, and it is there that the Lone Piners eventually discover her. The final chapter, of course, is the party to which some—but not all—of the Lone Piners' friends have been invited secretly by David.

I had been pleased when Mr Saville had decided to use Appledore again as the villains' hideaway, and it was appropriate that the first and the last book of the Lone Pine series should share this venue.

The letter continued,

> As you know *Home to Witchend* is to be published first as a paperback and indeed it may never appear at all in hardback, and this is due to today's disastrous situation in publishing. Practically no bookshops now stock children's fiction in hardback, because they stay on the shelves too long. Public Libraries no longer have the money to spend on new books and without much doubt the first sacrifices they make are in the children's section. Other difficulties are that there are not enough actual retail outlets for all children's paperbacks to be stocked and shown, and for that reason even Lone Pine is not likely to have all twenty titles on sale at the same time. But I shall be well backed by Collins when the time comes and *Home to Witchend* is published in October.
>
> Meanwhile, I would like you to know that your name will be mentioned in my acknowledgments at the beginning of the book. Your Index has proved invaluable to me, because I always knew that when I wrote the last book in the series, there would have to be some sort of get-together of the Lone Piners and their friends.

I was thrilled to read these words, as I had never dreamed that the labour of love that I had performed for Mr Saville for so many years would be acknowledged in such a public way.

I read on, 'It may be possible for me to show you a typescript of the whole book when it is written, so that you will be able to see how valuable your help has been.' I was familiar with typescripts and had seen a number of Mr Saville's books when they were at this stage. I can only describe them as being almost like a kitchen roll and most unwieldy to hold. These would be sent to me for their final check, which I carried out with diligence. I was fully aware of the trust placed in me and of the responsibility that I had to ensure that the books contained no errors. I was glad I might see the typescript of *Home to Witchend*. Of all the books that had been published during our long friendship, this was the one with which I had been most closely involved.

This letter finished with the almost inevitable personal touch that my friend knew I enjoyed. 'As I dictate this the sun is shining, although we still have some frozen snow about in the garden. You can imagine how the gales have been roaring over the Marsh down here, but for the last ten days or so the icy winds from the north east have been making even Winchelsea rather chilly.' I shivered as I read these words.

14 March 1978 was a red letter day in my interest in the progress of *Home to Witchend,* as I received these most welcome words: 'I've finished *Home to Witchend* and the last chapter is being typed now. Later on, when I've seen how many copies the Publishers want, you may borrow my typescript. Meanwhile I'm compiling, with the help of your Index, a list of the characters featured in *this* book and what other stories they appeared in.' He continued, 'I will send you a copy of my complete list for you to check later together with a copy of part of my Intro in which your name is mentioned.' The letter ends with, 'I'll send you the new Newsletter after Easter.' This was something that I was to look forward to, as I knew that it would contain the news for his readers that *Home to Witchend* was finished.

All the months and years of agonising over this book were ended, and the sense of relief that this was so turned to elation for Mr Saville. As always his mood affected me, as he embarked on the important step of giving this book the best launch possible. One of the ideas was to have a quiz based on the new book, as these had been so successful in the past. I was pleased to receive a letter from him in July 1978 which commenced, 'Yes—I would like to see your suggestions for an L.P. Quiz very much, thank you. I've forgotten the last one, but I'm now making plans with Collins for the launch of *Home to Witchend* and have an idea that a Quiz might go out with the October Newsletter. I'll discuss this with them as soon as possible and let you know.' He finished this letter, 'Yes, thank you. We enjoyed Paris and Brussels.' I was delighted to hear this, because travel always seemed to recharge Mr Saville's batteries and he came home with renewed and positive energy. I was so caught up in the exhilaration that I felt in my friend that at first I had not taken in the news of the postscript to this letter, which was dated two days later. I read, 'PS Have seen Collins who are most enthusiastic over the Quiz. We may circulate it at Schools and Book Fairs etc at end of Sept when *Home to Witchend* is published.' Ideas immediately came into my head at this news and I knew that compiling this new Quiz would be a top priority.

Because of the drama I almost missed the final sentence of this letter: 'Thought you would like this souvenir of the cover.' Mr Saville's envelopes invariably contained more than just a letter, and I had hardly been aware of the slim piece of card which was resting face down. I turned it over thinking at the time it was just like him to mention almost as an afterthought

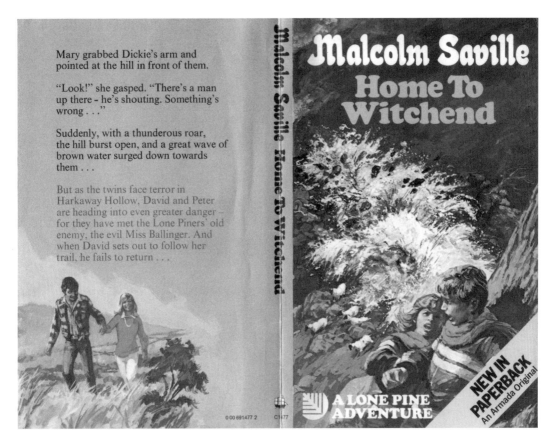

Mr Saville sent me this sample of the paperback cover to be used on Home to Witchend.

something as important as the new book's cover. I gazed at it with mixed feelings and almost with dismay. The characters depicted were unrecognisable to me as any of the Lone Piners, but, if this was the cover that Collins wanted, I had to be enthusiastic about it and accept it for Mr Saville's sake. I had to try to look at it through the eyes of young people at that time, and in doing this I realised that it was right for that market. It was bright and colourful, showing the twins in great danger. On the rear cover was a modern depiction of Peter and David on the gentle and rolling Long Mynd, and showed the happiness and harmony of that soon-to-be engaged couple. By return, I said all the right things about this cover, and Mr Saville said that he was pleased that I had accepted it. However, soon the almost inevitable words came from him and I was not surprised to read, 'We can't *do* anything about the new jackets but I agree that the characters as portrayed by the new artist are not much like my descriptions. The same designs are used for 3 editions including the paperbacks and are really to appeal first to the bookseller who is likely not to stock the books if he thinks the jackets look old fashioned! On the whole I think the modern child will like the new ones.' As always he was right. He knew perfectly well that it would not be my choice, but, if he could accept it, I must as well, and we would have to go forward into that new world, however reluctantly. This made me ashamed of my doubts and I vowed to promote this book with all the enthusiasm that I could. I suddenly realised that it was what was *inside* the cover that mattered, and I could give this my one hundred per cent support.

It was some time before I was to receive my signed paperback version of this book. In the interim period I cajoled Mr Saville to tell me what he had chosen for Peter's engagement ring. I asked if it would be sapphires to match her eyes, saying that I knew that David would never give her diamonds. This intrigued him and he asked how I could be so certain. I referred him to the relevant page in *The Secret of the Gorge*. Just after Jenny has found the Whiteflower diamonds, she urges Peter to try them on. 'Peter shook her head. "I'd like to hold them but I don't want to wear them. I don't think diamonds are for me."' Mr Saville checked his own words and was horrified to realise how easily he could have fallen into a trap of his own making. However, he still would not tell me what he had chosen and I had to wait and see. I was happy because this was more like my friend of old who would often tease me. He had never minded my constant barrage of questions about his work, nor my attempts to brainwash him into using my ideas. He knew that I did this because of my addiction to all that was Lone Pine. I could see that this book was going to bring lots of satisfaction into his life, and that also meant into mine. When my Armada paperback copy arrived, I resisted the temptation to read the last chapter first, and I was nearly at the end of the book before I learned that Peter's ring was to be an amethyst. I knew that Mr Saville was pleased when I said that he had chosen the right stone for her. Diamonds were much too hard for gentle Peter, but an amethyst was ideal.

I knew so much about *Home to Witchend*, but that did not impair the immense pleasure that I had when I started to read it. As I turned the pages, I wondered if readers ever thought of the hard work entailed in writing a book, knowing that this one in particular had caused so much anxiety for Mr Saville.

It was almost like meeting an old friend to start with a chapter starring Miss Ballinger; I have to admit to a great attachment to this wicked lady and her two contrasting accomplices. It was a poignant reminder of Mrs Thurston that these three should be ensconced in Appledore. For me the title of the third chapter 'The Gay Dolphin' was just right. This chapter was so beautifully written and said exactly all the things that I wanted said about Jon and Penny that it brought tears to my eyes. I had to let Mr Saville know this before I completed his story.

In the chapter, Mr Saville mentions what he called 'Penny's Wall' at the end of Trader's Street, which was a favourite place of the cousins.

> Here there was a low wall, always warm in the sunshine, on which she had often sat and looked towards the sea just a mile away beyond Rye Harbour. She stopped there now. The blue sky was already patterned with fleecy clouds. A gentle breeze from the south brought with it a faint savour of the sea, the saltings, and of sheep and the muddy banks of the river Rother as the tide slipped out.

The railway station at Rye plays a prominent part as the meeting place of Jon and Penny, as it does in this story.

Penny met him at the station as she had done so many times before. And as she waited on the platform she looked across the rails to the red roofs and grey walls of Rye clinging to the hill crowned by the great church. She remembered that Jon had always been waiting for her on the other platform when she came home to the *Dolphin* for the holidays. Although she was so often impatient with him; although he seemed to take her for granted and treated her as a schoolgirl and sometimes called her Newpenny because of the colour of her hair, she realised that her heart was beating faster just because his train was signalled and the level crossing gates were opening. She loved this station. The summer hollyhocks still stood like sentinels against the black fence. This old-fashioned little station was a place of happy arrivals and reluctant departures. Like life, she thought as the little train stopped with a sigh …

In the quiet of the evening Jon and Penny sit in the Gun garden. Jon tells her that David has been to see him that afternoon to inform him of his plans for Peter's eighteenth birthday party.

'He's got a wonderful idea. He's arranging a fantastic birthday party for her at Witchend and Seven White Gates, but he wants it to be a complete surprise to her. His idea is to get together as many relations and friends of us all and present them to her at the party. Charles and Trudie Sterling are lending us the big barn. The Morton parents will be at Witchend in a few days. We're invited, of course. David has already asked Mr Sterling and Charles and Trudie, and Mr and Mrs Harman know, and so do Mr and Mrs Ingles, who will put up some people who come a long way. All of them have been sworn to secrecy. We shall have a banquet in the big barn and then David is arranging a sort of "This Is Your Life" like the TV programme and he wants us to help. People like James Wilson and Judith. My mother and your parents—and that sheep farmer chap who we met when we went to Clun for the first time. Do you remember? David has already got a lot of promises but he wants us to think of some too, and it's vital that it must be a complete surprise for Peter … We shall give her presents and drink her health at what young Dickie will call "the fabulous feast" and then, after that, David will bring on all these other types, one by one, to wish her well … Wonderful idea, isn't it?'

I was gratified in later months to learn from Mr Saville that many of his Jon and Penny fans echoed my words of approval. Like the wise author that he was, he had listened to his readers and given them what they wanted. His reward was their praise.

I read about the familiar places and characters. I was pleased when the twins had the most exciting part of the story, set, as it should be, on the Long Mynd, which would always be associated with the name of Mr Saville.

This is what the twins saw when they were in Harkaway Hollow:

Then, with a thunderous roar, the high, steep bank on which the man had been standing burst open and vanished in a cloud of muddy spray. Rocks and huge clods of soil were blown into the air, and as the terrified twins cowered back under the tree, a great wave of water surged down the valley towards the junction above which they were crouching. The sound of the torrent was mixed with the cries of terrified sheep. They saw the white bodies of some of them rolling and bouncing towards them in the flood.

Of course there had to be a scene set on the Long Mynd. So often I have walked along its many tracks, but never without being thankful for my dear friend, because without him I might never have walked there at all. I comprehended how clever Mr Saville had been in tying up so many loose ends in such a satisfactory way. I could not be disappointed that the party for Peter takes place in the barn at Seven Gates rather than at Witchend, because this would hardly have been practical. Moreover, the barn at Seven Gates was almost as important a headquarters as the Lone Pine camp at Witchend. It was good that happiness should be shared in the shadow of Jenny's neglected mountain, and maybe it helped to dispel the myth of the many bad legends about it. I knew that the great feast would contain only simple food, as this was the way Lone Piners liked it.

Then came the magic moment when David slipped the amethyst ring on to Peter's finger.

There was not a sound as he took Peter's hand in his, and as she stood beside him he took from his pocket the amethyst ring and slipped it on the third finger of her left hand. She was not shy now and stood proudly by him as the cheers broke out …

Mr Morton stands and says:

'I want you all to know that David will now be studying and working with solicitors in Shrewsbury and so will be often at Witchend. And then one day, when these two are ready, our gift to them both will be the house we all love. I told them yesterday that home is Witchend.'

Almost everything is said to make a day that Peter would remember forever. This was as it should be, as in her quiet way she was the cornerstone of the Lone Pine Club. Although David was the captain and Peter the cook, in many ways it was fearless Peter who held the Lone Pine Club together. As I read the final words, I knew that this book had ended the series in the way that it ought to have done. Only Mr Saville could have brought in so many characters of importance in such a clever way. I was sorry that Jon and Penny did not have more prominence, but was satisfied with their appearance, which was almost a romantic cameo within the story. I had guessed that Mr Saville would make sure that we all knew that his favourite Jenny would become engaged, and that she would live happily ever after as a farmer's wife. I remembered that I had suggested previously that if Jon and Penny became engaged, Penny should have an emerald ring. Had this given the idea for Jenny?

I was pleased to read many of my little ideas mentioned in this book, such as the house

Appledore being the residence of the villains as in the first Lone Pine story *Mystery at Witchend*; Sally, the pony, enabling Peter to rescue David; Uncle Micah coming from Hereford now that the party was to be at Seven Gates and that invitations were also given and accepted by Agnes Braid and Alan Denton. Even after so many years, it always came as a shock to me that Mr Saville obviously valued what I said. I truly think that this was because over most of my life I had never wavered in my loyalty to him, everything that he wrote, and in particular the Lone Pine series. His characters became my friends, his venues places to be found and explored. I told him many times that no other author could write as he did, nor have such an affinity with his readers. I think he instinctively knew that my comments and ideas reflected those of the majority of his readers, and this is why he turned to me so often for my opinions.

Once Mr Saville stated, 'Old age is hurrying on—mine I mean!' For me he never grew old. He retained the secret of eternal youth by always finding life exciting, with an adventure around every corner. He had the intoxicating combination of being at heart a little boy, but with the wisdom that maturity brought, always accessible to his fans, reading their letters with interest and replying immediately. He invariably answered the telephone when I rang him and always thanked me for my call, as if he did not know that the pleasure had been all mine. He had a unique niche in the world of children's literature, which will never change. Good writing is not confined to the age in which it is written, but retains its excellence. I like to think that in many years' time the children who read these stories will derive pleasure, guidance and good moral standards in life, as I have done.

As always, I championed hardback books for people who wanted to keep their books for ever. I derived just as much pleasure in reading a book for the twentieth time as I did the first time. As a book became more familiar to me, it was like a good friend with whom I became ever more comfortable and happy. I knew that Mr Saville wanted hardback copies of *Home to Witchend* to be published even if only in a small number. I was so happy for him when he told me that he was having a small run of books printed in hardback, which he said he knew would please me. I assured him that it would.

At the beginning of December 1978 I received this wonderful letter, 'I'm sure you know that I am giving you for Christmas a specially bound copy of *Home to Witchend*. This was ordered for you—and a few others—weeks ago, but the books have not yet arrived from the Binders in Cornwall. I have asked them today to post you a copy *direct* unless the books are already on the way to me. Let me know when you have it and, after Christmas, either send it to me to inscribe, or I will send you a special inscription on a gummed label that you can stick in the book.' Almost before I could digest the exciting news, I received a further letter which read, 'I have just heard that your specially bound copy of *Home to Witchend* has been posted "express" direct to you from Cornwall. So you will get it in time for Christmas, after all. As you know, rather than risk the vagaries of the post, I did not have it sent here for you to sign*, so here is an "inscription" which you can stick in the book. Have a very happy Christmas in your Witchend home. You'll be in another one next Christmas. All the very best to you all and very special greetings to my most loyal friend.' I held the tiny paper between

* sic—but he clearly meant 'to sign for you'.

This is how Priors Holt ('Witchend') looks today covered with foliage in the height of summer.

my fingers and read the words 'Signed for Vivien by the grateful Author—Malcolm Saville, Christmas 1978.' I did stick this in the front of the book and Mr Saville quite understood that I would not trust it to the post by returning it to him. He had promised that he would mention me in the foreword of this book, and, always true to his promises, he did this. Knowing how fiercely possessive he was of his world-famous Lone Pine characters, I felt that to have my name forever linked to *Home to Witchend* was the highest accolade that he could bestow on me. He knew that I would fully appreciate his generous gesture and that I would receive it with humility.

The book, when it arrived, bore not the slightest resemblance to the chunky friendliness of the Newnes editions that I had known for most of my life. It sat easily between my hands, small and light with plain navy blue boards. 'Malcolm Saville—*Home to Witchend*' was printed only on the spine, in neat gold lettering. I had mixed emotions as I turned the stiff pristine pages—a book to be treasured. My joy was tinged with sadness knowing that this was to be the last Lone Pine story. I also had a sense of relief that the years of discussion and planning had finally culminated with this book. I knew that there were so few of these specially bound copies, and how fortunate I was to be one of its recipients.

This is an extract of what I read in the foreword.

I have many friends, old and young, to thank for their interest and help in planning this particular story. Over the years, hundreds of boys and girls have suggested the sort of adventure they would like the twentieth to be. A few early readers who have seen the series through have become my friends and have contributed to the planning of this story. And of these I am happy to acknowledge the help given to me by Vivien Turner, one of my earliest and most loyal of fans, who now has a small Lone Piner of her own. The details of the fictional characters and their relations, friends, and enemies at the end of the book have been compiled by her, and I am grateful.

It was fitting that this book should be written in the autumn of Mr Saville's life and encompassed all that was special in the Lone Pine series. The words of this final Lone Pine story held the same crispness as the first one published in 1943. They still managed to convey the poetry which took us to Witchend and Rye, so different from each other, but accurately brought to life by the pen of someone who loved them both equally. Mr Saville always wanted to share with his readers his love of these places. This generous quality that he had and his desire to give pleasure were so apparent and were recognized as such by young minds.

As I gaze retrospectively and with nostalgia at those precious years that were full of joy and laughter, I shall always be grateful that they were shared with my friend Mr Saville and that he allowed me to be a part of this final Lone Pine story—*Home to Witchend*.

Chapter X

Publishing and Publicity

'I promise you will never regret an interest in the printed word. Read as widely as you can and make books your friends.' Always believing implicitly in everything that Mr Saville said, I did this, and, as always, he was right. As the best adventure stories written for boys and girls were those of Mr Saville, I followed his advice to the letter and still do.

Almost from the beginning of our friendship, I was to learn that all authors view the world of publishing as being of paramount importance, and Mr Saville was no exception. In the early years George Newnes Limited published the Lone Pine stories as soon as they were written, and these required many reprints owing to reader demand. I am sure that those days were most satisfying for my writer friend; they certainly appeared to be a time when he did not have any publishing worries. Most of his letters contained news of his ideas for stories and, so important to him, who would publish them.

Maybe because children were maturing earlier than they did in the days when Mr Saville first started to write for them, or maybe because he wanted to give himself a challenge, he decided to write books for the older reader. These were the Marston Baines thrillers, the first of which, *Three Towers in Tuscany*, was published in 1963. Compared to his previous books, they were racy with lots of action in foreign exotic settings. There was a new group of people headed by Simon and Rosina, and Mr Saville's subsequent information leaflet (reproduced later in this chapter) gave a few lines on each of the books in print at that time, giving a promise of danger and of good triumphing over evil. He created an attractive potion with which to lure the older teenage reader. I would tease Mr Saville by saying that his three main heroines, Peter, Juliet and Rosina were all attractive blondes, to which he would defensively raise the flag for the redheads. In the spring of 1975 Mr Saville wrote, 'We hope to go to Luxembourg for a week or so … Luxembourg sounds like Marston, and I should do this book this year.' He did use this setting with exciting results; I always felt that his transition from children's author to one acceptable to young adults had been achieved effortlessly.

The most novel way that one of Mr Saville's books was promoted must surely have been when he was commissioned by the Children's Film Foundation to write a story in a setting that was unfamiliar to him, which would then be turned into a children's film. This is what happened with *Treasure at the Mill*, the location of which was Spring Valley in Essex. This unusual story of a search for a Cavalier's treasure featured the real-life family who lived at the mill, Merrilyn, Hilary and Harry Pettit, with their parents and their dog, Lundy. The story centres on the mill which has hidden a secret for hundreds of years. Water has a fascination for all children and Mr Saville had always cleverly exploited this component. The centrepiece of this gripping story is the chilly interior of the mill with its uninviting trough of cold green water, where the stillness is only broken by a steady insidious eerie drip that cannot be seen. As always, Mr Saville's book was meticulously researched and the reader benefits from learning how a water mill works, and being given a detailed diagram in the book. I was lucky enough to read this story at the right age, in 1957, the year that it

Above: Dustwrapper of Treasure at the Mill. *Below left:* Four and Twenty Blackbirds *was renamed* The Secret of Galleybird Pit *to modernise the title.*

was published. In the book, the stillness of the mill stands in sharp contrast to the tremendous motion of the turning water wheel, when the enemy is flushed out in a most satisfactory way to bring this story to its dramatic conclusion. Whenever I see the power of water during the rhythmic turning of a mill wheel, I automatically think of this story and know that 'the tail is up'.

The intriguingly titled *Four and Twenty Blackbirds* with its superb wrap-around dustwrapper (part of which is shown on the front cover of this book) was published in 1959 by George Newnes Limited and metamorphosed into *The Secret of Galleybird Pit* in1967. Feeling this to be a retrograde step, I proposed the return of the original title. Mr Saville sympathised with me and said that he felt the same, but if the book was to be in print then it had to be modernised and reluctantly he had agreed to certain changes. When

I commented to him that Lucinda must be a favourite name of his, he having used it for the heroine of this story as well as one of the characters, the delightful film star, who appeared in *Lone Pine London*, Mr Saville just smiled. I knew that he was pleased that I had noticed this. Whatever the title of this story, it contained all the Malcolm Saville ingredients for making it a special read. Within these pages we meet with Lucy, sensitive and wise beyond her years, who wishes to be liked, together with her younger brother, the unusually named Humf, who demands our admiration and respect as the story unfolds. It is set in a cold and snowy pre-Easter time and gave ample scope for Mr Saville to describe a little boy's fear at being lost in a blizzard. Readers are invited into the world of horse racing, with a description so vivid that we can almost smell the damp of the muddy earth and hear the hard drumming of horses' hooves as they thunder round the course. Readers will know that it was Mr Saville writing at his best when they read the final page.

Mr Saville had an almost childlike anxiety in wishing to know my opinion of books that he had written and of his ideas for new ones. Of all his books, he associated me most with the Lone Pine series. In a letter of August 1971 he said: '*Three Fingers* and, I think, *Rye Royal* are the most mature of Lone Pine adventures.' With this letter he sent me a mention of *Man With Three Fingers* made by a distinguished critic in *Signal,* a journal about children's books, which I commented on and returned to him. He was often to tell me that even the shortest written reference to his books was a great help to sales. Reviews began to take on a new dimension for me as I became aware of the machinations of the publishing world. I was also asked to comment on the Buckingham and Marston Baines series, and Mr Saville wrote: 'Collins want me to revive the Buckinghams and are reprinting the first with a new thriller about them set in Italy—*The Secret of The Villa Rosa*. You'll be relieved to hear that I'm about to start *Where's My Girl?*'

In November 1971 I received a change of address card informing me of Mr and Mrs Saville's move to Winchelsea on 2 December. I always felt that the following years spent at Chelsea Cottage were the happiest and most settled that Mr Saville had; I knew that he loved living in this particular corner of Sussex. I was concerned in this letter when he mentioned the difficulties of moving house and said: '*Where's My Girl?* hasn't got a chance and just at present I can't imagine that I shall ever write another book!' I sympathised with him over the trauma of a house move, but I knew that he would soon pick up his pen and be busily writing again. This proved to be the case and in April 1972 he wrote, 'I finished *Where's My Girl?* yesterday.' This letter was cheerful and optimistic and he ended by telling me that he received 'thirty-five letters this morning!' I knew that nothing pleased him more than to receive letters from readers and, however hard his work schedule, he always found time to reply, almost invariably by return of post.

In about 1962 the Hamlyn Group had taken over George Newnes Limited. In a missive to me of April 1972 Mr Saville's words brought sharply into focus how difficult life could be for him sometimes. He said, 'Publishing is a tough and sometimes cruel business and the fact is that the Newnes editions were selling too slowly to appeal to Paul Hamlyn when Newnes were absorbed by the bigger combine. They are not much interested in literary or moral merit. Only quick profit matters and I was *very* lucky to get the lot taken over by

Collins. No sooner does this happen than printers start to get a big rise every year so the cost of the "finished product" goes up and I am asked to write *fewer* words to save costs of labour, printing, paper and binding. The new cheap edition of LP is emasculated and I hate it, and have fought it, but frankly it was this or nothing. If I had not agreed, the series would have vanished except for paperbacks.' These sobering words made me vow to help my friend in every way to keep his old books in print and let any new ones start their life with a fanfare of trumpets and in a blaze of glory. I liked to think over the ensuing years that I helped a little. The last Lone Pine book published by Newnes was *Man With Three Fingers*. Collins published *Rye Royal* in 1969, *Strangers at Witchend* in 1970 and *Where's My Girl?* in 1972. *Home to Witchend* was published by Armada in 1978.

In May 1972 I received the news: 'We're going to Holland for ten days on 12 June with the Buckinghams in mind (Amsterdam will suit them).' In a later letter I was informed: 'Holland was interesting and Amsterdam surprising and fascinating. I shall certainly use the latter as a setting but I don't want to go back.' Mr Saville's letters were always a miscellany of varying topics, but when I read a line like '… in between struggles with the Buckinghams in Amsterdam' it made me realise how hard it was for him to devote all of his time to any one project. I sent what I hoped were soothing words, as I always did when he wrote in this vein.

Mr Saville's letters often contained news of his family, the many interesting places that they visited and the endless procession of visitors to their home. In May 1972 he mentioned almost as an afterthought, 'I'm working now on a new Sussex story in the "Brown family" series to follow *Good Dog Dandy*. These appear first in paperback.' Another popular series for younger readers is the Susan and Bill stories and I have a superb poster advertising the first four books that Mr Saville wrote about them (see overleaf). The number of projects that Mr Saville had going at any one time never ceased to amaze me; before he had finished one book he was thinking of the venue and plot of another. I knew how hard he pushed himself to keep all of his readers happy. So many of us had our favourite series and wanted him to write that next book that we just must have. Each letter had comments on a variety of books in varying stages of production and, until I opened the envelopes, I never knew what the next development would be.

Later in the year I received a letter which contained the words 'When I get proofs of *WMG?* I'll send them to you to read!' This was duly done and he wrote, 'Thank you for two letters and returning the proofs so quickly. I'm glad you liked *WMG*. I like the end and, as you know, I grow very fond of Jenny.' Naturally, I wanted to know about the dustwrapper and had reminded him that I much preferred Bertram Prance's depictions. Mr Saville replied, 'Bertram Prance has been dead for years and I agree that the Merlin pictures were awful. I don't think older children are keen on illustrations to fiction. "Kids' books", they say derisively and there is a danger that clothes etc date.' He said that he was very much at the mercy of his publishers. As he stated, 'It's just that a professional writer to succeed has to face the facts of publishing life and I've been in publicity nearly all my working life.'

November 1972 was the date when *Where's My Girl?* was set to make its debut and I almost think I was more excited than Mr Saville. He had been through this process with

WHY NOT READ THIS FAMOUS AUTHOR'S THRILLING STORIES ABOUT
SUSAN and BILL
— a boy and a girl who just can't help having adventures —

There are 4 of these exciting stories in print now, *all* for less than 50p, *all* in paperback and *all* published by KNIGHT BOOKS. Here they are listed below —

SUSAN, BILL AND THE WOLF-DOG

0 340 04022X
Price 30p

Susan and Bill meet for the first time at One Tree Hill. They brave an angry dog and win a very valuable friend.

SUSAN, BILL AND THE VANISHING BOY

0 340 040238
Price 30p

The Brooks and the Starbrights take Susan and Bill on a mystery holiday. A ruined castle and a mystery boy add to the excitement.

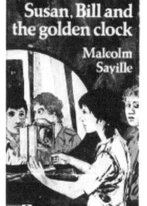

SUSAN, BILL AND THE GOLDEN CLOCK

0 340 205008
Price 45p

Susan and Bill are staying with the Frazers at Redmarsh Farm. They find a secret passage and catch a thief.

SUSAN, BILL AND THE IVY-CLAD OAK

Price 45p

0 340 205016

Bill starts a secret society which saves One Tree Hill from fire.

'I enjoy your books because of the way they are written . . . I feel it is possible they could come true to any person in every day life.' *Louise Bosworth*

'I have just read SUSAN, BILL AND THE WOLF-DOG. I liked the part when Susan was moving. The story sounds like it had just happened.' *Sarah Beardon*

'I think SUSAN AND BILL books are very interesting. The stories seem so real and when you're reading the book you feel as if you're joining in their adventures.' *Millicent Lyburd*

SUSAN AND BILL books should be available from your local Bookseller, but if you have any difficulty buying them, please write to KNIGHT BOOKS PUBLICITY, 47 Bedford Square, London WC1B 3DP.

 KNIGHT BOOKS Hodder & Stoughton Paperbacks

so many books, but for me each occasion I was able to participate in was thrilling, particularly when I had been closely involved with the story from commencement to fruition. It was not long before I was holding in my hands a pristine copy of *Where's My Girl?* with its gaily coloured dustwrapper that promised all the elements of excitement on Dartmoor. What meant most to me was what was written inside it: 'Signed for Vivien by her friend, the author Malcolm Saville.' At this time he also mentioned, '… have to go off tomorrow to N.E. London to speak to 400 children—arranged by the local library.' I knew that he welcomed any meetings that brought him into contact with his precious readers. This was the best way to promote his books and no-one could carry this out as well as he did.

Dustwrapper of Where's My Girl?

In the summer of 1973 I received a letter from Mr and Mrs Saville's holiday home in Amalfi, Italy, where Mr Saville stated: 'The country and coast is fantastically beautiful and I think Simon Baines and Rosina will have to visit it on their honeymoon. The book I am trying to write is the new Buckingham set in Amsterdam and I'm not concerned at all with Lone Pine at present. The Buckingham story is supposed to be published in the autumn so I'll have to start something soon but there is so much to see and so much to do with shopping and bargaining and working out the money.' On another topic he continued: 'We have no idea as to how many LP Clubs there are. We gave up the idea of a big, central club years ago because we can't cope with the work. We encourage readers to start their own clubs in school or amongst their friends and there is no way of keeping count.' He ended this letter by telling me that: 'I've been asked to be the "Guest of Honour" and make a speech at a "Banquet and Ball" at Bishop's Castle 400th Centenary of its Charter granted by Elizabeth I. More of this when I get back. Yes—I never mind coming home to Sussex. See what Mr Buckingham says in *The Long Passage*. He was an author and a Sussex man. Guess why?' The Buckingham quotation reads:

'I do want an idea for a new book,' he admitted, 'but then, of course, I nearly always do. More important even than that, though, we all want a change and I thought we'd combine the two. I'm going back to my own country. The South country. I want to see the sea again. And the Downs, too. I've been away from Sussex too long …'

I was kept informed of progress and was concerned to read in October 1973 the words, '… struggling with the plot of *Diamond in the Sky* but I've nearly finished this and hope it will do for the Buckinghams. I have to finish the book by the end of January so I shall be busy for the next three months. Christmas always interferes with authorship, I'm pleased to say …' He continued, 'We are going to London next Wednesday. I have to see Collins … This is my first visit for 4 months and there was a time [when I] went up once a fortnight. I don't suppose I shall enjoy it much.' I had noticed over a period of time how much Mr Saville disliked leaving his beloved Winchelsea, and how happy he always was to return to Chelsea Cottage which was now home. I was also interested to read, 'I am also becoming slightly involved in the battle which has to be fought against the suggestion that VAT may be added to the price of books—"A tax on literacy". The more people who write to their MPs on this subject the better!' He knew that I would do this for him, as I was now part of the campaign to keep children's books on the shelves and, in particular, his books. He continued, 'I've also written an article in *Books for your Children* and will send you a copy when it comes in—any day now, but like everything else the issue is "delayed".'

Often the envelopes from Mr Saville were bulky, which was when I knew that there would be an interesting enclosure. Amongst the contents of one letter was a copy of the latest Newsletter, which he sent at regular intervals to readers who requested it. It gave up-to-date news of the book that he was working on at that time, and of future projects, and also told which books were then in print. Readers were urged to have his books as Christmas or birthday presents, or to save up their pocket money and buy them themselves. If this were not possible, they were urged to read library books and, if the latest books were not on the shelves, to ask for them. He enlisted all his readers over the whole of the country in this way, to help with the publicity and availability of his books.

Publicity took varied forms; I have copies of some fliers for the Lone Pine books headed 'Malcolm Saville's Thrilling Lone Pine Adventures'. These told a little about the stories and showed pictures of the dustwrappers. There were also bright blue book markers with white writing (see opposite), which gave information about the Lone Pine Club and books.

These bookmarks were to promote sales after Collins took over publishing Mr Saville's Lone Pine series.

Overleaf: Lone Pine publicity fliers that Mr Saville sent to me prior to general distribution

15. **TREASURE AT AMORYS**
Jon and Penny are joined by the Mortons at the Gay Dolphin in Rye, and help to discover a Roman temple when helping a lonely old man who has befriended them. They meet some old enemies and the twins play a lively part in foiling them.

16. **MAN WITH THREE FINGERS**
Another Shropshire story. Tom, persuaded by an old friend that lorry driving will pay him better than farming, is tempted to leave Ingles. The lorry in which he is taking a trial trip is hijacked, and then his faithful Jenny and the other Lone Piners fight to keep him out of trouble, and help a friend to find a treasure.

17. **RYE ROYAL**
"Peter" comes for the first time to Rye's Gay Dolphin and helps the Warrenders and Mortons to solve the mystery of a missing Elizabethan document. The story features the famous "Rye Fawkes" Bonfire Celebrations.

18. **STRANGERS AT WITCHEND**
In this exciting story, Harriet Sparrow, the last member of the Lone Pine Club, comes to Witchend for the first time. With the twins, she befriends a runaway boy and they all become involved in a desperate adventure which culminates in the burning of a lonely cottage on the summit of the Long Mynd.

19. **WHERE'S MY GIRL?**
The Morton twins and David, "Peter", Tom Ingles and Jenny Harman from Shropshire find themselves at "Kings Holt" on Dartmoor. The old house has been converted into a Riding School Guest House, but the Lone Piners' suspicions are soon aroused. Host and hostess are too curious......Surely some of the visitors are unusual? ....Why does the Colonel spend so much time in his workshop carving model ponies?........And what is the fish van from Plymouth really carrying? And, most important of all, what happens to "Peter" and Jenny when they fail to return from a walk in Wistmans Wood? Both David and Tom have reason to ask,"Where's my girl?"

MALCOLM SAVILLE is a versatile and experienced writer. MYSTERY AT WITCHEND,the first Lone Pine adventure, was also the first of 75 books which he has written since. At one time in his career he was editor of a children's weekly paper, and the books he now writes prove how much he enjoys writing for young people; He also delights in 'places', travels widely and explores the setting of all his stories, the most popular series of which is undoubtedly LONE PINE.

He welcomes letters from readers about his work and will answer yours if you write to him- c/o Collins Publishers, 14 St. James's Place, London, SW1A 1PF

ALWAYS LOOK FOR THE
SIGN OF THE PINE

MALCOLM SAVILLE'S Thrilling
LONE PINE Adventures now
published by Collins and Armada

THE SIGN OF THE PINE which you see above is the symbol of the LONE PINE CLUB,which reminds tens of thousands of boys and girls — and their parents — of the adventures described in the Lone Pine Books by Malcolm Saville. Each of these takes place in a real part of England which can be, and often is,visited by Lone Pine readers.

There are 19 of these stories now, and as the first was published over 30 years ago, this immensely successful series is now well on the way to delight and enthrall three generations.

And this familiar sign stands not only for an exciting adventure, but also for the qualities of courage, loyalty, friendship and resource. The most important promise of the original Lone Piners was " to be true to each other whatever happens ". And so they have been. In many parts of the world today, boys and girls are founding their own Lone Pine Clubs based on these qualities.

 The LONE PINE Adventures by Malcolm Saville

1. **MYSTERY AT WITCHEND**
The exciting story of the founding of the Lone Pine Club in the wild highlands of Shropshire. For the first time we meet the Morton family — David, and the famous twins, Dickie and Mary, Petronella (Peter) Sterling and Tom Ingles, and read how they helped their country in time of peril.

2. **SEVEN WHITE GATES**
Another Shropshire story, set this time in the shadow of the grim, haunted Stiperstones, and the lonely farmhouse with seven gates. Features David, and Petronella "Peter" and, for the first time, red-headed Jenny Harman,the new member of the Lone Pine Club.

3. **THE GAY DOLPHIN ADVENTURE**
The scene changes to the romantic Sussex town of Rye, on the edge of Romney Marsh. Introduces Jonathan and "Penny" Warrender who meet, for the first time, David and the twins who help them in their hunt for smuggler's treasure from the famous old hotel called The Gay Dolphin.

4. **THE SECRET OF GREY WALLS**
Shropshire again, but this time the Lone Piners are joined by Jon and Penny from Rye. A new Lone Pine camp is established in the ruined castle of the little town of Clun. Here the Warrenders are enrolled as members of the club, and then help to foil a gang of sheep stealers operating from the house with grey walls.

5. **LONE PINE FIVE**
So called because it is the fifth adventure of the Lone Piners. The Mortons,"Peter," Tom and Jenny feature in a dramatic and exciting hunt for Roman treasure in the Shropshire hills, and face the dangers of an underground lake which overflows.

6. **THE ELUSIVE GRASSHOPPER**
This thriller, dealing with modern smuggling, opens in Paris where Jon and Penny are finishing an "educational holiday". They bring back to Rye with them the fascinating Arlette and, on the journey, recognise an old enemy. They send for the Mortons who stay at the Gay Dolphin and help them to solve the mystery of the Antique shop known as "The Grasshopper".

7. **THE NEGLECTED MOUNTAIN**
This is what Jenny Harman of the Shropshire Lone Piners calls the mysterious Stiperstones in the shadow of which she lives, and where this unusual and exciting story is set. Her friend Tom Ingles, the Mortons, and, of course, "Peter", become involved in a conspiracy concerning the drugging of guard dogs.

8. **SAUCERS OVER THE MOOR**
First seen over Rye by Jon and Penny, and again over Dartmoor where the Warrenders meet the Mortons and "Peter", these "Unidentified Flying Objects" are interesting others more sinister than the Lone Piners. An intensely exciting story set against a background known to thousands of tourists. The Lone Piners' second visit to Dartmoor is described in their 19th adventure.

9. **WINGS OVER WITCHEND**
The second Shropshire adventure to take place in the winter. Christmas tree thieves at work in the State Forest on the Long Mynd, a mysterious glider which only appears at night and a terrifying forest fire are dramatic features of this fast-moving story. Macbeth, the twins' Scottie dog plays an important part.

10. **LONE PINE LONDON**
Jon and Penny Warrender come to London to stay with the Mortons and become involved in a most unusual adventure concerning forged pictures. They meet again the young journalist James Wilson whom they were able to help in the adventure of "The Elusive Grasshopper", and Harriet Sparrow, a new friend of the twins.

11. **THE SECRET OF THE GORGE**
Shropshire again, but this time the scene is the deep gorge through which the river Teme runs on its way to Ludlow. "Peter", David, Jenny, Tom and the twins play the chief parts in this enthralling story of the hunt for the "Whiteflower Diamonds", the clue to which was found in an old sofa bought by Jenny's father at a sale.

12. **MYSTERY MINE**
A deserted mine on the North Yorkshire Moors near Whitby is the scene of this most unusual and topical adventure. Jon and Penny from Rye join the Mortons and "Peter" with Harriet Sparrow, who is now accepted by them all as a prospective member of the club. This is new country for the Lone Piners and they make the most of it.

13. **SEA WITCH COMES HOME**
David Morton is asked by a school friend who lives near Southwold in Suffolk to come and help him and his young sister to solve a distressing and urgent family problem. There is no time to call up the other Lone Piners, so David takes the twins as company for Rose, to investigate the mystery of the missing "Sea Witch" and her master. The terrific climax is founded on fact, when after a great storm, the sea breaks through the defences of East Anglia as it actually did in 1953.

14. **NOT SCARLET BUT GOLD**
The title of this story is the clue to a search for treasure hidden by an enemy spy in the Shropshire hills in the last war. It brings the Mortons up from London to join the local Lone Piners. An exciting and moving story as David and Petronella, when trapped in an old mine, discover what they mean to each other.

Malcolm Saville is a versatile and experienced writer. He is the author of more than eighty books — the first was *Mystery at Witchend*, the first *Lone Pine* adventure. At one time in his career he was editor of a children's weekly paper, and the books he now writes prove how much he enjoys writing for young people. He also delights in 'places', travels widely and explores the settings of all his stories, the most popular of which is undoubtably *Lone Pine*.

He welcomes letters from readers about his work and will answer yours if you write to him — c/o Armada Paperbacks, 14 St. James's Place, London SW1A 1PS.

ALWAYS LOOK FOR THE SIGN OF THE PINE

MALCOLM SAVILLE'S Thrilling LONE PINE ADVENTURES

ALWAYS LOOK FOR THE SIGN OF THE PINE

The sign of the pine is the symbol of the LONE PINE CLUB, and reminds hundreds of thousands of boys and girls — and their parents — of the adventures described in Malcolm Saville's *Lone Pine* books. Each story is set in a real part of England, which can be, and often is, visited by *Lone Pine* readers.

This familiar sign stands not only for exciting adventure, but also for courage, loyalty, friendship and resourcefulness. The most important promise of the original Lone Piners was, "to be true to each other whatever happens", and so they have been. Today, boys and girls all over the world are founding their own Lone Pine Clubs, based on these qualities.

Over two million Lone Pine books have now been sold, and there are twenty different stories for you to collect. The first *Lone Pine* book was published more than thirty years ago, so this immensely successful series now delights and enthrals a third generation of young readers. The *Lone Pine* adventures are published in hardback by Collins and in paperback by Armada.

Malcolm Saville's Lone Pine Adventures

1. **MYSTERY AT WITCHEND**
The exciting story of the founding of the Lone Pine Club, set in the wild highlands of Shropshire. The Mortons — David, and the twins, Dickie and Mary — Petronella (Peter) Sterling and Tom Ingles help their country in time of peril, in this, their first adventure.

2. **SEVEN WHITE GATES**
This thrilling story is set in the shadow of Shropshire's grim, haunted Stiperstones, and the lonely farmhouse with seven gates. David, the twins, 'Peter' and Tom find a new member for their club — red-headed Jenny Harman.

3. **THE GAY DOLPHIN ADVENTURE**
In the romantic Sussex town of Rye, on the edge of Romney Marsh, David and the twins meet Jonathan and Penny Warrender, and help them in their hunt for smugglers' treasure from the famous old Gay Dolphin hotel.

4. **THE SECRET OF GREY WALLS**
Jon and Penny from Rye join the Lone Piners in Shropshire, where a new Lone Pine camp is established in the ruined castle of the little town of Clun. The Warrenders are enrolled as Lone Piners, and help to foil a gang of sheep stealers operating from the house with grey walls.

5. **LONE PINE FIVE**
In the fifth Lone Pine adventure, the Mortons, 'Peter', Tom and Jenny are involved in an exciting, dramatic hunt for Roman treasure in the Shropshire hills, and are endangered by an underground lake which over flows.

6. **THE ELUSIVE GRASSHOPPER**
This thriller, dealing with modern smuggling, opens in Paris where Jon and Penny are finishing an 'educational holiday'. They return to Rye with the fascinating Arlette and, on the journey, recognise an old enemy. They send for the Mortons, who stay at the Gay Dolphin and help to solve the mystery of the antique shop known as 'The Grasshopper'.

7. **THE NEGLECTED MOUNTAIN**
This is Lone Piner Jenny Harman's name for the mysterious Stiperstones, in whose shadow she lives, and the setting for this exciting and unusual story. Her special friend Tom Ingles, the Mortons and 'Peter' become involved in a conspiracy concerning the drugging of guard dogs.

8. **SAUCERS OVER THE MOOR**
First seen over Rye by Jon and Penny, and again over Dartmoor, where the Warrenders meet the Mortons and 'Peter', these 'Unidentified Flying Objects' interest other more sinister than the Lone Piners. This gripping story is set against a background known to thousands of tourists.

9. **WINGS OVER WITCHEND**
Christmas tree thieves in the State Forest on the Long Mynd, a mysterious glider which only appears at night and a terrifying forest fire are dramatic features of this fast-moving Shropshire story. Macbeth, the twins' Scottie dog plays an important part.

10. **LONE PINE LONDON**
Jon and Penny Warrender visit the Mortons in London and become involved in a most unusual adventure concerning forged paintings. They meet again James Wilson, the journalist they helped in the adventure of *The Elusive Grasshopper*, and the twins make a new friend, Harriet Sparrow.

11. **THE SECRET OF THE GORGE**
'Peter', David, Tom, Jenny and the twins hunt for the 'Whiteflower Diamonds' in this enthralling story set in Shropshire, with a thrilling climax in a deep gorge, through which the river Teme runs on its way to Ludlow.

12. **MYSTERY MINE**
A deserted mine on the North Yorkshire moors near Whitby is the setting for this unusual and topical adventure for Peter, the Warrenders, the Mortons and the twins' friend Harriet, a prospective member of the Lone Pine Club.

13. **SEA WITCH COMES HOME**
David Morton has no time to take anyone but the twins when he rushes off to his schoolfriend's home near Southwold in Suffolk, to help him solve an urgent, distressing family problem — the mystery of the missing *Sea Witch* and her master. The terrific climax is based on fact, when the sea breaks through the defences of East Anglia after a great storm.

14. **NOT SCARLET BUT GOLD**
The Mortons join the local Lone Piners in a search for treasure hidden by an enemy spy in the Shropshire hills in the last war. David and 'Peter' are trapped in an old mine and here discover what they mean to each other.

15. **TREASURE AT AMORYS**
In this exciting Rye story, the Warrenders and the Mortons help to discover evidence of a Roman temple, when helping a lonely old man who befriended them, and the twins play a lively part in the foiling some old enemies.

16. **MAN WITH THREE FINGERS**
An old friend persuades Tom that lorry driving pays better than farming. But the lorry in which he makes a trial trip is hijacked, and the other Lone Piners fight to keep him out of trouble, and help a friend to find a treasure, in this exciting Shropshire story.

17. **RYE ROYAL**
During 'Peter's first visit to Rye, she helps the Warrenders and Mortons to solve the mystery of a missing Elizabethan document, in a story featuring the famous Rye Fawkes bonfire celebrations.

18. **STRANGERS AT WITCHEND**
In this exciting story, Harriet Sparrow, the new Lone Piner, first visits Witchend. With the twins, she befriends a runaway boy and they all become involved in a desperate adventure which culminates in the burning of a lonely cottage on the summit of the Lond Mynd.

19. **WHERE'S MY GIRL?**
The Mortons, 'Peter', Tom and Jenny are staying at a riding school guesthouse on Dartmoor. Strange goings-on arouse their suspicions and the Lone Piners are tumbled into exciting adventure. When 'Peter' and Jenny fail to return from a walk in Wistman's Wood, both David and Tom have reason to ask, "Where's my girl?"

20. **HOME TO WITCHEND**
The elder Lone Piners have now left school and discover, in this fast-moving story, what they mean to each other. Set mostly against the background of their beloved 'silent hills', in this story the Lone Piners unexpectedly face some old enemies and meet many old friends. The twins, of course, become involved in a terrifying natural calamity, but they all have thrilling parts to play in a breathless adventure, culminating in a glorious happy reunion — home to Witchend.

In January 1975 Mr Saville wrote: 'On January 1st, I consulted my records and found that I had received 3,250 letters in 1974. The publishing business is almost static and very worrying. Rising costs, labour troubles, paper shortage and in many cases declining sales are making publishers very cautious and Collins are no exception. They managed to get the Amsterdam book out at the end of November but that was really too late for Christmas sales.' This was a further indication of ominous storm clouds on the horizon of publishing and I closed my eyes to it as I did not like what it portented for my friend. As the years went by I became more aware of the endless struggle by Mr Saville to keep his books in print. I felt so strongly about this that I wrote to various publishers that I thought might help him, but sometimes it proved a difficult task.

I had long wondered whether there was a safe depository for the many and varied books that Mr Saville had written, and one day I was relieved to read, 'My executors have one copy each of every edition of every book I have written and they are kept by my daughter at Tunbridge Wells. None of those must be touched except for reference.'

There was other book news for me. I had known for a long time that *Jane's Country Year* was Mr Saville's favourite of his own books and I knew that he would be happy to be telling me, 'That comes out as a paperback on Feb 21st with a lovely coloured cover.' He continued, 'Next comes my new paperback *Eat What You Grow* and in June the first Armada paperback of [The] *Secret of Grey Walls*. Trouble is, Collins will not reprint immediately all those which go out of print and *Mystery at Witchend* is now out [of print] in all editions but I am fighting to get it back. I just don't understand what they are up to, but there's no doubt that they are very worried.' It never ceased to amaze me how he could work on so many projects at the same time. He informed me: 'I'm getting on slowly with my *Portrait of Rye*. I've been busy—and happy—compiling an anthology for Nelsons, which will be out in the autumn and I believe it's the sort of book you will like. At the same time comes a super, much revised edition of my life of Christ called *King of Kings* and I'm very happy about this.' This simple statement belied the enormity of the importance of this book to Mr Saville. His faith was the cornerstone of his life and I felt that no-one was more fitted to write about the greatest story ever than Mr Saville. I have a full page flier headed *Lion News* (see opposite), which shows the awesome cover that was used; I would urge every Christian to read this book. Sometime after its publication I was asked a question by Mr Saville:

Do you ever listen and watch BBC's 'Songs of Praise' on Sunday evenings? Next February (I think) the church will be Rye Parish Church and I (with 5 others) have been interviewed as members of the congregation. We each choose a favourite hymn. I have already been interviewed here, in our garden which was ablaze with roses, by Michael Barratt and am reading a few paragraphs from *King of Kings*. Another of those chosen is the artist of the Rye book who is also a Christian. So watch the *Radio Times* after Christmas!

Mr Saville's sincerity as a committed Christian was obvious to all who met him and reading from his own book would have brought immense satisfaction to him.

Lion News

MALCOLM SAVILLE
KING OF KINGS

NOW AVAILABLE IN PAPERBACK
Aslan Lion paperback £1.25

King of Kings tells the greatest story of all – the thirty-three years that changed the course of history; the life of Jesus Christ.

Familiar events and personalities live and breathe in this retelling: the excitement of a Passover Festival at Jerusalem; the growing opposition and intrigue of Pharisees and chief priests; Judas' betrayal and unbearable remorse; Peter's denial; the leaden hours of the crucifixion – and the incredulous joy of the friends of Jesus at his resurrection.

The facts come from the four Gospel records of the New Testament and Malcolm Saville uses his tremendous story-telling gifts to simply and effectively re-tell this exciting story. Powerful line drawings by Kathy Wyatt highlight the more dramatic moments.

- - - - - - - - - - - - - - -

AVAILABLE FROM YOUR LOCAL BOOKSHOP OR BY POST FROM ASLAN MAIL ORDER

    Name

    Address

Please send me .... copies of King of Kings. I enclose £1.40 per copy
(to include p & p)
Aslan Mail Order. Icknield Way, Tring, Herts.

Lion Publishing
Icknield Way Tring Herts HP23 4LE
Tel Tring (0442 82) 5151

Elsewhere Mr Saville revealed: 'Some people say that I ought to retire altogether from writing but I still feel that I have something to say to young people and while I am fit enough I want to make the best of my time.'

I was to read further disturbing words. 'It isn't only Collins finding life very difficult. I don't see the publishing situation getting any easier, but I am not going to write the 20th Lone Pine until I know whether they are going to keep the others in print. Nearly all authors are suffering in this way. My next Newsletter will tell you what I am up to, but I can tell *you* now that my *King of Kings* has been completely revised and illustrated and that I have just finished my anthology for Nelsons called *A Book of Seasons*. I shall finish *Portrait of Rye* within a week or two and I look forward to giving you a copy of that.' (I was thrilled to read these words, but neither of us realised then that it would be over twelve months before this book would be published.) 'The trouble now is *fiction*. Prices rising all the time and the money which libraries have to spend is being cut every week, but we are both well and busy.' In spite of a doubtful future that could affect the work that he loved, for the most part Mr Saville continued to be optimistic. Often he was the one who cheered me and told me not to worry or become downhearted, and just to continue to promote his books whenever I could.

A most important part of publicity was the dustwrapper, which publishers often send out in advance as part of the publicity material and, although I always argued in favour of the original style, I understood that the new modern versions were the ones acceptable at that time. Mr Saville once wrote to me, 'To my mind the best of the lot is Charles Wood's *Wings Over Witchend*' (shown on p162). The drawing of Peter on the dawn of womanhood shows a natural innocent beauty that would never be part of a modern cover, and we both regretted that this belonged to yesterday's world. The books that I have up to and including *Saucers Over the Moor* have dustwrappers and full page illustrations by Bertram Prance and these illustrations are how I always think of the characters. Mr Saville also liked Charles Wood's other covers; and I have copies of his *Seven White Gates* and *The Secret of Grey Walls* dustwrappers which state that the books' illustrations are by Bertram Prance. In later books such as *Not Scarlet But Gold*, *Treasure at Amorys* and *Man With Three Fingers* there are small illustrations over the chapter headings. None of the Collins books has any illustrations nor dustwrapper accreditations. I once mentioned the originality of the wrap-around picture on the dustwrapper of *Sea Witch Comes Home* (see opposite) and Mr Saville told me the story of how it came about: '*Sea Witch*. Yes, I took the colour snap of Walberswick. Newnes were so pleased that they enlarged this and then passed it to an artist who drew the "imaginary" figures on the enlargement and another artist did the lettering. I wish I could have got the complete original back but never managed it.' I knew that Mr Saville would have been delighted to be involved in one of his books in this new way. We agreed that the cover probably attracted young readers and in consequence enhanced sales of the book. In this same letter I had a mild reproof: 'Don't be too hard on Collins. They are in great difficulty as are many publishers of children's books with rising prices, labour trouble and the refusal of bookshops to stock children's hardbacks over a certain price. Collins are also moving office and factories to the country outside Glasgow and it will take them about a year! It doesn't really help to grumble at them … I'm having some talks with Collins about future policy soon.'

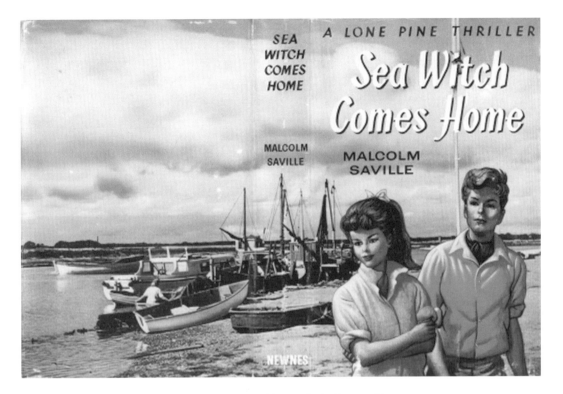

The dustwrapper of Sea Witch Comes Home

I thought hard for new ideas for publicity and also for diverting Mr Saville from the troubled world of publishing. As an avid reader, I spent a lot of time in my local library and therefore came to know the librarians. One who was particularly sympathetic to my reading habits was enthusiastic when I suggested asking Mr Saville to make a visit to the library to discuss his books and talk to the children. I knew that he would be visiting Shropshire later in the year when we would meet, so I thought that this would be a nice way to introduce him to Dudley. I waited anxiously to hear what he had to say about this suggestion and he wrote, 'It is good of you to mention me to your librarian and if she can arrange a talk to readers I should like to help her and she can certainly write to me. I don't want any "red carpet" treatment. I like talking to keen children and answering their questions and I like to help librarians too if I'm sure they are on the side of authors!' These words pleased me greatly, as they were much more like the cheerful Mr Saville that I knew so well.

In this same letter he elaborated, 'Sorry, if I sounded depressed before I left England. One of these days I will tell you more about the Rat Race of Publishing—but not now. At present I have six Publishers—no, seven!' When Mr Saville said that he had seven publishers, this should not have surprised me, as I knew that he had many irons in the fire at any one time and always gave himself a punishing workload. When he was not writing books he was promoting them. We once discussed this and he agreed that he was the person best able to do this and, as I told him, the person that readers wanted to meet. Mr Saville's life was scattered with promotional work, with many book signings, which even included the largest paperback shop in Brussels. His work at this time also continued with writing *Marston—Master Spy*, which I was told would be the last of this series. I was sad that this was to be the final book, but there would be seven sophisticated stories and Mr Saville had told me he wanted to finalise his various series. He had mentioned his increasing difficulty in formulating original plots. This is a publicity flier for this series:

THE MARSTON BAINES THRILLERS

by Malcolm Saville

Malcolm Saville has been delighting young people with his writing for thirty years. The Marston Baines thrillers are exciting, topical adventure stories featuring Special Agent Marston Baines, his nephew Simon, and his young friends Rosina, Charles, Kate, Annabelle, Pierre and Francesca. The novels are a fast-moving blend of high tension and romance. Each story is set in an evocative part of Europe which the author has visited for his researches.

There are six Marston Baines novels at present available and they are briefly described below. If you want to buy any and they are not stocked in your local bookshop, do insist that they order a copy for you, because they are all in print and published by Heinemann. Overleaf you will find some recent comments made by Malcolm Saville's young friends on their favourite Marston Baines thrillers.

THREE TOWERS IN TUSCANY
A political murder in Italy, the arrest of Marston Baines, and the mysterious disappearance of Rosina, lead Simon and his friends into a dangerous adventure.
£1.95

WHITE FIRE
Rosina is suspected of kidnapping a millionaire's son in a murder mystery which takes the Special Agent to the fascinating island of Mallorca.
£2.60

DARK DANGER
Francesca nearly becomes a black magic victim in this sinister story set in Venice and Rome.
£2.60

THE DAGGER AND THE FLAME
On holiday in the Dolomites, Marston's young friends discover a secret training centre for student revolutionaries. A most unusual thriller. £2.60

THE PURPLE VALLEY
Marston Baines and his friends find themselves involved in a plot to introduce an addictive drug into the universities of Europe. A hair-raising chase to Marsailles leads to a horrifying unmasking. £1.90

MARSTON - MASTER SPY
Why should anyone want to kidnap Marston Baines? Simon finds out when he follows the mystery to Luxembourg and finds himself caught in a complex web of evil. £3.50

..... and here are some extracts from the letters Malcolm Saville receives from his Marston Baines fans ...

"As a reader of the Lone Pine series, I was overjoyed to discover that WHITE FIRE was written by the same man! It was great, I felt I was really there. Sometimes I did not understand all the words, but I soon discovered them and I am glad you put them in. It helps with my reading age. I hope you will write many more books for people like me." Georgina Evans.

"The Marston Baines series is the best I have ever read. MARSTON - MASTER SPY could not have been better. What a grand finale for the superb little detective! The suspense and action was still going strong right until the last page. It sets an excellent example to many youngsters that we must fight evil all the way in today's tough society. Congratulations Malcolm! A first class book." Paul Hutton.

"I like the way you write about relationships. It is so important to make children aware of relationships and how their actions and inactions can affect others. Your novels show children how, and how not, to behave with their family and friends." David Heatley, Student Teacher.

"I completed PURPLE VALLEY this morning at quarter past twelve. I started at ten! It kept me in suspense right to the last chapter. How skilfully the book was written. It didn't get tedious or predictable as there was always a fresh surprise round every corner. The figurative language used was colourful and original and added to the spice of the book. Of all adventure books I prefer Marston Baines." Geoffrey Firth.

"I enjoy reading your books immensely. I have read five of the Marston Baines Secret Service novels. I find them very exciting and interesting and they teach you a lot about good and evil. I enjoyed the books because something different happens on every page. The characters are extremely good, especially Marston Baines the famous writer, who is a detective underneath." Angela Evans

In September 1976 Mr Saville informed me, '... what with one thing and another, as the years flash by I find that I have less and less time for writing books. There is so much else to do—garden, shopping, visitors and visiting, a pleasant social round and of course my wonderful fan mail which sustains me when my spirits are low!'

I was eager with anticipation when he continued with the words, '*Portrait of Rye* will, I hope, be published at the end of next month. We have had to wait over a year for the artist to finish twelve magnificent woodcuts. I shall send you a copy!' The next letter was contained within a bulky package which I hastened to open. The letter began, '*Portrait of Rye* is published next Monday and here is your copy—a pre-Christmas present. I hope it comes up to your expectation!' *Portrait of Rye* takes the reader on a series of walks through the streets of this historic Cinque Port. The text includes woodcuts by Sussex artist Michael Renton and a poem written at Mr Saville's request by Patric Dickinson. Local places of interest are also described. On reading this book, I found that its slim elegance contained a wealth of fascinating facts, and throughout showed Mr Saville's love for this unique town. The woodcut pictures were worth the long wait. This book bore the inscription, 'Signed for Vivien—most faithful of fans—by the Author, Malcolm Saville' and it was dated November 1976. I often wondered whether Mr Saville realised how grateful I was for the many kindnesses he did for me. He certainly knew that sharing his new publications with me in this personal manner pleased me in a way that no other gift could. My excited telephone call of thanks, and jumbled letter, must have convinced him, for the reply came:

Thank you for all you say about *Portrait*. Your comments are not only heart warming but some are very shrewd. I'm so glad you like Patric's lovely verse. He is a dear man—and such a good professional. I let him read my first chapter in typescript and asked him to write a farewell to Rye. He just nodded over his beer and the verses came three days later with a curt, 'If you don't like it I'll try again.' I did like it, and not a word has been changed. Occasionally you can hear Patric reading verse—sometimes his own—on Radio 3. At one time he was 'in charge' of all poetry at the BBC.

I continued to encourage and assist with publicity generally and to keep Mr Saville cheerful. I must have succeeded, because at the end of one letter he wrote, 'Thank you again for your two letters. You are much too flattering to me. Have you heard the comment made by one professional writer to another?—To hell with criticism. All I want is praise! We're all like that really.'

In March 1977 the publicity was continuing in its inevitable varied form and I was interested to read, 'A fortnight ago I went down to Devon and did three days at school and bookshops in aid of *Saucers Over the Moor* and *Where's My Girl?* which have just

been reprinted in hardback and, as you know, are set on Dartmoor. I also broadcast from Plymouth. Do you remember me showing you the Mithraic altar in Stone church on the Isle of Oxney?' (As if I could ever forget.) 'I've just been asked to open a Flower Show and Fete in Stone on a Saturday in July. And next week we have been invited to the Jubilee Celebration of the Romney, Hythe and Dymchurch Railway which you will also remember! To celebrate the occasion a new locomotive (steam) is to be named and will haul the guests to Dungeness and back.' I knew how he would love this and that it would bring *The Elusive Grasshopper* to life for him again.

Publicity came in all guises, and the information given promoting *Malcolm Saville's Country Book* (see opposite) was a delight for children of my generation. My copy of this book is rather battered, but it does contain some superb photographs of nature, and its inscription 'Signed for my friend Vivien by the Author, Malcolm Saville' ensures that it will stay with me forever.

A Carousel publicity poster that I have entitled Exploring Out-of-Doors (see below) shows five book covers including *The Wonder Why Book of Exploring a Wood* (1978), *The Wonder Why Book of Exploring the Seashore* (1979) and *The Wonder Why Book of Wild Flowers Through the Year* (1980). On the reverse side are nature drawings and a brief explanation of each book's contents.

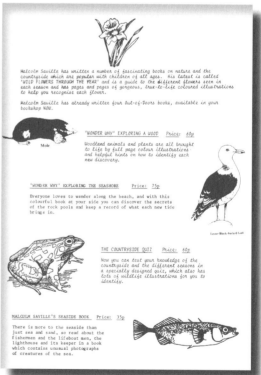

Publicity material for Malcolm Saville books

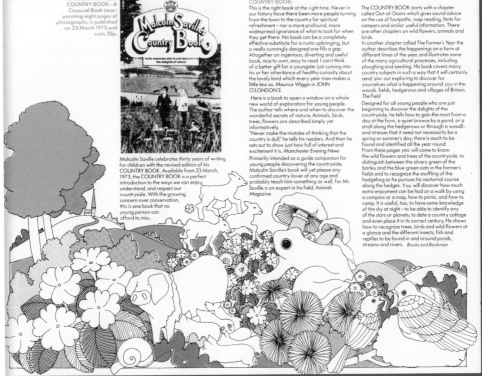

As time went on I began to notice subtle changes that caused me concern. Mr Saville's distinctive handwriting was not quite as strong as it used to be, and often he would mention that he felt tired. Sometimes I knew from the things that he did not say how concerned he was by the continuing publishing difficulties. I offered my help to him, in my secretarial capacity, to contact Collins on his behalf, but in March 1978 Mr Saville's letter contained this forlorn paragraph. 'I don't think it would help the situation if you wrote to Collins about hardbacks. Libraries can't afford to buy them and booksellers don't want to stock them when they can get paperbacks!' His letters invariably ended on a cheerful positive note and this one contained a promise, 'I'll send you the new Newsletter after Easter.'

I have before me a delightful caricature sketch of Mr Saville sitting cross-legged on a pile of books, reading from a large tome to a group of children crowded around him. Beneath him are the words 'Happy Christmas and Happy Reading from' followed by the unmistakeable signature of Malcolm Saville. It is reproduced on page 3 of this book. He explained its origin to me. 'I *may* have sent you my special Christmas Card last year. Forgive me if you've seen it before. It was drawn by a friend in the Savage Club for a menu card.' Certainly, it was an ingenious way to promote his work. When I said that this little drawing showed him at what I thought made him happiest, he agreed.

Mr Saville often sent publicity fliers and information sheets to me for my comments before they were distributed to his readers. In the autumn of 1981 I received the following sad epistle from him:

```
                    Surely not the end of
                    THE LONE PINE TRAIL

Malcolm Saville, author of the twenty popular LONE PINE stories, is
extremely sorry to hear that you are having difficulty in getting
the books you want to buy. All have been published in ARMADA
PAPERBACKS, but although they have been in continual demand for
many years, with over 2,000,000 copies sold, the Publishers have
decided that NOW is not the time to reprint them.

Please understand that this sad situation is NOT the responsibility
of the author who can only make a living if readers BUY his books!
So, if you are one of my faithful readers, I thank you now for your
loyalty to me, and your affection for my LONE PINERS.

If you feel that you would like to complain to the Publisher, and
ask for the books to be reprinted, the address to which you should
write is:-

                    The Editor, Armada Paperbacks,
                        14 St. James' Place,
                        LONDON, SW1A 1PS

                         Greetings from
```

The text opposite is formatted to imitate the original layout and would have ended with Malcolm Saville's signature although my copy is unsigned.

I was soon to receive Newsletter Number 25, dated autumn 1981, which was the last one I was to have. It contained a lengthy paragraph, similar to the one opposite, headed 'NOT THE END OF THE LONE PINE TRAIL', which set out Mr Saville's publishing problems with Armada and said that he hoped to find another publisher so that all of his Lone Pine books could stay in print.

Just before Christmas in 1981, I received another sad letter made so much more poignant when it should have been a happy time for families. It contained the news that I had been dreading for so long, but that I accepted as almost inevitable. I read with dismay, 'The blunt truth is that Armada have behaved disgracefully, and are not going to reprint any Lone Pine stories any more! They are apparently considered old fashioned in every way but we relied on their sales to supplement our pensions but I don't think I shall write any more fiction. Many loyal readers are writing to complain to Armada, and if you do the same don't tell them I suggested it! The fact is that publishing is in a fearful mess and the only children's books which are selling well are those with "TV coverage".'

In this letter I was pleased to read that he and Mrs Saville expected to visit their elder daughter, who lived in Connecticut, the following summer, as I thought that this change would do Mr Saville good. As I continued reading I realised that it would probably turn out to be quite a working holiday, as did most of his foreign travel. He added, 'It's just possible that I may also visit Canada, as I've got a Canadian publisher mildly interested in my work. He's already published in paperback *The Thin Grey Man*. We're hoping of course that he would like to take on Lone Pine, but I don't think that likely. And that reminds me to ask your help over a small matter. The Canadian chap is also interested in [my] life of Christ which you will remember is called *King of Kings*. A paperback edition published by Lion has just gone [out] of print and I'm trying to get together as many copies as I can to send to him so that he can test the market over there—I've got a few copies but if you do happen to see any in a shop do please buy them for me.' Although I searched, I was unable to find any copies. I recall exploring all the avenues for him and took the opportunity to promote his work. After many years of practice at this, I felt quite an accomplished promotions girl. He finished this letter by saying, 'I'm particularly proud of my *Words for All Seasons* and now that it is in paperback as well, it will reach a much wider public.'

Often I would receive information prior to a new book's first appearance and this edition of *Words for All Seasons* was no exception. I have a full-page information flier (see overleaf) bearing the words 'Lion Publishing Advance News' in bold lettering. There is a crest 'celebrating ten years of Christian publishing 1971–1981' together with the Lion logo. Rightly so, this flier gives unstinting praise to this anthology.

A New Year should be full of hope and anticipation of what was to come, but a missive written to me at this time by Mr Saville was almost an acceptance of his work being discarded in the publishing world, of which he was no longer a part. It began,

> I'm afraid that I can't match your splendid letter, but I do want to thank you for taking so much trouble and to make a few comments on the situation in the Book Trade since

N E W: A DELIGHTFUL ANTHOLOGY

Words for All Seasons
Chosen by Malcolm Saville
A Lion paperback, £1.50

Published 27 November 1981

Words are Malcolm Saville's stock in trade, the tools of his profession since he first became an author. All his life they have been for him an unfailing source of interest and delight.

In this book, appearing in paperback for the first time, he has gathered together some of the poetry and prose which has given him particular joy through the years. He writes, 'I hope to share with all readers, whatever their age, words which have enriched my life, strengthened my belief in childhood and youth, rekindled my faith in the eternal verities based, for me, on Christianity.'

Here is how a few papers have reviewed Words for All Seasons:

'Malcolm Saville's Words for All Seasons, which for him represents "a dream come true", is an anthology of prose and verse linking the seasons of the year to the seasons of our life: what gives this commonplace notion strength... is the author's total sincerity, humility and joy in living and language.'

Times Educational Supplement

'Unlike Eliza Doolittle in "My Fair Lady", I never tire of words - their subtle meanings, their sounds, their power to evoke memories of times and places, and to capture the essence of events. As a result I enjoyed browsing through this anthology.'

Country Life

'The poetry and prose... show a sensitivity to beautiful language, nature and the Christian religion.'

Church Times

Here now is an ideal book for all - a beautiful present, an anthology of prose and verse to be treasured and to delve into again and again.

Lion Publishing, Icknield Way Tring Herts HP23 4LE England Telephone Tring (0442 82) 5151

you are so kind to express concern about Lone Pine and my other books. Your assessment of the reading habits of children today is very shrewd. I've come to accept the fact that children, like your James, are being brought up in an entirely different world. I'm sure that even you who are young realise that TV in particular has a pernicious influence on the young. [I] realise this, and Lone Pine has been abandoned by Collins because sales were falling. They are not interested in moral principles but only on SALES as quickly as possible. They want TV coverage and their big success at the moment is 'Grange Hill'. So far as bookshops are concerned, all they want is *quick* sales and basically my books are out of date and old fashioned! Anyway I've had a good run and I don't suppose I shall ever write another story for children under my own name. My *Words for All Seasons* is, in a way, my 'Swan Song' and proves clearly in what I believe. You just won't see my books in shops any more because most of them are out of print and won't be reprinted because people don't *ask* for them. Truth is that the public—and in my case *parents*—don't *ask* in bookshops for the books they want. Booksellers can't afford to keep books that customers don't *ask* for. They only stock books that will sell quickly because they're on TV! It's good of you to suggest ways of 'helping' Lone Pine, but there's not much sense in trying to introduce them into James's school if there are only a few books available! By March I think they will all be out of print. Many parents, and children too, write to Armada and complain but nothing will make them change their minds because they publish 'Grange Hill' which is a big success. I fear that we have to face the fact that the standards of behaviour which I stress in my stories are now out of date and not in touch with reality and today's beliefs and practice. If your beliefs and standards are the same as mine—and I believe they are—you have a right to ask James's teachers what they are teaching him and are you in favour of what they are doing. As a parent and Christian you have a right to do this! Anyway I'm very proud of my *Words for All Seasons* and I do hope that it has given you pleasure and will do for many years to come.

I did derive much joy from this book which brought Mr Saville's career as a writer of books to a satisfactory conclusion. It was first published as a hardback in 1979

The cover of Words for All Seasons

to critical acclaim and appeared as a paperback by Lion Publishing on 27 November 1981. This anthology encompasses Mr Saville's Christian life with a mixture of his favourite prose and poetry, linking the pageant of the seasons of the year which run parallel with the seasons of life. The following are reviews for *Words for All Seasons* when it was first published in 1979. These were included in an Information Sheet which I received from Mr Saville:

The poetry and prose for this well-produced volume selected by Malcolm Saville show a sensitivity to beautiful language, nature and the Christian religion. Quite appropriately the sequence of readings, which can be used daily or read as any book is read, is divided into the four natural seasons of the year; and the significant human and Christian themes are worked into this.

In the section on spring, for example, there is a reference to childhood and Easter, as well as to the marvel of awakening nature. The poetry of John Clare and Ted Hughes mingle with the prose of Anne Frank and H V Morton. Delicate illustrations by Elsie and Paul Wrigley spice a meal that is both nutritious and delightful.

Church Times September 15 1979

A heart-warming Christmas gift is Malcolm Saville's *Words for All Seasons*. The veteran storyteller, whose understanding of the hearts and minds of young people has won him a huge and trusting following in many countries, presents a selection of poetry and prose which has given him especial pleasure during the best part of eighty years. Many a sympathetic chord is struck.

Living in Kent December 1979

This extremely attractive anthology of verse (and now and then prose) has a range that we might not expect from this widely popular author. And yet, why not? Saville himself describes it as 'a dream come true'. The poems, new and old for child or adult, track through the seasons, yet taking in everything that we might wish to find in poetry. Moderns include Seamus Heaney, Ted Hughes, Causley's thrilling 'On All Saints' Day', and some fine things from the little-known poetry of Mary Webb. 'Please enjoy it as much as I do,' writes Saville of one poem. I'll borrow the phrase for the book.

Newsagent and Bookshop September 20 1979

'... in the high pastures hundreds of lambs are bleating, and the bantums in our garden are hatching their first chicks'. I was reminded of these today when I received a very attractive new anthology by Malcolm Saville, *Words for All Seasons*, illustrated with fine line drawings, and published by Lutterworth Press. Here are the combined thoughts on the rhythm of the seasons in prose and verse from many sources, with thoughts also on the pattern and progression of life from youth to old age, and both are linked to the great Christian festivals. This would make an ideal present for Easter, for those who like to give a gift at this special time.

Anne Arnott's Diary in *The Sign* April 1980

Despite the glowing reviews for *Words for All Seasons,* my heart ached for my friend who now had to accept with disillusionment that his writing career, to which he had given his all, was at an end. Apart from his family and friends, children and writing books for them had been Mr Saville's motivation for living. It seemed to me that something died within him when he was discarded in this way and that his driving force and tremendous spirit began to dim. I reminded him many times of the exciting world of stories and new places that he had given to so many thousands of children, including myself, over the years that could never be taken away from us. He never disagreed with me, but I knew that nothing was quite ever the same for him again.

Winchelsea Church was important to Mr Saville and he took pleasure in showing it to me when I visited him. The story of Winchelsea Church, which he retold and revised at some point around 1978, is a thin volume of thirty-six pages with a quiet restful cover that is very fitting for him. It is a treasured memento of a happy visit to Winchelsea. Its inscription is appropriate to end this chapter and it is exactly right that Mr Saville should have the final word: 'Signed for Vivien my young, old friend! Malcolm Saville'.

The final books in the Marston Baines and Buckinghams series

Chapter XI

Mr and Mrs Saville

Initially Mrs Saville was, to me, a hazy person, to whom I rarely gave a thought. Of course, I had known of her existence as the dedicatee of *The Gay Dolphin Adventure* and, in later years, her husband's references to her as 'my wife' or 'Mrs Saville' in letters to me. It was when I knew that I was only moments away from meeting her as a guest in her home in September 1972, which I have described in Chapter I, that I realised how little I knew of her. After returning from our day spent visiting Lone Pine locations with Mr Saville, we were inside Chelsea Cottage and here was this lady coming towards me in friendly greeting. It was almost as if she were walking out of the shadows and becoming a person in her own right. She was smaller than I was with short hair that had an attractive curl and was greying slightly, just as my hair is now. She led us all into her sitting room and placed me next to herself near a table which was spread with a delicious tea on an exquisite white tablecloth edged in lace, while Brian and Mr Saville sat some distance apart from us. She smiled at me and her whole face lit up from her lovely eyes to her smile. It was then that I thought of Peter's first meeting with Mrs Morton, because I had the same feeling and 'within five minutes the two were like old friends.' From that moment, a special friendship started between us and, incredible though it may seem, the man sitting opposite me, who was now talking animatedly to my husband, became of secondary importance as we two women became acquainted.

Our hostess was asking about our journey to Hastings: what the accommodation was like that we had and were we comfortable there? As I told her of the flat near the East Hill lift, which gave magnificent views of the sea, I realised how much like her husband she was in appearance. It is often said that as people grow older within a happy marriage, they become alike, and this must surely have been the case with Mr and Mrs Saville. They were of similar height and build and both had the capacity of putting people at their ease and also of being genuinely interested in them. I was puzzled when Mrs Saville during our conversation made repeated references to 'Leonard' in a way that suggested I would know of whom she was talking. This was almost embarrassing, as I was quite certain that this was not a name that had been mentioned in Mr Saville's correspondence to me, but I did not like to show my ignorance. In my confusion I thought that she must be referring to my father, even while reasoning that she could not possibly know that my father's name was Leonard. It was only when she passed her husband a cup of tea and referred to him as 'Leonard' that I realised with incredulity that he was not Malcolm Saville, the author, to her, but Leonard, her husband.

Whilst sipping a welcome cup of tea on this perfect summer day and enjoying our sandwiches and cake, the four of us talked together. We discussed their family pets over the years. It seemed that Mackie's name was derived from that of a dog they had had, named Max or Maxie, and that they once had had a dachshund similar to the one that Peter gave as a surprise to her father in *Strangers at Witchend*. This reminded me of a photograph on publicity information for his *Country Book* that Mr Saville had sent to me, which showed himself with a dachshund. I asked whether this was their dog upon which Brock was modelled and Mr

Saville confirmed that it was. Mr and Mrs Saville also mentioned a pony that their children had enjoyed when young. This reminded them to ask whether we knew that it had been a film star together with child star Petula Clark during the filming of *Trouble at Townsend*. Of course, I knew of Petula Clark and I was interested to learn how she had enjoyed her stay in the country, which was so new to her, during this filming. It seemed that during this time she had become one of the Saville family without any apparent celebrity status.

By the time the tea things were put aside, I was quite relaxed and eager to answer Mrs Saville's enquiries about our new home and the alterations and improvements that we were having. She was sympathetic when I explained that the previous owner had only left his home, which he had called Woodsmoke, when unable to look after himself, but that we kept in touch with him until he died shortly afterwards, as I wanted him to maintain contact with the home that he had loved. Mrs Saville understood this and nodded, and I knew that she would have done the same.

Once, we glanced at our menfolk, who appeared oblivious to us, as from what we could hear they were deep in financial discussions, agreeing on how to solve the country's problems and realising that they shared the same choice of newspapers, particularly the *Telegraph*. Brian and I once went to hear a talk by the former Chancellor of the Exchequer, Roy Jenkins (now Lord Jenkins) and when I informed Mr Saville of this it prompted the following curt reply: 'I was amused by your comment of No Politics at Parties. I'm often told the same thing. As for Roy Jenkins—he's not a real Socialist but one of the tribe of humbugs who Vote Left and Live Right. But no politics in letters either!' This exactly echoed Brian's sentiments. It was a great bonus to me that Mr Saville and Brian were in such accord in righting the country's and indeed the world's wrongs. There were often messages for Brian in letters and this was one amusing aside: 'I wonder whether Brian has the same opinion of local Government Officers who call themselves Directors of Leisure and Recreation as I have? I think we can do without them. What this country needs is more hard work and less leisure! And who pays them?!' The letter continued, 'We look forward to seeing you both at Cwm Head on the 6th at about noon. We'll go and look at Witchend and perhaps get up on the Mynd after lunch and you can ask me as many questions as you like.' As a keen and, by his own admission, impatient gardener, Mr Saville was always interested to hear the fruits of Brian's labours. This letter contained the sarcastic comment: 'I hope Brian's vegetables are doing as well as mine in the flower beds. Has he asked the Director of Leisure and Recreation whether he can use the Sprinkler you gave him?'

I realised during this meeting that Mrs Saville was learning a lot more about me than I was of her; it seemed quite natural that I helped her to carry the used china to the kitchen and to look at their garden where she told me that they intended to grow vegetables as well as flowers. As we made things tidy I said what a delightful home they had in this ancient Cinque Port, which was close to their much-loved Rye. Mrs Saville told me that one of the reasons why they had moved to Chelsea Cottage was that it was a smaller property with a more manageable garden. From my own observations it did not seem small to me, but although I had written to Mr Saville at a variety of addresses, I had never visited the others. I did venture to say how surprised I was that they had had such an incredible number of house moves. Mrs Saville said that they probably had moved a lot more than most people. She seemed to cope well, even with a growing young family, and, what with travelling and house moves, they seemed almost nomadic to me. In time I was to realise that this lady seemed to take everything in her stride, but she did admit that it would be nice to be permanently settled in Chelsea Cottage.

When Mrs Saville began to talk about her family, the sharp ears of Mr Saville were immediately attentive. Before long they were both telling us how important it had been to them to give all of their children a private education, and how the success of Mr Saville's work had been paramount to this end. In fact, as they talked, it almost seemed the driving force for literary recognition. He must have been well satisfied that he was able to achieve this goal. My state education had been in the accepted orthodox way for many of my time. My only knowledge of boarding schools was acquired from the books that I had read, mainly the Chalet School series of Elinor M Brent-Dyer.

Chattering on about our day out, I said I was sorry that Mrs Saville had not been with us, and showed concern when her husband said that she had not been well enough to come. As I looked at her, I could see that she looked tired and I thought how good it was of her to welcome strangers into her home. When I said this to her, she said that we were not strangers and that all of her husband's readers were welcome. I thought then what a perfect wife she was for Mr Saville, as I could not imagine them ever turning anyone away. She probably would not have wanted to accompany us, as I am sure that there had been many similar outings with other fans over the years. She listened patiently as I related details of our treasure trail around the Isle of Oxney and was most interested in my opinion of Rye, upon which I was only too happy to eulogise. Brian and I told her of the excitement of entering Rye for the first time, and of the tense expectancy we had felt prior to finding 'Jon's Mill' and when I had climbed its steps in true Lone Pine tradition.

Eventually it was time to go, but not before Mrs Saville had made me promise to visit them again, either in Winchelsea or when they came to Shropshire, and of course I said that we would.

As I took a last look at the sitting room, I thought it was here that Mr Saville became the complete family man, a role which meant so much to him. I was sure that on

Chelsea Cottage. This photograph confirmed the friendship that was to last until Mrs Saville died. I am holding a bundle of work that Mr Saville had given me to do.

This garden photograph shows Mr Saville who took a great interest in all things that he grew, in particular vegetables and saladings. I cannot recall what he was thanking me for in the inscription on the back (shown below right), but I was delighted to have the photograph.

so many occasions this room would be filled with happy children. It would also be where fans would bring their books for signature, just as I had done, and would be made welcome, as we were. Before we left, Brian took a photograph of Mrs Saville with me in front of Chelsea Cottage. We looked at each other without speaking, knowing that we would like a photograph taken together. I felt that something special had happened and that we were going to be important to each other. I think that Mrs Saville experienced this also, and as we smiled our goodbyes I felt a rush of affection for her. I knew she probably knew quite a lot about me from the letters that I had written to her husband over many years, and, almost guiltily, I realised that I had rarely asked about her, as it was Mr Saville and his work that were my interests. As we said our farewells, I knew that nothing would be quite the same any more.

This lady was central to Mr Saville's whole world and she was now special to me. Future letters from me to her husband would have a message for her, which would be acknowledged. As I look at the photograph now, I see two people happy in each other's company who were in time to become close friends.

I remembered the saying that behind every successful man is a woman and I was certain that this was so in this home. It would be Mrs Saville who made sure that her husband had undisturbed time to write, and would see that the home ran smoothly, leaving him upstairs to create more of his enchanting world of make believe.

As well as messages written to me by Mr Saville, Mrs Saville started to add little notes to me at the end of some of his letters, which were a great source of pleasure to me. Her writing was to become as familiar to me as her husband's, and so much easier to read with its open characters. She had a genuine interest in all that I had to tell her, and always replied to what I had said, as well as telling me her news. Of course, her letters were different from those of her husband, being from one woman writing to another. I became familiar through her words with the names of her children and I began to feel that I knew them without ever having met them. Like their parents, they seemed to move round the country and abroad with apparent ease, but I knew that their visits to Chelsea Cottage were greatly looked forward to by their parents.

Although family members are the most important people in my life, and I am quite certain that this was so with Mrs Saville, sometimes we need help from other sources. Certain friends are there for particular situations. I realised over a period of time that Mrs Saville and I would not only share our joys and happiness, but also take comfort in the sharing of trouble. In July 1973, when Mr Saville was seventy-two years old she wrote these words to me: 'You will be sorry to hear that my husband is ill—has been more or less in bed for nearly a month—and so far in spite of countless tests of various kinds the doctors cannot find the root of the trouble, and so I cannot enlighten you more! I am waiting for the doctor now but in these days one feels they are doing you a favour coming to the house. We have had a consultant physician—and today I shall press for further advice—as there is really no definite improvement. However he is determined to come down for the Test match—that's a good sign.' These were stressful times for them, but there was always a tinge of humour. I smiled at the reference to cricket, which I knew they both enjoyed watching on the television. When I asked them once if Fred Vasson's love of cricket displayed a little part of Mr Saville in one of his characters, I only received a knowing smile. I used to tell them of my visits to our local county ground and how much I enjoyed the perfect English setting as much as the game. They were also interested when I told them that my cousin was married to a county captain who also became captain of England and I think they were rather envious of my constant supply of complimentary tickets.

In this letter, mention was also made of a long account of our holiday in Southwold, which I had sent them and which they both enjoyed reading. I was pleased to think that I was able to divert Mr Saville from his illness. After this letter I sent further holiday cards in an endeavour to cheer Mr Saville and a letter later that month from Mrs Saville started, 'Thank you for your card—Llangorse sounds a lovely place. I took your card into Mr Saville who has been in hospital eight days … They have found out everything that's *not* wrong.' Worrying months lay ahead but Mr Saville did return home and he did get well and all of this was put behind them.

The following year it was Mrs Saville's turn to help me in a most practical way. I had recurrent back trouble which I had mentioned to her and promptly came her help: 'I can write with real sympathy—for nearly twelve years ago we had a car accident in which I was badly hurt. Months afterwards, I began acute pains in my back and could *not* walk upstairs.' She told me of the consultant physician that she had seen: '… he found the injury at once (not without me yelling!) and after three very painful manipulations—he cured me completely.' Mrs Saville's words encouraged me and I soon became much better.

I was now the lucky recipient of letters from both Mr and Mrs Saville and it was interesting sometimes to read their different viewpoints on the same topics. These letters came from a variety of their holiday homes, but of all the places they visited I know that the one they loved most to be in was Cwm Head, the house near Witchend. I received this from Mrs Saville in May 1974: 'We have waited to answer your letter of April 24th until we could write from our beloved Cwm Head. We arrived last evening—and as is usual on these "Lone Pine" holidays my husband is working most of the day and certainly every evening so I am deputising for him and I hope you will not be too disappointed.' My companionable friendship with these two people was equal, but in such differing ways. Her letter continued,

> It's bliss to be here—this complete oasis of peace not only from urban noise but from all the troubles and problems: one feels mentally and spiritually refreshed once over the threshold of Cwm Head House. I wish you and your husband could have a visit here … Our first visit on arrival is to Priors Holt (Witchend) and to our amazement it is being completely rebuilt and added to. After our first shock of anger that anyone *dared* to touch Witchend, we are quite glad because within a few more years it would have been a ruin. Mrs Tyley (the owner of Cwm Head) tells us it has been renovated etc by a local man for his son's wedding present and that the son and his wife are dead keen on the place and love the garden and surrounding hills—so the house will be lived in and cared for. We cannot help feeling a bit sad that we shall not feel a particle of 'ownership', as we have done since 1941!! Some years ago we made enquiries about buying it but the authorities would not allow it to be used until basic necessities were installed and the owner refused to do these—evidently he was waiting for his son to marry. It is all 'mod cons' including bringing the electricity to the house at vast expense.
>
> We are sitting before a big log fire. It is certainly colder here than in Sussex but all the afternoon we were in this very delightful garden basking in hot sun—indeed we *both* slept.
>
> We took the car up Burway this morning and had a grand walk on the top of the Mynd past the gliding station (ugh) and on to the patch which was Pole Cottage—burned down a few years ago (*Strangers at Witchend*).

Above: The Long Mynd. Below: The Gliding Club - inspiration for Wings Over Witchend

The dustwrapper of Wings Over Witchend

This amused me as I knew that neither Mr nor Mrs Saville liked the gliding station, but, as I had reminded them before, if it had not been there, it is unlikely that we would have had *Wings Over Witchend*.

Mrs Saville told me of the comfort that she found from knitting and sewing and that her twelve-year-old granddaughter would be receiving a pale blue sweater for her birthday gift at the end of June. I pictured her in the garden at Cwm Head busily knitting and often, as she told me, sleeping, but always content just to be there. She also mentioned in this letter, 'Just about a year ago, Mr Saville started his mysterious illness and it's wonderful to see him now. All his energy and zest for life has returned. We have much to be thankful for.'

In the summer of 1974, Mrs Saville told me that their elder son had moved to Brussels where he had an appointment and that she had been sad to say goodbye to him and his family. She said that in the future, when they visited them, '… we shall go and see all the Waterloo museums—though English people say, "There's so much of Napoleon one would think *he* had won the battle."' She mentioned that 'the weather has not been conducive to bathing—and I have only been in the sea three times!' I told her in my next letter that I thought that she was brave as, although the sea often looked inviting, it was rarely warm.

Sometimes Mrs Saville mentioned her husband's work, and of great interest to her, as well as us, was his book on vegetable produce, *Eat What You Grow*. I was amused when she told me that, '… large herbaceous borders are sprouting long lines of radishes, various kinds of lettuce, spinach, carrots etc. We have runner beans stringing up on the fence behind all the roses and we are putting out tomatoes on our return.' I was also amused to learn that they 'siphoned off the bath water and bailed out most of the washing up water'. It was obvious that the plants thrived on this nourishment.

It was with shame that I had to tell her that our efforts, although enthusiastic, were not particularly rewarded. Our most successful fruit, our strawberry plants, were eaten by unwelcome visitors to our garden during the night and, however hard we tried, we never seemed to be able

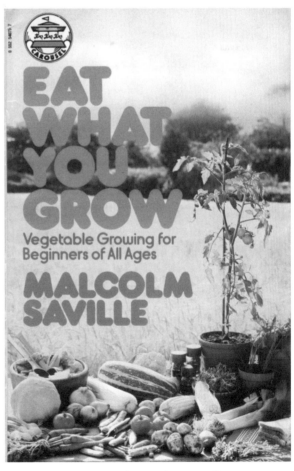

The cover of Eat What You Grow

to protect them. Our three apple trees, with fruit tasting delicious, much like a Cox's orange, were devoured before they were ripe by the ever-present squirrels, who to this day show no fear of me however loudly I shoo them. I had told Mrs Saville that we expected great results of our carrots, as they were growing in neat lines of sturdy feathery leaves. On pulling these in anticipation of their consumption, we were dismayed to find all the growth above ground, and the miserable specimens beneath were hardly an inch long. Our radishes hardly fared any better, and we would have been disheartened if it had not been for our runner beans. Year after year we had great success with these and they gave us many healthy meals.

Brian was tactfully told by Mr Saville that he must read carefully *Eat What You Grow*, which was then finished and due to be published in the spring of 1975. Mrs Saville mentioned the Amsterdam story of the Buckinghams which they hoped would be ready for Christmas. She also told me, 'At the moment, my husband is busy with *A Portrait of Rye* and he is finding it fascinating visiting the old streets, the museums and delving into the history. He is taking walks from Rye to nearby villages as so many people like to explore beyond the town and so far, this kind of book has not been attempted—it is *not* a guide book. We shall send you a copy *when* it appears—about a year's time.'

Mrs Saville was delighted when James was born and knitted a white cardigan for him, which, as he was a winter baby, was not only attractive but exceedingly useful. I knew that she was pleased when I told her that it was in constant use until, as babies will, he grew out of it. It was she who requested a photograph of him which was gladly given, and from this dear friend I received much good advice when problems arose. With her and my mother, I was well blessed. We had anxious times when James developed croup, but she reassured me by agreeing with my doctor, that he would grow out of it when he was seven years old. To a fairly new mother this seemed an awful long time to wait. Mrs Saville comforted me with soothing but helpful words, and in one letter she wrote: 'Oh dear, I am speaking really like a grannie but we too, had fearful crises of health with our two elder children.' I never thought of Mrs Saville as a grannie and yet she was probably a gorgeous mixture of grannie, mum, aunt and sister. To me she was simply a treasured friend who became the recipient of so much of my day-to-day life. She continued, 'It's easy for me to say "keep cheerful" and we here will remember James and his parents in our prayers.' The final paragraph of this letter read, 'This letter is from us both and brings our love and continued thoughts for a complete recovery of your son.'

Of course, James did get better and grew into a sturdy little boy who gave us all joy. Mr and Mrs Saville continued their life in Winchelsea, and they told me of the changes in their garden as the seasons progressed. There were visits from family and friends and fans, as well as their many travels abroad. I received letters and postcards from Amsterdam, Italy and France, as well as the familiar ones from Winchelsea and Shropshire. In one letter Mrs Saville told me, 'We go to Paris on May 31st and after a week, on to Brussels—we are going across the Channel by hovercraft! We have been all ways and decided to experiment with a new mode of transport.' I told her that I had travelled with a friend to France on a hydrofoil, which is a most exhilarating form of transport, and I remember to this day skimming lightly over a calm sea, watching the creamy foam trailing behind us, and feeling the gentle warmth of an early morning sun as St Malo came into view. At a later date Mr Saville was to ask me for a detailed report of this visit as he said something including this method of travelling just might suit 'Marston'. Mrs Saville knew how much I loved to hear about their home town and she told me that 'Winchelsea is looking so glorious here and our garden is giving us immense pleasure. As usual we have had a stream of visitors—very pleasant but very exhausting!' She also added, and this was quite normal: 'As usual Mr Saville's terribly busy—I seem to see less of him now than when he was going to London.'

Brian and I were settled in our home by this time and enjoying the challenge of turning the wilderness of our neglected garden into something that would give us pleasure and a safe place in which James could play. The happy letters between Dudley and Winchelsea continued, as well as invitations to visit proffered by the four of us. The cosy harmony of our friendship was to continue for many years, until tragedy for our families meant that life would never be the same for any of us again.

Despite being a small family, ours was close knit and although my mother had been ill for a number of years when she died suddenly in May 1981 it was a time of incalculable sadness for us. I wrote of this to our friends far away in Sussex, in hurt bewilderment that my mother had to die so young and knowing that James would be too young to remember her. This was almost the greatest heartbreak of all. I have their replies before me now. From Mr Saville: 'We were shocked to hear of your dear mother's death and know how much you will miss her. It will be some comfort to you to remember that she knew and loved James. I'm sure you will be a great help and comfort to your father. Meanwhile we send you our love and sympathy.' And from Mrs Saville: 'We received your letter yesterday—having been sent on from Chelsea Cottage—and this comes with love and sympathy—the loss of your mother to whom you were so devoted and such a loving daughter—your father will rely on you for help and support in the coming weeks and no doubt James will help to comfort him—children can be a tremendous help to the older generation.' Both of these letters in the familiar handwriting commenced with 'My dear Vivien' and gave me something good to cling to. They always called me by my full name as did my parents, but it was never as a sign of displeasure, although most people used the obvious diminutive. Likewise, to me and Brian, they were always 'Mr and Mrs Saville' and in our long friendship with them we never lost the respect that we had for these people.

In both of these letters was news that, in my misery, took a while to sink in. The words before me from Mr Saville were: 'Your letter reached us safely here in Tunbridge Wells, but we have been house hunting in the Lewes area and no post was forwarded there.' From Mrs Saville I read, 'I shall not write of our worries but at present our home is in store and we are living in our daughter's home and a flat in Lewes.' I registered on both letters that the Chelsea Cottage address was crossed out, being replaced by a new one in Tunbridge Wells. My friends could hardly know it, but their news helped to take my mind from my own loss. I knew that the ten years that they had spent in Winchelsea had been happy ones. Instinctively I had always felt that it would be their final home. I knew from experience how traumatic it was to move from a well-loved home, as we had done this at a much younger age, and the upheaval that their move would create was not lost on me. Mrs Saville shielded me from her worries as she felt that I had enough of my own, but life goes on—it has to—and Mr Saville was clever enough to know that including me in his work was the best antidote for me. He asked me to visit as many bookshops as possible and request that they stock any of his books that were currently in print, if they did not already do so. I was asked to make a list of my findings and this did keep me busy. In helping my friend, I dwelt less on my loss. He had been right to give me the job—after many years he knew me so well. I was more than a little sorry to know that I would never receive letters again from Chelsea Cottage, but it was not too long before a new address in Ringmer, Lewes was to become familiar.

I learned that 'This house is modern in a very pleasant setting with a *small* garden.' This implied that one of the reasons for the move was that Chelsea Cottage and its garden were too large for them. It seemed incredible to me that ten years ago Mr and Mrs Saville had moved to Winchelsea for a similar reason. Where had all those years gone to? I felt that Mr Saville settled far more quickly than his wife, having his work in which to immerse himself, it being a perfect distraction for him. He told me, 'As I look up from my desk now I can see the lovely curls of the Sussex Downs against the skyline.' I knew that he wanted me to envisage what his new room, where he did his writing, was like. He told me that 'Ringmer is more than a village now, although older inhabitants are furious if one hints such a thing!' He also added, 'There are lots of children here, which is a great change from Winchelsea.' His observations of these young people would probably one day have become part of a new story. He continued, 'We are settling down here but my wife misses her friends very much.' These words saddened me, for I was sure that Mrs Saville would be feeling adrift now that she was away from Winchelsea. I know myself that getting older makes it harder to adjust. Stubbornly we cling on to what we know and love and any changes are viewed with doubt and mistrust.

However, there was other news from my friends that I knew would have taken their minds away from their house move. I was told, 'We've had other worries too as our younger daughter who lives just two miles away in Lewes has just had a very serious operation.' The letter continued, 'She is coming out of hospital this weekend and you can be sure that we are thankful to be so near her now. We should have had many problems if we had still been in Winchelsea!' In a letter dated December 1981 was the statement, 'Obviously we haven't had a proper holiday this year and we are rather tired.' I thought at the time that these words stated how we all felt at the end of what had been such a distressing year for us all. It was three years since the publication of the final Lone Pine story, *Home to Witchend*. It was also at this time that Mr Saville learned that the Lone Pine stories were no longer to be reprinted.

1982 started well with this news: 'Thank you, our daughter is making progress and is now home. She is very brave but I'm sure she has several difficult months ahead. I'm sure however that she will be able to drive their car and we all have to be very thankful.' News continued of their daughter and Mrs Saville told me how courageous she was in coping with her new life, which was just as I would have expected of a child of theirs.

Life went on and we all adjusted to our new situations. I continued to help Mr Saville as much as I could. I thought we were all a little subdued, as it was hard not to look back at previous losses and anxieties and to wonder what the future held.

Letters arrived from Mr Saville, always a mixture of family news and work and invariably ending, after 'Love to you all from us both', with a distinctive 'Malcolm Saville'; and how could I be prepared for the time when they did not come any more?

I was to receive a letter from Mrs Saville in January 1983 which contained devastating news. I noticed with concern that her firm clear handwriting was not as steady as it had been. This is the sad news that I read: 'I am not really sure if you know that my husband died on June 30th last, after a short illness. He had a heart attack and went: a great mercy for him. He would have hated to be an invalid. For me and the children it was shattering and I have been ill more or less ever since.' This man who had been in my life since I was a young girl was now gone forever. In a small way I had been part of his working life, and I will always be grateful for this. Our family lives had also touched, and knowing the man was almost of greater importance to me than his books. He had shared with me the joys and heartaches of family life. As long as I could remember I had turned to him for guidance and advice and he had always given it. After many months I stopped looking into the empty void resulting from his death, because he would not have wished this, but he would have wanted me to help the person who would miss him most of all.

Mrs Saville told me in a later letter of selling the house in Ringmer and that she had had a fall and fractured her wrist. The letter continued, 'Alas! I have had a slight stroke affecting my right leg and we realised that for the present I could not manage a flat …' (Mrs Saville sustained this while she and Mr Saville lived in Ringmer.) She knew that I would be interested in her new home as I liked to picture it, and she told me that the rest home, which her younger daughter had found for her, was in a beautiful Victorian house which had been redecorated and restored. She said, 'I have a big room—my own furniture—telephone—"tele"—etc and I can be as independent as my legs allow me! My life has altered so completely I dare not look ahead but live from day to day.' She stated with typical common sense and determination: 'My job is to get mobile again—I am not worried about my wrist. You can imagine the gap after fifty-six years of happy marriage and companionship—I try and concentrate on the happy times we had together and all the fun.'

I wrote to the new address, and anxiously awaited a reply. It commenced, 'At last I am answering your letter. I have simply not had the heart to reply to so many lovely letters—have just existed from day to day—but I know it's selfish and it's no good wallowing in self pity, so who better to start with than Malcolm's faithful friend.' These words made me tearful, but they were true. I had been her husband's faithful friend and I would be hers.

I read: 'I am pretty well in myself but shall never regain the mobility I had before the stroke—it was a _really_ minor affair and only affects my right leg so I walk with a stick out of doors. My real worry is my increasing arthritic condition—that's Anno Domini!!' It cheered me that she still retained her sense of humour. I appreciated the effort that it must have taken to send me such a long letter when she said: 'I find it difficult to write letters—however as you see, I _can_ write, and fairly legibly. Reading is my great solace and I _do_ enjoy certain programmes on the television. I love the cricket in which Malcolm and I shared so often.'

She told me that she spent a week with her daughter-in-law in Rye, and I knew that that would have given her great comfort. She always told me how fond she and her husband were of her, and also how much she had enjoyed her visit with her granddaughter Amanda, who at that time had just finished her first year at Cambridge. Time had gone quickly since I had read in 1976: 'On Tuesday we go to Brussels for six days so that we may attend our granddaughter Amanda's Confirmation.' I was so pleased that Mrs Saville was beginning to take an interest in life again and I knew that the best solution for her pain was being with her family. She told me that her elder daughter and husband would be celebrating their silver wedding anniversary in July and that there was to be a big family buffet luncheon in their garden. This reminded her of a similar celebration that the family had had in 1976 to celebrate her and her husband's golden wedding.

Even after her husband's death, his books were still a great bond between us and I was delighted to hear this news, 'A few weeks ago a new edition of the Lone Pine books was launched—hardbacks—very well done—and the agent proposes to issue two a year. John Goodchild is the publisher—price £5.95. Isn't it awful? But it's well produced, well illustrated and not *cut* in any way. Anything like this reduces me to tears and yet I should be proud and thankful and of course I am.' I was, too, and responded encouragingly about this, as I knew that such good news of her husband's books would cheer her. She mentioned a long weekend which she had spent with her younger son and told me of her grandson who was '… nearly fourteen—he is *very* adolescent so his parents tell me!' It gladdened me to hear this amusing aside. She continued, 'Some years before *you* have that hurdle to jump—I shall look forward to hearing about James's school—Is he keen on sport and has special hobbies?' I was always delighted to tell her of James's progress and of all the happy times we had when he was young.

She asked about our holidays and acknowledged our love of Wales. I always told her of visits to Shropshire, as I knew that this would rekindle happy memories. Mrs Saville wrote, 'Yes, my dear, Shropshire played a very dominant part in our married life. Alas, it's so far away for the rest of the family. We toyed with the idea of Church Stretton to retire but very sensibly we decided against it—life would have been even more complicated if I had been left there, on my own. I really feel our move to Ringmer was a big mistake. We both disliked it and we became unwell, though not *ill* almost as soon as we got settled.' Such words were so sad to read. '… it was a mistake. We should never have left … but it was all done for the best. I must not look back.' Towards the end of her letter Mrs Saville mentioned her husband and said, 'I could not wish him back. He would have hated living like an invalid—we women are more resilient!' This was much more like the friend that I had known for so many years. When she ended with a request for a family snap, I was only too happy to send one to her.

At the top of all of these letters was clearly printed the telephone number where Mrs Saville could be contacted and I often took advantage of this. These calls were to give us both immense satisfaction, when we chatted about the small inconsequential things of daily life as good friends can. It invariably turned to 'Do you remember?' and we had such happy times reminiscing. There was always so much to say that I would grow anxious of tiring her. She was most insistent that I was not doing so and that it was wonderful to hear from me. To her I was a voice from the past. I was alarmed when once she said it was as well that I could not see her as she was sitting with tears pouring down her face. I was concerned that I had done something to upset her, but she said I had done nothing at all. It was just that over the years her husband's fans had come and gone as they grew up, but I never did and now I was the only one left who kept in touch with her. This is when I started to cry and for a while we just sobbed down the telephones to each other. I promised that I would never lose contact with her. More tears were shed when I told her that we were reading her husband's books to James. We encouraged his interest by saying that we could take him to all the places in the books, and that the author had referred to him as 'a small Lone Piner'. I said that she must not cry and that her husband would not have wished me to make her unhappy, but she assured me that they were tears of joy and said how glad her husband would have been to have had news of one of his youngest Lone Piners. These telephone calls and letters gave us both comfort, but it did sadden me that I must accept Mrs Saville's encroaching age.

I was concerned when Mrs Saville's address changed yet again and she wrote to me from Rottingdean. She told me 'I am settled here but not at all happy. I ... did it for the best and financially I am better off but Tunbridge Wells is so big and impersonal and now I am very handicapped.' She told me of a bad fall which had upset her confidence, and also the sad words, 'I still feel lost without my dear companion of so many years but I am luckier than some who have no close family and whose friends are as old as I am.' There was plenty of family news, and she told me of her elder daughter's daughter who '... is to be married in May—great excitement all round. She will be living in Australia after the wedding for at least two years.' It seemed to me that the family tradition of moving around was continuing. Mrs Saville asked about my family and enquired, 'Is James computer mad like most of the young? I do not understand it at all and don't try. No doubt you and Brian have to be clued up in this respect.' I quickly assured her that neither of us was clued up, but James was computer mad and we were concerned about the time that, out of choice, he would spend logged on. She took an interest in James's hedgehog and wanted to know of his progress on the recorder, which he was learning at school. She always asked after my father who enjoyed cooking and generally keeping house, tending his garden and driving his car, but she said of him, 'I call 75 young. My husband was 81 when he died and I am 80 plus.' Mrs Saville gave me more news that she knew I would be pleased to hear. 'I hear regularly from Mrs Tyley at Cwm Head—what lovely memories it has for me—I am *so* glad you saw it and also our home and Rye. I have so much to be thankful for. I can read and learn and talk but no longer can I run!! I have altered your telephone number in my book—I have had my own telephone installed in my room—a great boon—learn through experience!' She asked, 'No chance of you coming to Eastbourne for your holidays? It is not far from here and lovely to see you.'

I think Mrs Saville became resigned to staying in Rottingdean and always made the best of her situations. I was happy to read words like 'It is a glorious spring morning and I am enjoying the sun in my room.' She invariably managed to make me laugh and in one letter said 'Here am I, a very old lady with good eyesight, excellent hearing—still a capacity for chatter.' She continued to ask us to visit and said that her younger daughter would arrange things and that we could stay with her at the Garden House. I thought this a most kind offer, but I never knew whether her daughter even heard of it. I regret that we never managed this holiday, but with an elderly father, a young son and a husband who seemed to spend all of his time at his office, these things were not easy to arrange.

Mrs Saville always retained the capacity of being interested in other people and I would recount our daily lives to her. This was her response to James's reading habits: 'How splendid that James is becoming interested in Lone Pine books and that Brian is willing to read them.' I always asked after Mrs Tyley whom I was told asked kindly after me. Mrs Saville added, 'Yes, I *do* hear from Mrs Tyley. They sold Cwm Head last autumn [and moved to] Church Stretton as they have both given up driving. It is very unlikely I shall get to Shropshire again as the younger generation go abroad for their holidays.' She told me of Brighton and requested that I visit as it was only fifteen miles from where she lived. She said, 'I'd say come by train, but a car would enable you to see interesting places—ME!!' and then: 'Although it is May' she said, 'I have put on my electric fire—it is suddenly bitterly cold!' In this letter she said, 'Very best luck for you.' She ended, 'Greetings and love from your friend Dorothy'. This letter dated Sunday 4 May 1986 was the last that I was to receive from Mrs Saville, and I think its ending says more than anything I can about how deep our friendship had grown. Initially, her letters had ended 'yours sincerely' and then 'yours very sincerely' until they became 'yours affectionately' and finally ending, 'with love'.

Mrs Saville and I still remained in contact as there was always the telephone. Then came yet another move for my friend, this time to Lewes and a letter that I received from her younger daughter, 'I am writing for my mother Mrs Saville as she can no longer write letters or use the phone. However she does love to hear occasionally and I will certainly let you know how she goes on. She was eighty-nine last month and really it is just old age. She remembers you and sends her love.' Of course, I was to continue to write to her and send her Christmas and holiday cards until one day I received the inevitable letter, in August 1987, from Mrs Saville's younger daughter. I was sad to read, 'Dear Vivien, In case you didn't see my mother's death in the paper last month I thought I would write and let you know that she died peacefully in her sleep on June 14th. It was in every way a marvellous release for her. She had never come to terms with my father's death or very old age, and we were glad for her. I was able to read the letter you sent for her to her and she was very pleased to hear from you and to hear all your news. Your friendship and loyalty to her after my father's death was much appreciated. I hope all goes well with you and yours. Yours, Jennifer Mettyear.' I had noticed that both of Mrs Saville's daughters' writing was similar to hers, but with none of the distinctive unique style of their father. What I said in reply to this letter I do not recall, but I doubt whether it could have adequately expressed my sense of loss of what this dear lady had come to mean to me over so many years. Having her friendship had made the pain of losing Mr Saville that much easier.

After my mother's death I had turned to Mrs Saville and, as well as being my friend, she almost became a surrogate mother. We had laughed together and cried together and I knew that no-one could ever replace her. Even now, the memory of Mr and Mrs Saville and the happiness that we shared still remains with me. They never lost their zest for living and always remained young at heart. I am glad that they both knew how much they meant to me, because this will help me in the years that lie ahead, now that they do not share my life.

After so long my many memories of Mr Saville are as fresh and bright today as ever. I could never imagine my life without him having played such a prominent part in it. There is so much that I remember—his strong purposeful walk, the smile that lit up his whole face and the way that he listened intently to everything that I had to say. His joy of living that ran alongside the high standards of behaviour that he set for himself which never faltered. Our friendship was such that he knew that he could always tease me without me ever taking offence. He had always been kind, courteous and protective of me—quintessentially an English gentleman.

Mr Saville's reimbursement for a life given over in such a great part in writing for children was the hordes of young people writing to him or knocking on his door. Most of all, he awakened the spirit of adventure in their hearts, and a longing to explore the countryside and wild dramatic places. Inevitably, parents were forced to listen to their children in their wish to be taken to many of these possibly hitherto unknown places, and so a new world was opened up for them. Mr Saville's writing was like a stone dropped into water giving rise to ever-widening circles. I knew that he was often surprised at the phenomenal success that he enjoyed. However, he never forgot that with success came responsibility and he never failed any one of us.

Mrs Saville once wrote to me 'I know how fond you were of my husband and his books'—and I was.

MALCOLM SAVILLE TODAY

The Malcolm Saville Society was formed in 1994 in appreciation of the author and his work. Members of the society receive four magazines a year. There are three editions of *Acksherley*, for which members are encouraged to write articles. These range from descriptions of visits to locations to discussions on the importance of Mr Saville's books in the various readers' lives and are often accompanied by photographs. Throughout the year, a variety of weekend meetings are arranged. The most important of these is the annual gathering, details of which are contained in the fourth magazine, the *Souvenir Programme*. The society also holds a variety of competitions and quizzes. Names and addresses of society members are contained in the publication *Peewit* where many give details of any specific Malcolm Saville interest, ie a particular series or a location site, as well as other interests and favourite books.

The society has a wide selection of merchandise available in a variety of colours and sizes, which includes t-shirts, a cap, fleeces and an attractive Lone Pine badge. It also has its own library which contains many Malcolm Saville books in more than one edition and provides a valuable lending service for members. A book search facility, although not a direct activity of the society, specialises in searching for Malcolm Saville titles.

The success of the society is due to the hard work and the dedication of its members who are always happy to welcome new faces at any of its gatherings. Mr Saville would feel honoured and delighted that a society flourishes in his name and that people are being encouraged to enjoy his books and to visit the many places about which he wrote. Since its inception, society membership has grown, and in the current edition of *Peewit* there are nearly 500 members. The society can be contacted at www.witchend.com

With the renewed interest in Malcolm Saville's books there is an increased demand for new, uncut editions of his books. This service has been provided by Girls Gone By Publishers which produces books of the highest quality in their original forms. Their Malcolm Saville editions are complete and unabridged, have interesting introductions by a Malcolm Saville expert, and show all the original illustrations. They are produced at affordable prices which makes it possible for many collectors to own books which were previously scarce and often prohibitively priced. Information and publicity fliers are circulated with several fan magazines. Mr Saville never underestimated the need for his books to be reasonably priced so that they could reach a wide market. The Girls Gone By publications of his books would please him greatly and he would know that they could not be in better hands.

So far Girls Gone By have reissued the following Malcolm Saville titles—*Mystery at Witchend, Seven White Gates, The Gay Dolphin Adventure, The Secret of Grey Walls, Lone Pine Five, The Elusive Grasshopper, The Neglected Mountain, Saucers Over the Moor, Wings Over Witchend, Strangers at Witchend* and *Where's My Girl?* with more scheduled to come. Girls Gone By can be contacted at 4 Rock Terrace, Coleford, Bath, BA3 5NF, UK. Tel: 01373 812705; e-mail ggbp@rockterrace.org website: www.ggbp.co.uk

ANSWERS TO THE FIRST QUIZ

1. It had yellow, not red, berries
   Not Scarlet But Gold

2. Dickie, Mary and Mackie
   Mystery at Witchend

3. In a cave in the Gorge
   The Secret of the Gorge

4. Penny
   Treasure at Amorys

5. Tom
   Lone Pine Five

6. Paris
   The Elusive Grasshopper

7. Stolen sheep
   The Secret of Grey Walls

8. A cave in the Stiperstones
   The Neglected Mountain

9. Guns
   Where's My Girl?

10. nt 8 April 7 and 15 6 10
    The Gay Dolphin Adventure

11. Peter and Tom
    Seven White Gates

12. Primrose Wentworth
    Wings Over Witchend

13. Johann Schmidt
    Not Scarlet But Gold

14. Mr Channing
    Sea Witch Comes Home

15. Dan and Mrs Sturt
    Saucers Over the Moor and
    Where's My Girl?

16. Jon
    Lone Pine London

17. Miss Ballinger's Antique Shop
    The Elusive Grasshopper

18. Robens and The Doctor
    The Neglected Mountain

19. Tom and Ned Stacey
    Man With Three Fingers

20. The Cellar under Mrs Flowerdew's house
    Rye Royal

21. The mine on Yorkshire Moors
    Mystery Mine

22. Camber Castle
    The Gay Dolphin Adventure

23. Charlie Smith
    Strangers at Witchend

24. Colonel Longden
    Where's My Girl?

ANSWERS TO FUN QUIZ

1. Mr Green
2. Jenny
3. Jon
4. David and Peter
5. Cats
6. Mr Cantor
7. Jenny
8. Jacob
9. Tom and Peter
10. Burton
11. Jon and Penny
12. Guns
13. Jon and Penny
14. Jenny
15. Dickie, Mary and Mackie
16. Mackie

ANSWERS TO *HOME TO WITCHEND* QUIZ

1. Dartmeet
   Saucers Over the Moor

2. Fenella
   Home to Witchend

3. Harriet
   Lone Pine London

4. One hundred and ninety-nine
   Mystery Mine

5. Reuben
   Home to Witchend

6. Heron's Lodge, Walberswick
   Sea Witch Comes Home

7. Powerless Percy
   Lone Pine Five

8. '… about twenty large uniformed men'
   The Elusive Grasshopper

9. Bell Cottage, Traders Street, Rye
   Home to Witchend

10. 'Slinky' Grandon
    The Elusive Grasshopper

11. Jenny
    The Secret of Grey Walls

12. Peter
    The Neglected Mountain

13. Appledore
    Mystery at Witchend

14. In a field in Winchelsea. Jon
    The Gay Dolphin Adventure

15. Amethyst
    Home to Witchend

16. Harry Sentence
    The Secret of the Gorge

17. The Second Saucer
    Saucers Over the Moor

18. Witchend
    Home to Witchend

19. Harkaway Hollow
    Home to Witchend

20. Fenella
    Seven White Gates

21. Hollyhocks
    Home to Witchend

22. Peter
    Wings Over Witchend

23. Peter and Jenny
    Where's My Girl?

24. In the cardboard food carton
    Strangers at Witchend

25. Josef
    Home to Witchend

26. Major Bolshaw, Amorys, Stone-in-Oxney
    Treasure at Amorys

27. Jem Clark
    Not Scarlet But Gold

28. Mr Dank, Swift and Sure Transport Company
    Man With Three Fingers

29. The old-fashioned sofa
    The Secret of the Gorge

30. Mrs Flowerdew
    Rye Royal

Girls Gone By Publishers

Girls Gone By Publishers republish some of the most popular children's fiction from the 20th century, concentrating on those titles which are most sought after and difficult to find on the second-hand market. Our aim is to make them available at affordable prices, and to make ownership possible not only for existing collectors but also for new collectors so that the books continue to survive. We also publish some new titles which fit into this genre.

Authors on the GGBP fiction list include Angela Brazil, Margaret Biggs, Elinor Brent-Dyer, Dorita Fairlie Bruce, Christine Chaundler, Gwendoline Courtney, Winifred Darch, Monica Edwards, Josephine Elder, Antonia Forest, Lorna Hill, Clare Mallory, Dorothea Moore, Violet Needham, Elsie Jeanette Oxenham, Malcolm Saville, Evelyn Smith and Geoffrey Trease.

We also have a growing range of non-fiction titles, either more general works about the genre or books about particular authors. Our non-fiction authors include Mary Cadogan, James Mackenzie, Brian Parks, Stella Waring and Sheila Ray. These books are in a larger format than our fiction titles, and most of them are lavishly illustrated in colour as well as black and white.

For details of availability and when to order (please do not order books until they are actually listed) see our website—**www.ggbp.co.uk**—or write for a catalogue to Clarissa Cridland or Ann Mackie-Hunter, GGBP, 4 Rock Terrace, Coleford, Bath, BA3 5NF, UK.

Illustration from The Elusive Grasshopper *by Malcolm Saville*